# MURDER AMONG
# THE MIGHTY

# BOOKS BY
# JAY ROBERT NASH

Fiction

ON ALL FRONTS
A CRIME STORY
THE DARK FOUNTAIN

Nonfiction

DILLINGER: DEAD OR ALIVE?
CITIZEN HOOVER
BLOODLETTERS AND BADMEN
HUSTLERS AND CON MEN
DARKEST HOURS
AMONG THE MISSING
MURDER, AMERICA
ALMANAC OF WORLD CRIME
LOOK FOR THE WOMAN
PEOPLE TO SEE
THE TRUE CRIME QUIZ BOOK
THE INNOVATORS
ZANIES
THE CRIME MOVIE QUIZ BOOK
THE DILLINGER DOSSIER

# MURDER AMONG THE MIGHTY

## CELEBRITY SLAYINGS THAT SHOCKED AMERICA

BY

## JAY ROBERT NASH

Delacorte Press/New York

Published by
Delacorte Press
1 Dag Hammarskjold Plaza
New York, N.Y. 10017

Manufactured in the United States of America

First printing

Book Design by Elaine Golt Gongora

**Library of Congress Cataloging in Publication Data**

Nash, Jay Robert.
  Murder among the mighty.

  Bibliography: p.
  Includes index.
  1. Murder—United States—Biography.
  2. Crime and criminals—United States—Biography.
  3. Victims of crimes—United States—Biography.
  I. Title.
HV6245.N39  1983   364.1′523′0922  [B]   82–17314
ISBN 0–440–05956–9

This book is for
Neal and Joan Amidei

# THE CASES

# ACKNOWLEDGMENTS

I wish to express my deep gratitude to my research associate, Cathy Anetsberger, who labored long and conscientiously in archives and libraries on this book's behalf, as well as obtaining and processing important graphics herein reproduced. Again, my tireless typist, Sandy Horeis, provided superb work in manuscript preparation.

Many friends and associates were extremely helpful in providing printed material, graphics, and correspondence, plus memorabilia in this work. They include Neil and Vicky Nash, Jack Jules Klein, Jr., Leonard Des Jardins, Phil Krap, Edgar Krebs, Jerry Goldberg, John McHugh, Mary and Tom McComas, Bob Howe, Curt Johnson, Marc and Judy Davis, Bill and Edie Kelly, Dan McConnell, Jim and Edie McCormick, P. Michael O'Sullivan, Sydney Harris, Hank Oettinger, Bob and Linda Connelly, Jack and Gladys Conroy, Ray Peekner, Bud Freeman, Bruce Elliot, Arthur Kluge, Michaela Touhy, George Spink, Karen Connor, Les Susman, Arnold L. Kaye, Raymond Friday Locke, Mark and Lois Jacobs.

Sources particularly helpful in providing all manner of graphics include Cinemabilia of New York City, the New-York Historical Society, the Chicago Historical Society, the Chicago Public Library, the New York Public Library, Kiki Dokas and Bill Kelly of Wide World, and Pete Gregory of UPI. Newspaper librarians were especially helpful, including Lynette Francis of the *San Francisco Chronicle;* Susanna Shuster, editorial research librarian for the *Los Angeles Times;* Dorothy Frazier of *The Denver Post;* and the librarians of the *Chicago Tribune,* the Chicago *Sun-Times, The Atlanta Constitution, The Philadelphia Inquirer, The Washington Post,* and *The New York Times.*

Of particular help were the district attorneys' offices in Atlanta, Chicago, New York, Washington, D.C., Philadelphia, and Los Angeles, who provided trial transcripts and other pertinent data to the cases covered herein. Librarians and archivists throughout the United States aided the research for the book greatly and include Anne Salter of the Atlanta Historical Society; Kevin

## ACKNOWLEDGMENTS

Carey of the University of Illinois Library; Melanie Dodson and Rene Dedonato of Northwestern University Library; Jerry Delaney of the Chicago Public Library; Peter Weil, microfilm, and the staff of the Newberry Library; Pat Wilcoxon, Joseph Regenstein Library, University of Chicago; the staff of the John Crerar Library at Chicago's Illinois Institute of Technology.

I wish also to thank specifically Rich Kaplan of the district attorney's office in Chicago and Sergeant Anthony Consieldi of the Chicago Police Department for their help.

# PREFACE

This book is not only a natural outgrowth of my writing and research in the crime field over the last decade but a work that logically stems from yesterday's and today's headlines. The stories here deal with murder or attempted murder and present some of America's famous and sometimes infamous citizens, past and present, as slayer or victim. All manner of celebrities—from bankers to doctors, from movie stars to politicians—have captured the attention of the public with their involvement in that most heinous of crimes, murder. Their lethal acts have, in reality, enlarged their images as celebrities. The individuals depicted here, both good and evil, are, after all, products of our national imagination, but they loom so large in our mind's eye that they take on, through the various tricks of publicity, legends that even the stark reality of homicide cannot easily destroy.

Even in their final acts of killing or being killed, these high-positioned creatures of the mind play out their parts with lofty drama—for the most part ever-mindful of their social place, their status among the heavens, some even keeping a jaundiced eye peeled for their niche in history, no matter how infamous that footnote might be. It is status that obviously propelled many portrayed herein into murder, as it did Mark David Chapman, the killer of John Lennon, who actually lived the singer's life for years before slaying him. As Lennon's most devoted fan, Chapman imitated the Beatle almost to the last physical detail; he was a self-styled clone who even married a woman of Japanese extraction as had Lennon, and only days before he murdered his idol, took Lennon's name to add to his adopted personality.

This was a case of personality envy that became a murderous mania. The same could be said of Dennis Sweeney, who murdered his political mentor, activist Allard Lowenstein. Lowenstein failed in Sweeney's strange imagination to live up to the image that Lowenstein himself had implanted in his protégé's mind. A similar identity problem existed in the mind of Paul DeWit, slayer of Chicago drama coach and onetime voice of "The Whistler," Everett Clarke.

Even among the rich, money is often a prime motive, as in the case of Dr. Bennett Clarke Hyde who, in 1909, embarked upon the wholesale slaughter of his in-laws so that his wife could inherit a fortune and Claus von Bulow who, from 1979 to 1980, injected his wife with insulin in order to obtain the millions she had left him in her will.

Money, though in slightly lesser amounts, was also the motive in the slayings of Mrs. Theresa Mors in 1924 by onetime boxing champ "Kid McCoy"; New York's "Mr. Big," gambler Arnold Rothstein in 1928; Atlanta banker Henry C. Heinz in 1943; film star Sal Mineo, who was stabbed to death in Hollywood in 1976; and physician-writer Michael J. Halberstam, who was killed by superburglar Bernard Welch in 1980. A lack of money, on the other hand, brought about the misguided-mercy murder of Nellie Chapin, wife of the editor of the New York *World* in 1918. Money mixed with sex in the killings of silent screen star Ramon Novarro in 1968 and newspaper heir John S. Knight III in 1975, although these were essentially homosexual killings.

A case where hatred for homosexuals and a lust for power combined to create murder was the slaying of San Francisco Mayor George Moscone and Supervisor Harvey Milk by former Supervisor Dan White in 1978—a double killing that led to enormous riots. Political power was also clearly behind the murder of Detroit's popular radio announcer Jerry Buckley in 1930 and, in the same year, the very public murder of *Chicago Tribune* reporter Jake Lingle.

Love or the lack of it has produced a preponderance of celebrity killings in the United States, from cheating wives and husbands of the famous and rich to the eternal and lethal triangles. Here the reader will find the fascinating stories of New York robber baron Big Jim Fisk, killed by a onetime associate in 1872 over the affections of Fisk's straying mistress, the notorious Helen Josephine "Josie" Mansfield; the berserk millionaire Harry K. Thaw, who shot to death America's most prominent architect, Stanford White, in 1906, because he had once sexually enjoyed his wife, Evelyn Nesbit, "the girl in the red velvet swing"; Webster Guerin, killed by his forsaken mistress Dora McDonald, the wife of Chicago's crime czar, in 1907.

It was also love corrupted by jealousy that brought about the stabbing death of Lana Turner's lover, hoodlum Johnny Stompanato, in 1958, and it was love turned to raging homicide that sent actor Tom Neal to prison in 1965. It was the scorning of a woman's love (and the loss of a considerable inheritance) that drove Jean Harris to send several bullets into her estranged Lothario, Dr. Herman Tarnower, in 1980.

Status, money, power, sex and love—these are the basic ingredients of the murders depicted in this book, common to the thousands of murders that occur each year in America but totally uncommon in that these killings enveloped our gods and goddesses, making them oddly mortal but no less captivating. In the end, overshadowing the crimes themselves, we are left with personalities that continued to blind the public eye long after their luster faded and their stars exploded in our fragile human universe.

—Jay Robert Nash
*Chicago*
*1982*

# MURDER AMONG THE MIGHTY

# 1872

## EDWARD S. "NED" STOKES

### SLAYER OF BIG JIM FISK

Jim Fisk was all brass. A towering 250-pound giant, Big Jim began his career as a circus roustabout and barker. During the Civil War he bought and sold war contracts, ignoring regulations for the most part and bribing officials who objected to his underhanded methods. Following the war Fisk traveled the South, where he purchased huge amounts of confiscated cotton at depressed rates. He was the epitome of the hated carpetbagger; the jeers and taunts of defeated Southerners bothered him not in the least.

Once again in New York, Fisk befriended and became the partner of a man with his identical lust for money and power, Jay Gould. The thirty-year-old Fisk happily became the front man for Gould in their nefarious Wall Street enterprises. On his own Fisk bought controlling interest in the Fall River and Bristol steamboat lines, designing his own elaborate gold-braided uniform and appointing himself an admiral. Vain, egotistical, and forever strutting his self-importance, Fisk, like Gould, had his covetous eye on the railroads, any railroad that could be purchased for little money and through a great deal of fraud.

His opportunity came in 1867 when he and Gould befriended the unscrupulous millionaire Daniel Drew, a onetime drover who had made his first fortune by watering livestock and selling the bloated steers for much more on the hoof than they were worth. Drew made Fisk and Gould directors of his Erie Railroad, knowing full well that Commodore Cornelius Vanderbilt, who already owned the New York Central, was trying to swallow every railroad in the East. He wanted everything on rails between Chicago and New York, as well as the entire Eastern seaboard of railway systems, under his control. Erie was the holdout.

1

Thinking Drew was a friend and confidant, one who was giving him tacit approval to buy controlling interest in Erie, Vanderbilt began to purchase huge blocks of the railroad's stock. The real controllers of the line, Fisk and Gould, merely issued more freshly printed stock, flooding the market. This was, of course, in the days when few or no controls were exercised upon such flagrant business practices. Within months the Erie stock, once valued at $19 million, was inflated to an unreal $57 million through the bogus stock of Fisk and Gould.

When told that Vanderbilt would continue to buy Erie stock, Big Jim Fisk bellowed: "If this printing press don't break down, I'll be damned if I don't give the old hog [Vanderbilt] all he wants of Erie!" Vanderbilt finally discovered what was going on and caused authorities to act. Process servers broke into Gould's office in New York just as the robber baron fled out a back exit to join Fisk. Both men escaped on the night ferry to New Jersey, carrying more than $6 million in greenbacks stuffed into heavy carpetbags, most of the loot being Vanderbilt's cash.

The two much-wanted men, joined by a nervous Daniel Drew, hid in a hotel called Taylor's Castle in Jersey City. Fisk hired more than a hundred armed bodyguards to protect them. The hotel was so heavily patrolled that guards renamed it "Fort Taylor." Thugs from New York sent by the Commodore to retrieve his money were beaten back from Fort Taylor, often by Fisk himself, who led his army of goons into club-wielding battle.

Though the stock swindle was nothing more than a bold theft, Fisk promoted his actions and those of his partners as a noble cause célèbre, giving boisterous press conferences in which he played the role of the businessman as martyr. Said Big Jim to the newsmen: "The Commodore owns New York; the Stock Exchange, the streets, the railroads and most of the steamships there belong to him. As ambitious young men, we saw there was no chance for us to expand."

"Why then, Mr. Fisk," asked a pugnacious newsman, "did you not stay in New York?"

"We came over here [to New Jersey] to grow up with the country," replied Fisk with a wide grin. "Yes—tell Mr. Greeley from us that we're sorry now that we didn't take his advice sooner—about going West."

Though Big Jim found his scandalous scam amusing, Gould,

Left: *Big Jim Fisk in 1867 when he became Jay Gould's partner.* Right: *Josie Mansfield, the love of Big Jim's life.*

the tight-lipped, dark-eyed schemer, was annoyed to distraction at having to stay in New Jersey. He spent hours writing down schemes to best Vanderbilt in the "Erie War" and then tore up his notes into hundreds of little pieces of paper, kneading these into balls as he plotted his next move. Old Daniel Drew was entirely disgusted with the larcenous young men and complained that he was a virtual prisoner in New Jersey.

Jay Gould suddenly left in the middle of the night with $1 million stuffed into a bag, going secretly to upstate New York, taking a hotel room in Albany under an assumed name. He had a wild and brazen plan in mind, but it would take time to enact.

During Gould's absence Jubilee Jim, as Fisk was known to New Yorkers who cherished his extravagant ways, sent for the love of his life—not his wife, Lucy Moore Fisk, who had married him at age fifteen, but his ravishing dark-haired mistress, Helen Josephine "Josie" Mansfield. Josie took up residence in Taylor's Castle, and Jim sported her about Jersey City. Newsmen flocked to their sides and delighted in reporting to their readers how Josie's clear gray eyes would captivate any male, describing her "daz-zling white skin" and her "buxom beauty." As usual, Fisk bought jewels and furs for Josie and hired maids to wait on her at all moments of the day.

In Albany, Jay Gould went about his stealthy business. He approached the most corrupt senator of the state legislature, one William Marcy Tweed, later to be the head of Tammany, becom-ing the notorious Boss Tweed, the ultimate practitioner of cor-ruption and graft. Gould, through Tweed, simply bought the state legislature in one of the most blatantly unscrupulous moves of the century. Some of the legislators charged as much as $70,000 for their votes, others asked a mere $5,000. Tweed himself re-ceived $100,000. The state officials then voted approval of Erie's bogus stock—including an enormous block of shares still in the hands of Gould and Fisk that gave them control—making the once useless certificates genuine in one corrupt sweep of legisla-tive action.

Fisk and Gould returned to New York triumphant and still in charge of the Erie Railroad. Fisk strolled the Manhattan streets, loudly bragging of his victory, spending his money freely. He gave huge amounts to charity to offset the image of his real character, that of a dandified crook with a beaming smile.

Vanderbilt still had his lawyers on the trails of the Erie execu-tives, but he tired of the game. He would stop filing suits against Drew, Fisk, and Gould, he said, if the lot of them would return approximately $4.5 million to him. (Vanderbilt had lost almost $7 million to the hustlers and was willing to split the difference, allowing with grudging admiration his enemies to realize about $2.5 million profit, plus the millions they had gleaned on the open market.) The trio met at the Commodore's Washington Place residence and agreed to the restitution. They were still many millions ahead and would continue to control Erie.

With this newfound fortune Fisk and Gould promptly set about to corner the gold market. Gould bribed President Ulysses S. Grant's brother-in-law, Abel R. Corbin, to be a spy inside the White House, obtaining details on the country's gold reserve and on whether or not the Grant administration planned to release any government gold in the near future. When Fisk and Gould learned that Grant intended to keep a lid on the gold reserves, they began to buy up the $15 million in gold then in circulation.

Both men were careful to assign agents to buy the gold for them without signing a single purchasing order.

As Gould manipulated the gold purchases Fisk inveigled President Grant on board his luxury yacht, *The Providence.* Resplendent in his admiral's uniform, Fisk wined and dined Grant, pumping him for information on the U.S. gold reserve. Grant shrewdly puffed on his cigar and freely drank Fisk's liquor but refused to utter a word about gold. During this vexing confrontation Big Jim's new aide, Edward S. "Ned" Stokes, was on hand to cater to Grant's every desire. Stokes, a shrewd and calculating young man, watched Jubilee Jim closely as the robber baron attempted to manipulate the President; he watched and admired, but three years later he would face his mentor with a gun in his hand.

Agents for Fisk and Gould bought public gold rapidly, driving up the price from 133 to 165, then sold out quickly, leaving other investors ruined when the government suddenly released an enormous amount of gold on the open market; Grant had outguessed the robber barons. When prices collapsed on "Black Friday," September 24, 1869, hundreds were left penniless. Brokerage firms by the scores were ruined and several investors and brokers committed suicide or went mad.

Fisk and Gould had again made a killing, pocketing an estimated $10 million each. Gould secreted his loot as usual. Fisk spent his millions lavishly. He bought Pike's Grand Opera House at 23rd Street and Eighth Avenue, then the most fashionable area in New York. He moved into the luxurious quarters in the Opera House, installing his mistress Josie in her own four-story brownstone some doors away.

The robber baron not only saw Josie regularly but kept a string of show girls on hand and was seen driving through Central Park with as many as six beautiful women clustered about him in his enormous carriage. Everything about Jubilee Jim was extravagant. He wore a new suit of clothes each day, and bedecked himself with diamonds, so that he glittered like a Christmas tree when appearing in public. (The youthful James Buchanan Brady read about Big Jim and later outstripped Fisk as a gem-wearing dandy, becoming "Diamond Jim" Brady.)

Fisk backed musical reviews and operettas at the Opera House, personally selecting the girls who would appear in the chorus. Most of these beauties became part of his ever-widening harem.

The tycoon, according to Matthew Josephson, "loved the crush of crowds, loved to move among the admiring glances drawn to him, dressed in a scarlet-lined cape, a frilled shirt over his expansive bosom, in the center of which sat the immense flashing diamond sparkler of wide fame."

The gaudy, crude, uneducated, but always colorful Big Jim was a hero to most of New York. From a boy laborer he had grown up to best the greatest fortune-holders of the day. A New York *Herald* reporter, drenching Fisk's character with florid prose, likened the robber baron to "the sweep of a fiery meteor, or a great comet . . . plunging with terrific velocity and dazzling brilliance across the horizon, whirling into its blazing train broken fortunes, raving financiers, corporations, magnates and public officers, civil and military, judges, priests, and Presidents." Fisk became "Prince Erie" and lived up to the image of a royal money merchant with great verve, partying most of the day and night, usually with his adored Josie Mansfield.

One evening when Prince Erie was in a generous mood, he decided to share the dazzling sight of his mistress with his now trusted junior partner, Ned Stokes. The onetime aide had risen rapidly under Fisk's guidance, investing heavily in Big Jim's schemes and reaping huge fortunes himself. Stokes was completely unlike Fisk. He was well-educated and cultured, and displayed impeccable manners. Further, he was, according to one report, "so handsome that it was painful . . . women, quite naturally, found him irresistible." Josie was no exception. She fell in love with Stokes on the night Fisk brought him to dinner.

Stokes discreetly traded deep glances with the mistress but remained aloof; in the weeks to come he would visit her secretly, even though he knew well her scandalous past—that she had been divorced at an early age, had appeared in some risqué if not bawdy musicals, and had served a short apprenticeship in one of the more elegant New York brothels.

Although the lovers took the necessary precautions, Fisk learned of Josie's disaffection through one of the many agents he employed to spy on her. He exploded, stating publicly that Josie was an ungrateful courtesan, and that his friend Ned Stokes was nothing more than a backstabbing blackguard. Throughout this bombast Mrs. Lucy Fisk told reporters that her marriage to Big Jim was secure, that she "owned the man."

*Ned Stokes shoots "Prince Erie" on the grand staircase.*

Big Jim suddenly accused Stokes of embezzling stock funds he owned jointly with the junior partner. Stokes retaliated by suing Prince Erie for slander. Not to be outdone, mistress Josie, who had completely gone over to Stokes but felt that she was losing a great fortune in Big Jim, sued Fisk for alienation of affection. Fisk then brought suit against Stokes on charges of blackmail.

Stokes was brought to trial first and on January 6, 1872, was questioned so unmercifully by Fisk's lawyers that he almost attacked the attorney. He checked his fierce temper, however, until some hours later. At that time he was dining at Delmonico's when he learned that a grand jury had indicted him for blackmail. He jumped up and raced back to his hotel, where he retrieved a four-chambered Colt revolver. The seething lover then visited Josie and learned that Fisk would be entertaining Boston guests at the Broadway Central Hotel. (Josie made a point of keeping tabs on Big Jim's movements.)

Going immediately to the richly appointed hotel on lower Broadway, Stokes climbed the grand staircase, lurking at the head of the stairway, and waited for Jubilee Jim. Promptly at 4 P.M., Big Jim Fisk entered the hotel and started for the staircase. He wore his usual cape and top hat. Jubilee Jim hummed confidently as he began to mount the stairs. Looking up, he was startled to see Stokes standing at the top of the stairs, a revolver in his hand pointed directly at him.

"I've got you at last!" roared Ned Stokes, aiming the weapon.

"What?" bellowed the incredulous Fisk.

"Now I've got you!"

Prince Erie looked about frantically for aid, spotting a terrified clerk standing nearby. He called out: "For God's sake, will no one help me?"

At that moment Stokes fired twice; the first bullet struck Fisk in the arm, the next buried itself deep in his bowels. The robber baron collapsed on the stairs as Stokes fled out a rear exit. Hotel employees rushed forward to catch the toppling form of Big Jim. He insisted on walking to a room upstairs, where doctors were summoned. An operation was impossible, doctors concluded. The strain of that climb, Fisk's own bravado, undoubtedly caused his end the following day when he simply bled to death.

As Jubilee Jim lay on his deathbed he called for Josie, but his mistress refused to visit him. Fearing for her life, she packed her bags and fled her Fisk-owned mansion with the cash, jewels, and finery her onetime lover had bestowed upon her. Lucy Fisk did arrive in time to kiss her errant husband farewell. She stepped sobbing from the death room to tell reporters that Big Jim "was such a good boy."

It was only a matter of hours before the handsome Ned Stokes was apprehended. He was quickly brought to trial. Josie begged

*Jubilee Jim in his casket, and his wife in tears. "He was such a good boy," she said.*

for his life from the witness stand. The jury could not agree on a verdict and Stokes was tried again, this time convicted of murder and sentenced to hang. His lawyers, however, won a new trial on a technicality, and following this third trial, Stokes was found guilty of manslaughter. He was given six years in Sing Sing.

Lovely Josie saw him to the station with his guards, kissing Stokes passionately and telling him that she would wait for him. She did not. A few weeks later Josie obtained a theatrical manager, who arranged for her to tour Europe as a lecturer. She gave astounding talks on her celebrated love life, earning a great deal of money, especially in Paris, where she became the rage for a while. She settled down there, living to the age of eighty and dying in a small Left Bank flat in 1931. There were pictures of *both* Stokes and Fisk above her deathbed.

Ned Stokes, murderer, emerged from Sing Sing as a minor Broadway celebrity. He spent his considerable fortune in one bad investment after another until he bought a piece of the illustrious Hoffman House, which he managed. The luxurious spa became the meeting place for every stellar notable in New York, and Stokes again grew wealthy, hobnobbing with Diamond Jim Brady, P. T. Barnum, Edwin Booth, and John "Bet a Million" Gates.

Josie's lethal lover never sent for her, even though he knew her whereabouts. Ned Stokes died unmarried in the comfort of his own mansion in 1901. On the table next to his bed was a four-chambered revolver, the very weapon he had used to kill Prince Erie.

# 1893

⟨⟨⟨⟩⟩⟩

## CARLYLE HARRIS
### KILLER OF
### A SECRET WIFE

Life was a free and easy thing for Carlyle W. Harris. He had been raised in a comfortable, luxurious home as an only child. His mother, Hope Ledyard, was a well-to-do author and lecturer and doted on his whims. His grandfather, Dr. Benjamin McCready, was a rich, well-established physician and teacher in New York who advanced Harris all the funds he required to enter medical school. Before he was twenty Harris envisioned a future bloated with fame as a doctor, wealth to serve his materialistic bent, and a fashionable marriage that would win the nodding approval of his rather snobbish family.

Harris also believed that attractive females existed to serve his sexual needs, and he played the lecherous rake at every opportunity, having one careless affair after another, discarding with regal disdain any girl who became annoying. He and some of his classmates formed something called the Neptune Club in Asbury Park, renting rooms where gambling, drinking, and the company of whores was the order of each evening. Police broke up the raucous club one night in 1890, arresting Harris as the person responsible for the illegal activities since he was the club's secretary-treasurer. The smirking youth was locked up in a cell overnight and indicted the following morning for "operating a blind pig and a poker joint." He was never prosecuted; his family paid a fine and Harris went back to his fleshpots without remorse.

In a short time the philandering medical student was back to his old haunts and ways, enticing young girls to apartments he rented by the week and where he held his assignations. On separate occasions two young women, Harris later stated, became indignant at being compromised and demanded he "do the right thing." He married them out-of-state, Harris said, and then abandoned them. No records of these unions, however, exist to verify Harris's boasts, made while he awaited electrocution. Such braggadocio was second nature to the vainglorious student. As Edmund Pearson later remarked in *Murder at Smutty Nose:* "[Harris] was at that age of cruelty, between eighteen and twenty-four, when many clever egoists blossom into their greatest activity."

Part of the student's activity was a beautiful but simple girl of seventeen named Helen Nielson Potts, whom he met at an afternoon social in a New Jersey hotel. Helen, from a middle-class family in Ocean Grove, was a student at the Comstock School for Girls at 32 East 40th Street in Manhattan, where she also boarded. Harris and Helen began to see each other regularly, with Mrs. Potts giving her sanction to the friendship.

The couple spent so much time with each other that Harris neglected his studies at the College of Physicians and Surgeons. Suddenly, Harris got the notion to marry Helen and whisked her off to City Hall, where an alderman of his acquaintance married them on February 8, 1890. They gave their names as Charles Harris and Helen Nielson, the latter being Helen's middle name. They kept the marriage a secret at Harris's insistence. He was afraid that his grandfather would learn of his "dirt common" bride and cut him out of the large family estate. Helen continued to attend school.

Mrs. Potts learned of the marriage and asked that Carlyle make the union public. The student nervously stalled her, fearing that Mrs. Potts would expose his secret marriage to his relatives. Months went by and Helen informed her fidgeting husband that she was pregnant. Harris performed an abortion on her. When she became pregnant again, Harris prevailed upon Helen's uncle, a doctor, to perform another abortion. Now Mrs. Potts demanded that Harris tell his family about his secret wife.

Trapped, Carlyle Harris began to scheme a way out of his dilemma. He privately reveled in his quick-thinking abilities and concluded that his own inventiveness would deliver him from the vexing Mrs. Potts and her daughter. His idea was, quite simply, to murder Helen Potts Harris in such a way that he would never be detected as the killer. He would let medicine be the slayer—specifically, morphine.

Helen agreeably and unwittingly aided her darkly brooding husband in his killing plan when she complained of headaches, asking that he prescribe something. Carlyle was happy to do so. On January 20, 1891, Harris presented Helen with a box of four capsules that bore the label of the reputable pharmacy of Ewen McIntyre & Son on Sixth Avenue and 56th Street. The capsules, ostensibly a harmless type of aspirin, each contained 4½ grains of quinine and 1/6 grain of morphine. Harris kept two more of these capsules on his person. Into one of the four capsules in the box, Harris had injected enough morphine to kill half a dozen secret wives.

Why Harris had kept two capsules was his little stroke of genius. He reasoned that if Helen took the poisoned pill first, second, or third, the remaining pill or pills would be examined and prove to be harmless. If the poisoned pill was the last of the four Helen consumed, he would quickly supply the last two capsules and any investigation would prove them harmless also, all six having been issued to him by the pharmacy. It was a foolproof plan, he was sure.

On the day Carlyle gave his wife the capsules, he left for Old Point Comfort, Virginia, on a vacation. He told Mrs. Potts that he was going away to think out how he would introduce his secret spouse to his family since "no other way can be found to satisfy your scruples."

Helen took the pills for her headaches—Carlyle later stated that these headaches stemmed from malaria, although his wife had never manifested any symptoms of that disease. She awoke at 10:30 P.M. on January 31, 1891, in her room at the Comstock School, calling in agony to a roommate, Miss Carson. "I feel numb," moaned Helen. "I feel as if I were choking."

She asked that Miss Carson rub her head, which the roommate did. After some minutes the stricken girl said: "I can't feel your hand on my forehead."

"Try to go to sleep," soothed the roommate.

"If I do," Helen replied in a muffled tone, "it will be the sleep of death." Then she said cryptically: "Do you suppose that that medicine Carl gave me could do me any harm?"

When Helen began to breathe with great difficulty and was unable to speak further, the principal, Lydia Day, was summoned. Miss Day found Helen paralyzed and unconscious; she called for the school physician, Dr. E. P. Fowler. The doctor arrived before midnight and carefully examined the girl. He noted that the pupils of the comatose Helen were no larger than pinheads. He found that Helen's skin was cold to the touch and had turned somewhat bluish.

The experienced Fowler knew the telltale signs of narcotic poisoning. He began to work feverishly over the prostrate girl, administering atropine and caffeine. He also summoned more help; Doctors H. Baner and B. L. Kerr responded quickly to his call. For hours the physicians worked to save Helen's life, laboring in relays. One of the doctors found a small pillbox, empty. On the top of the box were the words "C.W.H. Student. One before retiring."

The initials, Helen's classmates said, stood for Carlyle Harris; Helen had talked of her "Carl" often, but as her fiancé, not her husband. Harris, who had returned from his brief vacation by then, was sent for by Dr. Fowler. He appeared at the school at dawn, entering Helen's room where the doctors were still working on her.

Fowler held up the pillbox and said to Harris: "We have a frightful case here, and there must have been some very great mistake. What did those capsules have in them?"

The pills were harmless, Harris told the doctor, they were "for malaria, for headache, for insomnia, and the like." He detailed his prescription of quinine and the small amount of morphine in the capsules.

Fowler was puzzled. "One sixth of a grain of morphine or even one grain of morphine could not produce this condition. We have here one of the most profound cases of morphine poisoning that I have ever seen." The physician then reasoned that the druggist had made a mistake, a terrible error in which the proportions of the drug had been reversed. He sent Harris off to Ewen McIntyre & Son to check. The medical student was back shortly, stating: "The druggist has made no error, according to the records I've just seen." He was lying, of course. Harris had not gone to the pharmacy but merely strolled around the block slowly.

"Are you a physician licensed to practice?" Fowler asked Harris.

"I am a medical student but I signed the prescription," Carlyle admitted with a shrug. (Such practices by medical students were not uncommon in that regulation-free era.)

Suddenly Harris's face flushed scarlet as he stared at the physicians working on Helen. "Doctor," he asked Fowler, "do you think anybody can hold me responsible for this?"

"Right now, I'm not concerned with responsibility. I'm only concerned with reviving this patient."

For three hours Harris lounged about the bedroom, performing odd chores for the doctors but only when asked and in a plodding, seemingly uncaring manner. Sitting in a corner, Harris blurted: "Perhaps a tracheotomy operation would help."

Fowler gave him a withering glance and remarked: "That's ridiculous. It would kill her."

Exhausted and running sweat from their labors, the three doctors finally leaned back from Helen's immobile form, defeated. It was 11 A.M. "Well, it's no use," Dr. Fowler said, "she is gone."

"Is she dead, Doctor?" asked Harris, a nervous edge to his voice.

"Yes."

"My God, what will become of me?"

Fowler studied Harris's handsome face, thinking the student's statement slightly suspicious.

Harris then went on quickly to say that he had been "somewhat interested in the girl. I was thinking we might become engaged after she graduated this year."

"Go and say your goodbye to her," Dr. Fowler told Harris, and he and the other physicians moved away. Harris, Fowler took grim note, merely stood over Helen's body and stared down dumbly, showing not the slightest trace of emotion. As he followed the doctors into the hallway he passed Miss Day and said in a flat voice: "I'm sorry for that girl."

Some minutes later Harris stood briefly outside the school on the sidewalk with the three doctors. He turned to Fowler and repeated his nervous inquiry of hours earlier, saying: "Doctor, do you believe anyone can hold me responsible for this?"

Dr. Fowler only stared at him for a moment and then walked away.

Mrs. Potts appeared at the school that afternoon after being called from her New Jersey home. She knew all about Carlyle's prescription, and in her deep sorrow she could only wonder at the terrible blunder that had been made. She felt that the pharmacist had inserted too much morphine into the prescription, but the druggists at Ewen McIntyre & Son were not charged. Harris was rebuked for prescribing medicine without a license, then the matter was dropped "in consideration for his feelings [bereavement]."

Oddly, Mrs. Potts kept the knowledge of her daughter's secret marriage to Harris to herself. Further, she told the coroner, Louis Schultze, that Helen had suffered from heart disease since childhood. The coroner, wanting to avoid any expense for the city in an extended autopsy and investigation, closed the case with the words "unfortunate accident," concluding that either the druggist had erred, which was doubted, or that most probably Helen had taken all the pills Harris gave her at once, ignoring his instructions of "one before retiring."

The body of Helen Potts Harris was shipped to New Jersey and buried on February 7, 1891. She would have remained at rest in the earth, a victim of an "accident" instead of murder, had it not been for the inquiring mind of a zealous reporter for the New York *World,* which then specialized in sensational news.

Ike White, doing a follow-up story for the *World,* interviewed Dr. Fowler, who told him how strangely Harris had acted, perhaps suspiciously, at the time of Helen's death. White began to investigate the student's background and soon discovered his police run-ins as a member of the Neptune Club, his many affairs, and the record of his secret marriage to Helen. He next went to Mrs. Potts and got her to admit that she had lied about Helen's heart condition. The woman merely wanted to avoid any scandal about her daughter's secret marriage. "I was confused," said Mrs. Potts. "I thought it was better that way."

Almost immediately after White's story about Harris's background broke in the *World,* District Attorney Delancey Nicoll ordered that Helen's body be exhumed and an extensive autopsy performed. Dr. Allan McLane Hamilton performed the autopsy, and one of the leading toxicologists in the country, Dr. Rudolph Witthaus, analyzed the remains for poison. He found morphine in all the organs he examined, and no sooner was Dr. Witthaus's report filed than Carlyle Harris was arrested for murder.

The medical student was cooperative with arresting officers. He told them that he had heard that there was "some discrepancy" with the remains of Helen Potts and he was just that moment going to authorities when policemen appeared at his door. He was jailed while his mother hurried off to retain the best defense attorney in New York, William Travers Jerome, to champion her "angel boy." In the weeks of the long trial Mrs. Harris was to tell newsmen that her Carlyle was incapable of killing anyone, that he was the perfect young man, just as he had been the perfect child. "His mother," one report had it, "who lectured to Sunday schools and temperance societies, used to introduce the subject of 'Carl' as an example of what might be accomplished, by proper religious training, to develop a really good boy."

Prosecutor Francis L. Wellman, the deputy district attorney, was unflinching in his zeal to convict Harris. Carefully he built up a staggering case of circumstantial evidence. He eliminated the theory that Helen had committed suicide, proving her to have been a happy, outgoing person who optimistically looked forward to marrying "her Carl." He put the two druggists from Ewen McIntyre & Son on the witness stand. Both explained that it was impossible for them to have made a mistake. Wellman then recounted Harris's wild womanizing and his secret marriage to the victim. A friend of Harris's took the stand and quoted the accused as having said that he "would kill her [Helen] and himself rather than have the marriage made public."

Another damning witness was a girl Harris had been seeing almost up to the time of Helen's death. The girl testified that Harris wanted her to "marry an old man with money." Following this marriage, the witness insisted, it was Harris's plan to give her "a pill" to be administered to her spouse that would "put him away, leaving the money to us both."

Jerome fought valiantly for his client, but at every turn the prosecution eliminated each possible reason for Helen's death except for morphine poisoning. Moreover, when Harris produced one of the remaining pills he had ordered for Helen—he said he had lost the other—the capsule worked against him and for the druggist. The pill was examined and proved that the druggists had been precise in their work and that the morphine poisoning had to have been the doing of none other than the calculating medical student.

The defense countered weakly with some medical experts who suggested that Helen Potts Harris had died of an obscure kidney disease. This possibility was eliminated quickly by Wellman, who offered up the meticulous autopsy made on Helen's remains, one that showed no evidence of any such disease.

The trial, which had begun in January 1892, dragged on for weeks before Judge Frederick Smyth. It concluded with brilliant summations by both Wellman and Jerome. But it was too much for the defense attorney; as he was returning to his table in court after his final address, Jerome gave a great sigh—some said of disappointment in his hopeless case—and fell to the floor in a dead faint. Most attributed Jerome's collapse to exhaustion. The sight shocked all in court except Carlyle W. Harris, who merely glanced to the floor at the man who had tried to save his life, and then clucked his tongue and appeared annoyed, a reaction not lost on the jury members riveting their eyes upon him.

Within a short time after retiring, the jury returned with a conviction of murder in the first degree, a deliberation that was unexpected by most, who thought Harris would escape the web of circumstantial evidence that had been spun about him. He was sentenced to death.

Harris was calm and collected about the decision, maintaining his innocence as he was returned to jail to await execution. His lawyers appealed the case but the court of appeals sustained the verdict without one dissenting vote. In delivering the opinion of the higher court, Judge John C. Gray stated: "Taking them in any combination, is there anything to help out the presumption of the defendant's innocence, and do not every incident and fact, with greater or less significance for a chain of circumstantial evidence, which subjects and holds him to the consequences of an intentional destruction of the life of the woman, to rid himself of whom no other way seemed open? I can reach no other conclusion."

Neither could New York's Governor Roswell Pettibone Flower, who refused to commute Harris's death sentence. The medical student would die on schedule, as precise a one as that he had ordained for Helen Potts. While awaiting execution, the convicted killer steadfastly maintained his innocence. Algernon Blackwood, then a reporter who covered the Tombs, often saw Harris in his cell. He later recalled in *Episodes Before Thirty* "the face gazing at me through bars [which] would often haunt me for days. Carlyle Harris, calm, indifferent, cold as ice, I still see, as he peered past the iron in Murderers' Row, protesting his innocence with his steely blue eyes fixed on mine." Blackwood, who was later to become a popular novelist, would profile Harris as "Max Hensig" in *The Listener.*

Exhausting every legal move to save her son, Mrs. Harris visited her "angel boy" on May 8, 1892. Harris played the martyr for his mother and then walked calmly to the execution room, standing before the electric chair. "May I speak?" he asked the warden.

"Go ahead."

"I have no further motive for concealment," said Harris in a clear, strong voice, "and I desire to state that I am absolutely innocent of the crime for which I am to be executed." Without further comment the medical student sat down calmly in the electric chair and, after the straps were applied, waited patiently for the current.

Judging from the incredible ego of Carlyle Harris, his final lie was nothing more than a self-triumph in denying satisfaction to those who had convicted him. If nothing else he had convinced his mother with his last words that he was, indeed, a sacrificial lamb to the berserk rage of an unthinking society.

Mrs. Harris had had her son's casket prepared a week in advance of his execution, and as it was lowered into the grave, newsmen noticed a bronze plaque affixed to its top, which read:

CARLYLE W. HARRIS

MURDERED MAY 8, 1892

AGED 23 YRS, 7 MOS, 15 DAYS

"WE WOULD NOT IF WE HAD KNOWN"

Mrs. Harris was later to write a book entitled *The Judicial Murder of Carlyle Harris.* It was not a best seller.

# 1906

## HARRY K. THAW
## THE MILLIONAIRE MURDERER

Wholly unlike the simpleminded gold digger portrayed in *Ragtime,* showgirl Evelyn Florence Nesbit was a clever vixen who schemed her way into two fortunes and, through incredibly involved intrigues of her own subtle design, brought about one of America's most scandalous high society murders.

Evelyn Nesbit began with no fabulous destiny in mind, only the thought of survival plagued her and her mother. Mrs. Winifield Nesbit moved to New York from Pittsburgh in 1899, her son, Howard, and fifteen-year-old Evelyn in tow. Oddly enough, the man who was to make Evelyn's name a household word through his wild actions and murderous whims, Harry Thaw, had lived in the same town, Pittsburgh, where Evelyn had once lived—he in a towering, sprawling Victorian mansion, she in a slum.

A tenement slum was also the first home the beautiful Evelyn Nesbit occupied in New York. Her mother was all but penniless, a widow with no way to support herself, or so she later stated. She intended all along to put Evelyn's great beauty to work for her. "You're just like a picture," Winifield Nesbit constantly told the fifteen-year-old Evelyn.

Mrs. Nesbit dragged the girl from one theater to another, offering her up as a child prodigy to managers who said no before Evelyn ever opened her mouth to sing or recite lines. Though a beautiful child, Evelyn had little talent. Further, managers feared having their theaters closed by agents of the Gerry Society, who had successfully prevented underage children from appearing in productions. (Paradoxically, this was an era in which thousands of small children were worked close to death for twelve hours a day in sweatshops.)

Next the Nesbits made the rounds of producers' offices and met with talent agents, but to no avail. One producer, a man named Fisher, took one look at Evelyn and then said to Mrs. Nesbit before showing her the door: "Madam, I'm not running a baby farm."

The Nesbits went hungry, their clothes got threadbare. Still Mrs. Nesbit refused to give up. She had no choice, really. Bruce Sanders was to write in *Murder My Love* that "to move out of New York would have cost more than to continue living on their debts and some scraps of extended credit."

Finally, Mrs. Nesbit managed to have her attractive child pose for some calendar artists and magazine illustrators. The girl became so popular that she was earning all of $15 a week, a handsome income even for an adult in those free-lunch counter days. Evelyn's soft hazel eyes, luxuriant long dark-brown hair, her almost perfect and delicate features, along with a fast-maturing body of voluptuous proportions, soon caught the eyes of such top illustrators as Archie Gunn, James Montgomery Flagg, and Charles Dana Gibson, who made her a "Gibson Girl" in one of his magazine cover sketches.

Inside of two years Evelyn had landed a job as a member of the dancing sextet in *Floradora,* an ongoing variety show that Florenz Ziegfeld was later to emulate. By the time Evelyn joined the troupe, it was a tradition for a Floradora Girl to marry well, wedding either a nobleman or a millionaire, or both. Evelyn proved to be the most popular girl in the show. Critics raved about her remarkable beauty, and stage-door Johnnies fawned over her. Irvin S. Cobb thought she was "the most exquisitely lovely human being I ever looked at—the slim, quick grace of a fawn, a head that sat on her flawless throat as a lily on its stem, eyes that were the color of blue-brown pansies and the size of half dollars, a mouth made of rumpled rose petals."

She was called "the most beautiful woman in the magazine world," and one enamored editorialist likened her to the Venus de Milo, although Evelyn, even in her late teens, was much more amply endowed than that legendary statue. It took no time at all for Evelyn to realize that her beauty was her passport to riches, and after dating several prospective husbands, she fell madly in love with a strikingly handsome actor named John Barrymore, just then beginning his legendary career. Mrs. Nesbit quashed that romance promptly after discovering that the young Barrymore was rich only in family heritage. Through Edna Goodrich, another chorus girl in *Floradora,* Evelyn met the prestigious and gifted rakehell, architect Stanford White.

Evelyn was a shrewd girl by the time she met White. Her later court admission, acted out with embarrassed blushes, that detailed White's insidious deflowering of her virginity, was undoubtedly one of her best performances. The truth was that she literally stalked the red-haired, 250-pound voluptuary, much to his edification, of course. A millionaire many times over, the designer of New York's most impressive structures, including the Century Club, Madison Square Garden (the original, not the present-day edifice), and the magnificent Washington Square Arch, White was the very essence of success and fame. The fact that White was married and had a grown-up son at Harvard worried Evelyn and her mother not a bit. In fact, Mrs. Nesbit made a point of encouraging her daughter to spend time with the great womanizer, for a price, of course. White paid Evelyn $25 a week. He called it a subsidy to her budding theatrical career. Mrs. Nesbit lamely referred to the stipend as an "escort fee."

White, in addition to a palatial home and sprawling offices, maintained private lodgings in the Madison Square Garden building and several other luxuriously appointed domiciles the newspapers would later label "love dens." White's Winter Garden studio had a large room with mirrors everywhere and a red velvet swing in which his lovely Evelyn often sat. He would swing her toward the high skylight as her skirts billowed, allowing White's eye for flesh to get its fill.

On many occasions the architect would give Mrs. Nesbit hundreds of dollars to return to her Pennsylvania home while he remained to "chaperon" Evelyn. One such time White insisted that Evelyn have her portrait taken while wearing nothing more than a skimpy kimono that showed her inviting form as she curled up upon a bearskin. Later that night White took her to a society party, then back to his Madison Square Garden penthouse, where Evelyn drank so much champagne that she passed out.

"When I woke up all my clothes were pulled off me," she was to tell a horrified court, "and I started to scream. Mr. White got up and put on one of his kimonos which was on a chair. I moved up and pulled some covers over me, and there were mirrors all

*Architect Stanford White at the zenith of his spectacular career.*

around the bed. . . . Then I looked down and saw blotches of blood on the sheets. Then I screamed and screamed and screamed, and he came over and asked me to please keep quiet, and that I must not make so much noise. He said, 'It's all over, it's all over.' "

The loss of her virginity to the libertine White did not compel Evelyn to shun his company. Throughout 1902 she went everywhere with the architect, traveling to such out-of-town resorts as Saratoga and Atlantic City. She continued her theatrical career, appearing in *The Wild Rose* and other musicals. About this time another strange millionaire entered Evelyn Nesbit's life, Harry Kendall Thaw of Pittsburgh.

Where White was an insatiable satyr and skirt-chaser and spent most of his time ogling the long legs of chorus girls from his reserved footlight tables, Thaw sought not to appreciate but to punish. A raving sadist, the Pittsburgh tycoon loved nothing better than to whip a young woman raw. He was known in New York's Tenderloin as "Mad Harry." Most of the women he ravaged were willing victims; he paid handsomely to exercise his perversions.

Thaw had been strange since childhood, unbalanced, his father thought, full of quirks and tantrums. He was somnambulistic, "excessively nervous," according to a private tutor, and "was subject to outbursts of uncurbed animal passion. . . . [He] had St. Vitus Dance and used baby language as late as seven."

At sixteen Harry entered Wooster College, but his weird conduct unnerved and frightened his teachers. One, Charles Koehler, remembered how Thaw would "walk in a zigzag manner . . . his capacity for concentration was weak." In his father's mansion Harry had fits of anger where he would yank the tablecloth from the dining room table and kick food into the fireplace. He attended Harvard briefly but was expelled for "immoral practices." One report had it that he had sexually attacked several other male students.

During his twenties Thaw became the complete wastrel, lavishing fortunes on show girls and prostitutes alike, once giving a dinner for more than a hundred "actresses" of dubious pursuits at $400 a plate. He loved attention, and his escapades were self-designed to snare the limelight; he drove a cab wildly down Broadway once, smashing it through a plate-glass window. On another occasion he rode a horse up the stairs of the Union

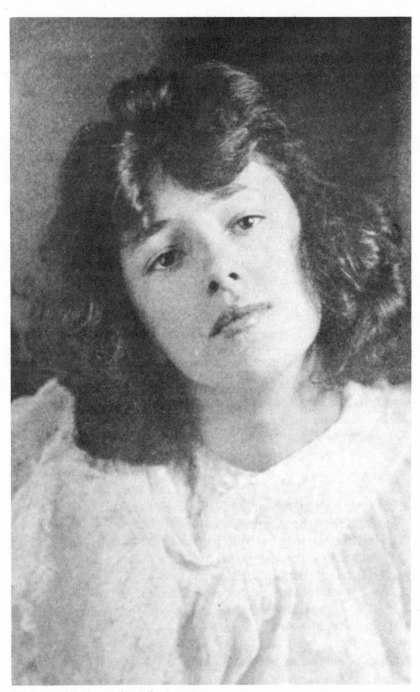

*The beautiful Evelyn Nesbit, White's mistress.*

League Club. When restrained by an officer, he sneered: "I am Harry Thaw of Pittsburgh." He lighted his cigarettes with ten-dollar bills. His pasty, puffy, and generally featureless face had two glaring wide eyes and full, sensuous lips that often parted into a maniacal-looking grin, one that made his entire person seem the embodiment of madness.

Thaw was the heir to a $40 million coke fortune but his father, William Thaw, fearful of what his unhinged son might do with such money, left him only a $2,500-a-year allowance for life when he died. But Mary Copley Thaw, William's second wife and Harry's mother, saw to it that her favorite child had all the spending money he required, giving him $80,000 a year as a supplement to his allowance, an enormous fortune at that time.

When not wrecking restaurants, carriages, and expensive shops, Thaw spent his energy in abusing women. "The Pittsburgh Queer," as Harry was named by Broadway show girls, was at first a charming escort, but his mood and manner would change abruptly. One of his many female companions before meeting Evelyn was Ethel Thomas. Miss Thomas dated Thaw in July 1902 until she fell afoul of the beast lurking in Mad Harry's boyish body. She brought suit against the millionaire, claiming he had attacked her.

"At first he lavished much affection on me," said Miss Thomas in her complaint.

> He took me on automobile rides, to theaters and other places of amusement, and bought flowers and jewelry for me. . . . One day, however, I met him by appointment, and while we were walking towards his apartment at the Bedford, 304 Fifth Avenue, he stopped at a store and bought a dog whip. I asked him what that was for, and he replied laughingly, "That's for you, dear." I thought he was joking, but no sooner were we in his apartment and the door was locked than his entire demeanor changed. A wild expression came into his eyes, and he seized me and with his whip beat me until my clothes hung in tatters.

Miss Thomas was given a handsome settlement by Thaw's lawyers and sent on her way. Mad Harry decided that he would concentrate his energies on women from the lower class, those who would not be so willing to drag him into court lest their own scarlet pasts be exposed. Thaw went to the large brothel run by Madame Susan Merrill, renting several rooms from her, using the alias of "Professor Reid."

Young girls not too particular of their company were advertised for by Thaw; he promised in print to make them stars of the theater. Once Harry had enticed the girls to his rooms in the bordello, he stripped them, tied them to furniture, and applied his whips. Mrs. Merrill estimated later for authorities that Thaw had paid 233 girls—most between the ages of fifteen and seventeen —approximately $40,000 so he could indulge his peculiar perversion. The bordello madame said she had had enough one night when the piercing shrieks of "Professor Reid's" victims brought her on the run. "I could hear the screams coming from his apartment and . . . I could stand it no longer. I rushed into his rooms. He had tied a girl to the bed, naked, and was whipping her. She was covered with welts. . . . I found others writhing from punishment. Thaw's eyes protruded and he looked mad."

In 1903, just after having met Evelyn Nesbit, Thaw, still playing the gallant gentleman and hiding his real nature, promised to show the famous chorus girl the grand sights of Europe, saying that he would marry her if she would sail with him. She did, much to her regret. Upon her return Evelyn went to Stanford White, telling him that Harry had performed unspeakable acts upon her person, chiefly tying her to the bed while in their stateroom and whipping her until she bled. He had whipped her throughout Europe, she said, and even whipped her while they were scaling a mountain in Switzerland, then ravished her on a snowy cliff.

White, who by then expressed genuine love for his wandering show girl, advised Evelyn to swear out an affidavit concerning Mad Harry's transgressions. She did, showing the document to Thaw and demanding he make a huge settlement or face charges in court. Harry paid her more than she demanded, so much that the pernicious Evelyn went back with him instead of returning to White, as she had promised the architect she would do. The show girl went on a second European trip with the mad playboy, and again he repeatedly attacked her. She returned alone to America and took a leading part in a new musical, *The Girl From Dixie*, vowing never to see Harry K. Thaw again.

The Pittsburgh millionaire was relentless. He appeared in Evelyn's theater dressing room on Christmas Eve, 1903, carrying flowers and diamonds and, weeping his apologies, begging the girl to marry him. He promised her half his fortune, when he inherited his father's millions. Evelyn asked White for advice, and the architect told her to forget Mad Harry. There is some evidence to prove that Evelyn was actually attempting to make White jealous enough to leave his wife and marry her. When he did not, one story relates, she flew back to Thaw, accepted his ring, and married him in a lavish ceremony.

Evelyn Nesbit Thaw continued to see Stanford White long after her marriage to Mad Harry. She was seen dozens of times to enter White's lodgings, staying for long periods of time. Although she never spoke of these clandestine meetings, it was thought that Evelyn was still trying to extricate herself from Thaw's clutches, but would not leave his millions unless she was assured that the millions of Stanford White would come to her. When White continued to rebuff her, she retaliated by manipulating Thaw's berserk rage in White's direction.

At her husband's later trial Evelyn insisted that Thaw was insanely jealous of her former relationship with White, that he exploded at the mere mention of the architect's name and demanded that Evelyn describe in detail every move she had made with the fifty-two-year-old roué. He also insisted that Evelyn refer to White not by his name but as either "The Bastard" or "The Beast" and that she point out White to Thaw whenever she spotted the architect in public. At such times Evelyn was required to say, for propriety's sake, "I have just seen the B." or "The B. has just come into the restaurant." It is equally possible, given Evelyn's nonstop Arabian-nights descriptions to her husband of her sex life with White, that she created those stories to goad Thaw into action, seeking retribution against a man who was by then escorting new show girls through his glittering night-life world.

Thaw's rage was at fever pitch by June 25, 1906. He had intercepted a basket of roses and a note from White to his wife and thought the architect was attempting to steal Evelyn away. He did not know that Evelyn had visited White's studio earlier that day when the architect was not in, and that White had sent the flowers as a way of expressing his regrets for not having seen her.

That night the Thaws were dining out. Harry watched Evelyn wriggle into a white satin Directoire gown, newly purchased for that evening and designed to accent Evelyn's voluptuous form, a gown that one reporter later described as "squeezing out breasts and emphasizing the curving line of hips and buttocks."

Thaw paced the elegant (and the most expensive) suite in the Hotel Lorraine. He said nothing to Evelyn about having intercepted White's flowers and note. He went into his dressing room and took out a pistol from a leather box, slipping it into his inside suitcoat pocket, then put on a heavy overcoat, even though it was quite warm outside. Such out-of-season apparel, however, would draw little attention to Mad Harry, who was known for his eccentric behavior.

While Evelyn finished dressing, Thaw walked over to Sherry's restaurant to have a few drinks. Evelyn and two friends, Thomas McCaleb and Truston Beale, joined him in about an hour and the foursome went on to dinner at Cafe Martin.

Thaw appeared calm after having three more drinks and remained sober, according to witnesses. He was careful to count out his change from the hundred-dollar bill he gave the waiter for dinner. Just then Stanford White walked by Evelyn's table without acknowledging the Thaw party. Evelyn spotted him, then whispered in Harry's ear: "There goes the B." Thaw nodded.

At nine o'clock the Thaws and their guests arrived at the Winter Garden Theater, which was on the open rooftop of the building. They were to view the opening of a new musical, a frothy comedy entitled *Mamzelle Champagne*. The musical, most of the first-nighters agreed, had little to offer in originality. Harry Short sang one of the lead numbers, "I Could Love a Thousand Girls," and Viola de Costa, the star of the show, failed to surprise the audience as she emerged from the top of a cardboard bottle of Pommery Sec.

Those sitting next to the Thaw party later stated that when Stanford White entered in midshow alone, and made his way to the stageside table reserved for him, Harry Thaw became visibly nervous, so agitated that he squirmed in his seat, grimacing in the direction of White. During the performance Thaw got up nervously and wandered through the audience, stopping briefly to exchange a few words with acquaintances. As he was doing so a chorus of leggy girls wearing brief costumes and pink tights danced to the footlights, brandishing foils and singing a number called "I Challenge You to a Duel."

Albert Payson Terhune, a correspondent for the *Evening World* who had been assigned to review the musical, noted with curiosity how Thaw began to pace back and forth in front of White's table, the architect taking no notice of him. "Every time he passed the table," Terhune later recalled in *To the Best of My Memory,* Mad Harry "would pause to glower furiously down at the ostentatiously oblivious oldster. I knew both men by sight. I knew, as did many another observer, the reason for that dramatic glower."

The chorus went on wiggling their behinds and then turned to point their foils in mock threat to the audience, braying:

> I challenge you,
> I challenge you,
> To a duel, to a d-u-e-l!

It later seemed to some that the words of the song provided a bizarre cue for Harry Thaw to release his pent-up rage against the man he hated most on earth. Suddenly, Thaw stood granite still, then pulled out his pistol just as White, eyes popping, mouth gaping, began to rise. (The architect was once quoted as having said about Thaw: "That dude won't attack me with a pistol. He hasn't nerve enough. All he is trying to do is scandalize me.")

Thaw aimed the weapon directly at White's head, holding it only a foot from the florid face of the startled architect. He fired "three times in slow and rhythmic succession," according to Terhune. White's face was blown away, along with the top of his head. In a grotesque reflex, White's body jerked upward almost to a standing position for a moment, then collapsed to the table, which tipped and spilled him onto the floor.

Everyone present froze in horror. The chorus girls stared bug-eyed, motionless. The conductor of the orchestra held his baton ramrod stiff in the air. During the awful silence Harry Thaw calmly raised his pistol over his head, breaking the cylinder and releasing the unused bullet, which rattled to the floor. A woman at the back of the theater finally managed a piercing scream that triggered pandemonium. The once respectful, sedate audience turned into a shoving, wild-eyed mob, stampeding toward the exits in panic. The stage manager raced out front, waving the chorus girls offstage. He leaped upon a table and shouted to the orchestra: "Go on playing, damn you! Bring down the curtain!"

A doctor forced his way through the crowd to bend over the fallen form of Stanford White. White's features were a blackened, shredded mass of distorted flesh, a huge pool of dark blood spreading before them. He was obviously dead. The physician looked up to see Thaw still standing over the body, a twisted smile on his pasty face.

One of the uniformed theater guards came forward and carefully took the pistol out of Thaw's hands. "He deserved it," Thaw said to the guard. "I can prove it. He ruined my wife." (Some reports later stated that Thaw said "life.") With that, Mad Harry turned on his heel and briskly walked to the elevator lobby, where he met Evelyn. Reportedly she had not seen the shooting but had left the boring musical with her companions, thinking the absent Harry had done the same. Upon hearing the shots, she had turned back to see Thaw standing over White and then watched her husband as he walked toward her through the panicking crowd.

Gerald Langford in *The Murder of Stanford White* quoted Evelyn as saying to Thaw at the moment: "Good God, Harry! What have you done?" But Terhune, an eyewitness to the killing, claimed that Evelyn blurted: "Oh, Harry, I never thought you'd do it that way!" The implication in the latter quote is, of course, that Mrs. Harry Thaw had full knowledge that her husband intended to murder Stanford White but was merely unsure of the method Mad Harry would choose.

Thaw was incredibly nonchalant, telling his wife: "It's all right, dearie. I've probably saved your life." He embraced her and kissed her passionately. In his almost incoherent autobiography, *The Traitor,* published twenty years after the shooting, Thaw rationalized the murder as a chivalric act designed to save the honor of future females. At the time Thaw recalled how, immediately after killing White, his chief concern was being attacked by White's friends. "A man, a dozen men might have maimed me," Thaw wrote, "cut off the light, allowed him to escape and rape more American girls as he had; too many, too many, as he had ruined Evelyn." This, then, would be the hard line of his shabby defense. He had struck for home and family, for the virtue of American womanhood.

A policeman summoned by the management arrested Thaw

quietly at the elevators. The killer did not resist and went meekly along with the officer to street level. Once outside, Harry Thaw pulled a hundred-dollar bill from his pocket, saying: "Here's a bill, officer. Get Carnegie on the telephone and tell him I'm in trouble." (Thaw's sister, Margaret, was married to George Lauder Carnegie, the man to whom he had undoubtedly referred; another sister, Alice, had also married well, becoming the Countess of Yarmouth.)

The two walked casually through the Tenderloin for several blocks, finally turning in at a precinct station. Thaw told a desk sergeant that he was "John Smith, student," and that his address was "18 Lafayette Street, Philadelphia." He was nevertheless quickly identified as Harry Kendall Thaw and was arrested on a charge of murder.

"Why did you do this?" the desk sergeant asked Thaw.

"I can't say," Mad Harry shrugged, and then lit a cigarette, smoking it casually as he was led to a cell. He asked for water and a cigar. A guard gave him both. Thaw puffed rapidly on the stogie, filling his cell with smoke and saying: "That's a fine cigar, officer. I've always heard that policemen smoked good cigars. Now I know it."

The news of the killing electrified the country. Nothing like it had ever been seen in America, at least in public. A millionaire had murdered another millionaire over a show girl. The day laborer and the female sweatshop worker marveled at the thought of these superior beings, the rich, indulging in the low and pedestrian act of murder. The crime itself affected national thought, which had for decades held America's rich as sacrosanct and beyond reproach. With three shots Harry K. Thaw had tumbled the image of his own class to the gutter. Moreover, when the sordid backgrounds of Thaw, White, and Evelyn Nesbit were made public, the reaction of the average citizen went beyond shock. There was a mass disillusionment with the wealthy class.

The rich had long been held up as the epitome of righteousness, idealistic grace, and high morality, or at least that was the image the rich had successfully projected through the days of John D. Rockefeller, Andrew Carnegie, and J. P. Morgan. But the Thaw-White murder scandal changed all that with blinding proof that the rich were a self-indulgent lot of practicing perverts, corrupted to the core by money, reinforcing long-held suspicions that could

*Harry Thaw, the day after he killed Stanford White.*

not earlier be uttered, out of Edwardian propriety, by the struggling masses of the lower economic depths.

Now an avalanche of scorn and ridicule was heaped upon this
aloof breed of superhumans, and oddly, the victim received most
of the pent-up rancor of the press and public alike. White was
pilloried by newspapers charging him with being the worst kind
of wanton libertine, a rake, a lecher, an immoral beast who
dressed in a tuxedo and traded on his architectural fame to seduce
naive virgins, to rape innocent-eyed daughters, sisters, and wives,
before laughingly and viciously discarding his victims.

In the weeks that followed his execution by Thaw, only a few
of White's friends thought to speak against the grain of public
opinion whipped up by the press. The distinguished journalist
Richard Harding Davis did publicly champion White, but his
voice was a lone cry in a din of mass condemnation. Writing in

*Collier's,* Davis stormed against the "yellow press" that described White "as a satyr. To answer this by saying that he was a great architect is not to answer it all . . . what is more important is that he was a most kind-hearted, most considerate, gentle and manly man, who could no more have done the things attributed to him than he could have roasted a baby on a spit."

Not so, thundered back New York's *American,* stating that White's so-called studio in the Winter Garden Tower was nothing more than a love den, and that "he needed the studio for the purposes that have been so abundantly revealed in the disclosures following his tragic end." A *Tribune* reporter interviewed a cabman who had driven the millionaire architect to many of his assignations, or so he claimed. The *Tribune* quoted the cabman as saying of White: "I knew that fellow would be killed sooner or later, but I thought it would be a father who would do it, not a husband."

Meanwhile, the remains of the much-lambasted Stanford White were buried at St. James churchyard on Long Island. More than two hundred mourners, mostly the cream of New York society, attended. Mrs. Stanford White was present to contradict rumors that she and her famous husband were separated at the time of his murder.

The attack on the dead man continued unabated. New York's pompous self-appointed censor, Anthony Comstock, stepped forward to tell eager newshounds that he had been investigating the scandalous and secret love life of White for almost two years at the request of none other than that protector of American womanhood, Harry K. Thaw. Stated Comstock:

> [Thaw] seemed to think White was a monster who ought to be put out of the community. . . . On the strength of his information and from that received in anonymous letters which corroborated Thaw's statements, I endeavored to get the truth about White. . . .
>
> I looked up several of the girls whom Thaw said White had ruined. Several of them were underage and of respectable families. I interviewed some of these girls and obtained statements from them. But when it came to preparing a case against White, many difficulties confronted me. Family influences were instrumental in checking some of the girls

from consenting to appear in court against White. Some of the girls were spirited away. The result was that, although I was morally convinced of White's guilt, I had no substantial evidence to offer in a legal action . . . I was therefore compelled to drop the idea of having White indicted. My ill success in not bringing White to trial seemed to depress Thaw. As to whether I believe this depression caused Thaw to murder White, I do not care to say. Never, however, in all my investigations did I hear anything against Mrs. Thaw and, everything I heard about Mr. Thaw himself was highly commendable to him.

Francis P. Garvin, assistant district attorney, had had enough. He exploded at reporters shortly after White's burial: "It is ridiculously easy to besmirch the character of a dead man who cannot reply or institute a suit for libel!" The campaign to smear White's name, as Garvin and others knew, had been instituted by none other than Mrs. Mary Thaw, Harry's obsessively devoted mother, who, upon hearing of her son's arrest for the murder, screamed: "I am prepared to pay a million dollars to save his life!"

Evelyn Nesbit Thaw, the centerpiece in the murder scandal, seemed enthralled at the idea of the attention she would receive during the long trial that loomed before Mad Harry. She, too, busied herself in dirtying the history of her onetime lover-mentor White, then played the staunchly devoted spouse, telling Francis Garvin at Thaw's hearing before a grand jury: "You may send me to jail but I will not testify against my husband. I will never do anything to harm Harry, and you may as well understand that now."

Harry, while awaiting trial, was far from harm in the Tombs. He complained about drafts and was given the most comfortable cell the jail had to offer. His private butler brought fresh linen for his specially installed bed, and a clean suit of clothes each day. His meals were catered from the best restaurants in town, particularly selected from the rich menu of Delmonico's, Thaw's favorite dining spot. He was given wine and champagne while guards looked the other way, tucking into their pockets ten-dollar bills that Harry had thrust upon them.

Evelyn and Mrs. Thaw were suddenly seen everywhere together, presenting the noble portrait of family unity, even though

Harry's mother had disliked the Nesbit girl from the beginning, thinking her a music-hall lowlife. She gave Evelyn large amounts of cash, buying her allegiance to her mad son, promising her a great fortune following the trial, when her boy would be safe from the executioner, provided Evelyn "did her part" in freeing Harry.

According to Evelyn's rambling memoirs, *The Story of My Life,* Mrs. Thaw kept a tight rein on Evelyn, escorting her everywhere, watching her every move, attempting to control each word dripping from her sensuous mouth. When Mrs. Thaw caught Evelyn chatting with a police officer at the beginning of her son's trial, she chastised her daughter-in-law: "Evelyn, how can you speak with these people? Don't you realize the social position you hold?"

"What kind of story do you imagine it would make," replied Evelyn, "if I turned up my nose at men whose social position is, at the moment, infinitely superior to Harry's?"

Thaw's trial began on January 27, 1907, before New York Supreme Court Justice James Fitzgerald in New York's Criminal Courts Building. Thaw had repeatedly admitted his guilt, telling District Attorney William Travers Jerome before the trial: "I saw him [White] sitting there, big, fat and healthy, and I thought of Evelyn, poor delicate little thing, all trembling and nervous." The army of lawyers hired by Mrs. Thaw collectively pled their client not guilty. (It was not necessary under New York law to plead their client guilty "by reason of insanity.") Of the five distinguished attorneys representing Thaw, the most illustrious was Delphin Delmas, an old-fashioned political orator (who had once made the nominating speech for William Randolph Hearst for the presidency) who was known as "The Little Napoleon of the West Coast Bar." The San Francisco legal giant had been given an initial fee of $50,000 by Mrs. Thaw.

Mary Thaw went on acting the protective mother as the long and tedious procedure of selecting jurors ensued. "If it takes the fortune of my entire family to clear him," she said, "every dollar we possess will be used to help Harry regain his freedom."

The famous legal lion Jerome was enraged at this statement and the special treatment Thaw received in jail. "With all his millions," roared Jerome, "Thaw is a fiend! No matter how rich a man is he cannot get away with murder—not in New York County!"

Once the trial was under way, Jerome severely cross-examined Evelyn after she had testified on Harry's behalf, detailing his devotion to her, his high-mindedness, his dedication to the purity of the American home and the moral well-being of women in general. Evelyn told the D.A. the sordid story of her romance with White, but the details were thought to be so shocking that she whispered these in Jerome's cocked ear. (Reading the sensation-packed news of the trial, President Theodore Roosevelt called the testimony "filth" and advised the newspapers to discontinue covering the trial, advice that was ignored.)

One newspaper that had not sided with Thaw in the killing was *The New York Times*. During the trial it pointed out that Mrs. Evelyn Nesbit Thaw was not the innocent young thing despoiled by a monster, as Harry's lawyers tried to portray her to the jury, having her wear sailor blouses and Buster Brown collars in court. In addition to Barrymore, White, and Thaw, Evelyn had had intimate relations with several New York men of stellar reputation, including George Lederer, producer of *The Wild Rose*, whose wife, Adele, won a divorce based on allegations that Lederer had spent intimate hours with Miss Nesbit in New York hotels from October 1, 1902 to March 25, 1903. The *Times* also pointed out that James A. Garland, a wealthy businessman, had taken Evelyn on yachting trips in 1901 and the show girl had been named as a corespondent in Mrs. Garland's subsequent divorce.

District Attorney Jerome was relentless in his condemnation of Thaw, providing expert medical witnesses to state that the Pittsburgh millionaire was certainly sane when he killed White. Delmas and company provided an equal number of medical men to state otherwise. The wily Delmas then advanced the unheard-of mental disorder he called "Dementia Americana," a neurosis that had afflicted his client at the time he killed White. Delmas explained that "Dementia Americana" was a neurosis exclusive to American males who believed that every man's wife was sacred, and that the killing of anyone violating this credo was a standard compunction on the part of those suffering the neurosis. It was, of course, grand gobbledygook, but the jury bought it—or, at least, five members did to the point where the jury could not reach a decision.

A second trial a year later proved much more successful for Delmas's imaginative "Dementia Americana." The jury found

Thaw "not guilty, on the grounds of his insanity, at the time of the commission of the act."

Thaw, protesting that he was sane, was nevertheless sentenced immediately; he was to be confined in the New York State Asylum for the Criminally Insane at Matteawan. Three hours later he was put aboard a train heading for the lunatic asylum. Evelyn saw him off at the station. "I will not go there," yelled Thaw to his lawyers as guards restrained him. "I don't want to go to Matteawan."

One of his lawyers, Daniel O'Reilly, asked sardonically: "Where did you expect to be sent? Rector's or Martin's [restaurants]?"

From the moment Thaw arrived at the asylum, Mrs. Thaw's battery of attorneys began ambitious attempts to get him freed, summoning new medical experts to declare him sane. Mrs. Thaw had spent almost $1 million in the defense of her son and would go on spending tens of thousands of dollars to pry him loose from the asylum. Seven years later, in 1913, Thaw escaped from Matteawan, bribing guards to let him loose. He fled to Canada, where he was captured by none other than William Travers Jerome and New York deputies.

Evelyn Nesbit Thaw was not idle during Harry's confinement. She went on vaudeville tours almost immediately after Thaw had been sent to Matteawan, earning a good deal of money as she sang and danced. Patrons payed staggering admission prices to gape at the girl who had caused the great society scandal, rather than to appreciate her limited talents.

While Thaw was incarcerated, Evelyn gave birth to a child, naming Thaw its father. Thaw raged that such a claim was impossible; he was a prisoner in a lunatic asylum. Evelyn smiled prettily to newsmen and insisted that she had bribed Matteawan guards many times so that she could spend nights with Harry. The child was never recognized by the Thaw family.

In 1915, Mrs. Thaw's indefatigable efforts to free her son were rewarded. He was adjudged sane and released. Once free, Thaw disowned and divorced Evelyn, and within a year was again in trouble, charged with horsewhipping a teen-ager named Frederick A. Gump, Jr. He settled a large sum on the Gump family, but further transgressions forced authorities to return Thaw to Matteawan. He was released again in 1922.

*Reunion of Mad Harry and Evelyn in Atlantic City in 1926, twenty years after the murder of White.*

Thaw went on whipping and beating women and boys, paying off claims whenever threatened with arrest or suit. In 1926 he was in Chicago, where his ex-wife was singing in a small cabaret under the name of Mrs. Harry K. Thaw, her most popular number being "I'm a Broad-minded Broad from Broadway." Evelyn had recently tried to kill herself, gulping down a bottle of Lysol, but recovered. Thaw visited her in the hospital and some weeks later saw her again in Atlantic City, where she was working in a nightclub. He came in one night with three women, drank himself into a stupor, then went into a rage when given the bill, kicking over the table during Evelyn's act and stomping out. Later, Thaw appeared to reconcile with his onetime spouse, escorting her and her fifteen-year-old son, Russell, about Atlantic City.

The meeting brought about a news conference in which Evelyn said: "Well, it's all fixed. Harry and I are going to live together in the suburbs here as soon as I can sell my own house. I think most people, especially women, have pity on me deep down in their hearts. They know what a hard time I have had." She went on to say that Harry would not only return to her but take care of "our son, Russell."

Thaw, however, was only indulging his whims, as usual. He

went off to his fleshpots, abandoning Evelyn and her son. Evelyn drifted about the nightclub circuit after that, a forlorn creature. Said Stanley Walker of her in *The Night Club Era:* ". . . whatever glamour Miss Nesbit once had was gone. She was a tired, nervous little woman trying to make a go of a tearoom just off Broadway in the West Fifties. She passed most of the Prohibition era in cabarets in Atlantic City."

Thaw, wearied by his incessant perversions and a life-style that would have killed most men by the age of forty, suffered a massive heart attack in 1947, dying in Miami on February 21, at seventy-six. His obituary commanded little space in the press.

Evelyn Nesbit went through another marriage and an on-and-off divorce with one Jack Clifford (real name Virgil James Montagni) before retiring to southern California to paint seascapes. She was interviewed in her old age and asked about the famous red velvet swing in Stanford White's studio of those long, gray decades earlier. "I never heard of it," she responded. She was shown her testimony at the trial of Harry Thaw. "I guess my memory is no longer all it should be," she said with a laugh.

Shortly before her death on January 17, 1967, in Santa Monica, California, the eighty-two-year-old Evelyn admitted the reason for the scandalous murder of Stanford White by a lunatic she wielded as an avenging angel. She remembered rummaging through White's desk in his studio once when the architect was out. "I came across a little book in which he had recorded the birthday of every pretty girl he knew. I became violently jealous. . . . Like a silly child I wanted to make him jealous of me."

# 1907

## DORA FELDMAN MCDONALD
### MURDER FOR LOVE

Michael Cassius McDonald, or "Big Mike," as he was universally known in Chicago, where he ran every crooked enterprise from 1877 to 1907, was a man plagued with women troubles. Big Mike's word on the streets and in government offices was law, but in his own home he was ignored, bullied, and deceived by three different wives who made his life miserable and lonely.

To the outside world Big Mike represented anything but the gullible cuckold. (Edna Ferber would later use McDonald as a role model for her larger-than-life gambler in *Showboat*.) Born only a few miles from Chicago in 1839, McDonald began his miscreant career by fleecing midwestern railroad passengers in small con games, graduating to the Mississippi riverboats and rigged card games for high stakes. During the Civil War, Big Mike found bounty jumping so profitable that he organized his own ring of phony army-enlistees who were paid $500 for joining the Union ranks, deserting, then returning to Chicago and enlisting again and again to collect the enlistment bonuses. Following the war McDonald invested his illegal nest egg in a Chicago gambling den on Dearborn Street, going into partnership with one Dan Oaks. He prospered quickly and opened up another gambling hall, then a third. By the early 1870s, McDonald was one of the wealthiest men in Chicago. He backed Harvey D. Colvin, a fellow gambler, in his bid for the post of mayor in 1873, and when Colvin won, Big Mike virtually owned the city government.

"He never held office," wrote historian Richard Little of McDonald, "but he ruled the city with an iron hand. He named the men who were to be candidates for election, he elected them, and after they were in office they were merely his puppets. He ran saloons and gambling houses, protected bunko steerers and confidence men and brace games of all kinds without let or hindrance."

In 1875, McDonald opened a colossal gambling emporium on Clark Street called The Store, which was the gambling center of the Midwest and brought even more gold to Big Mike's burgeoning coffers. He cut a handsome figure in the finest tailor-made suits money could buy. His carriages, along with the many mansions he owned at one time or another, rivaled anything owned by the McCormicks, the Fields, and the Potter Palmers.

Big Mike hated policemen. He had been harassed by cops throughout his mercurial career. Once a social worker approached him, asking him to donate two dollars for the burial of a cop. "Good," snorted McDonald, "here's ten dollars. Bury five of 'em!" Eventually the gambler bought the entire police force, paying the policeman on the beat more than his weekly salary to look the other way as McDonald's army of con men fleeced thousands of visitors, especially in the red-light district, Chicago's notorious First Ward, which was the center of vice and gambling from the 1880s to 1912 when evangelists forced authorities to close up the area.

Big Mike McDonald became omnipotent, and "for years he was in and out of Chicago's enterprise as well as its scandals," wrote Lloyd Lewis and Henry Justin Smith in *Chicago: The History of Its Reputation*. His riches stemmed not only from his enormous gambling empire but from vast tracts of real estate he owned in the heart of Chicago's downtown, from profits generated by his daily newspaper, *The Chicago Globe*, and from his secret partnership with the corrupt traction king, Charles T. Yerkes. In the latter capacity he helped to build the famous elevated train (the "El") that would eventually encircle the Loop.

"As an executive of vice and crime," Finis Farr wrote in *Chicago*, "McDonald ranked with Jonathan Wild of eighteenth-century London. Both men held that there must be an unvarying tariff on all sales of stolen goods, proceeds of gambling and returns from prostitutes and blackmailers." The con men, thieves, and courtesans on McDonald's payroll—and that included all who wanted to work in those capacities, since Big Mike monopolized all crime in Chicago—were allowed to keep 40 percent of their profits. He took the rest, giving 20 percent to the police and keeping the balance in a private fund that was used to buy city officials, judges, and juries.

It was McDonald who told Chicago's mayor, Carter Harrison, to go ahead with the World's Columbian Exposition of 1893. The fair served as a hustler's paradise in that tens of thousands of innocent visitors were conned, bilked, and compromised in McDonald's gambling and vice dens, bringing the crime sachem even more millions.

Though Big Mike maintained a low profile during his reign, he occasionally appeared in public, attending city social functions. At these times newsmen flocked to him, grateful for any quote he might bestow upon them. Reporters credit McDonald with the statements "Never give a sucker an even break" and "There's a sucker born every minute," albeit these oft-repeated quips have been attributed at one time or another to P. T. Barnum, Texas Guinan, W. C. Fields, and Wilson Mizner.

It is fair to state that McDonald proved to be a classic "sucker" himself when it came to women. His marital relationships were hardly brimming with bliss. Most claimed that Big Mike's obsessive work in developing his gambling empire was to blame, that he had left his wives alone at home too much and they, in turn, spent their idle hours pursuing other men. Little is known of McDonald's first wife, except that on more than one occasion the crime czar caught her dallying with some of the sharpers who worked for him. She died of unknown causes shortly before the Chicago Fire of 1871. Mary Noonan became Big Mike's second wife sometime in the early 1870s, and she proved to be a firebrand.

A cop accidentally stumbled into Mary's kitchen during a rare raid on Big Mike's (Clark Street) gambling joint—the McDonalds then lived above the gaming emporium—and Mrs. McDonald promptly shot him through the head. She had little to fear, however, since Big Mike's political clout was by then enormous. According to Herbert Asbury in *Sucker's Progress*, "McDonald's influence was sufficient to bring about her arraignment before a judge who held that she was justified in killing the invader of her home." The mother of his two children, Big Mike reasoned, would be less inclined to display her volatile temper in a house far removed from his gambling operations. He built a giant mansion for Mary on Ashland Avenue, one that equaled any domicile

Left: *Big Mike McDonald, Chicago's crime czar in 1907.* Right: *Mary Noonan, Big Mike's second wife, unfaithful but much loved.*

constructed by Chicago's superrich, replete with exquisite furnishings and an army of servants.

The home life was not for Mary Noonan McDonald. In 1886, Mary somehow managed to meet a shifty character named Billy Arlington, a minstrel singer with the Emerson troupe. One evening Big Mike returned home from his underworld labors to discover that Mary had run off with Arlington. Through his network of spies he soon learned that Mary and her lover were living in San Francisco. McDonald raced west, breaking into Mary's suite at the Palace Hotel, finding her with a terrified Billy Arlington.

Pulling forth a pistol, McDonald intended to kill Arlington on the spot. As the singer cringed and wailed for mercy in a corner, Mary dashed forward, standing in the way, pleading with great tears: "Mike, for God's sake, don't shoot! Take me back! For the love of God!"

Mary's invocation of the Almighty touched the gambler's heart; he was a devoutly practicing Catholic despite his criminal pursuits. He solemnly put away his weapon, took Mary into his arms, and returned with her to Chicago. As a way of guaranteeing her fidelity, McDonald ordered built in his own home an expensive chapel where Mary could pray each day for salvation. Further, Big Mike asked young Father Joseph Moysant to visit Mary twice a week to take her considerable confessions.

The assistant rector of the Catholic Church of Notre Dame did visit the errant Mary, and once too often; Mrs. McDonald ran away again in 1889, this time with Father Moysant, traveling to Paris. Mary lived in France with the defrocked priest for six years before Father Moysant had second thoughts and left her, to enter a monastery.

Repentant, Mary returned to Chicago, sending word to Big Mike that she was back. McDonald's reply was that he never wanted to see her again, let alone hear the mention of her name. She was a woman alone, Big Mike's emissary informed Mary, McDonald having gotten legally divorced in her absence. Moreover, the millionaire crime czar refused to allow Mary to see her two children, because of "her bad influence." This from a man who controlled all organized crime in Chicago. The softhearted gambler, however, did provide for his ex-wife by giving her enough money to buy a small boardinghouse on the near West Side of the city. She did not see her children until they were adults. And she never saw Big Mike again until the day of his death. "I don't want to be bothered again by that woman," McDonald had instructed his henchmen. At the time, McDonald had enough to worry about in pleasing his third wife, Dora Feldman McDonald.

Big Mike had met Dora in 1898. He had gone to a burlesque house and was smitten instantly when seeing the buxom blond Dora dance before the footlights. He escorted her about town for several weeks before she told him that she was married to a ballplayer named Sam Barclay. "But Sam's not much of a husband," Dora hastily added. "He's never home and sees a lot of other girls."

Dora's marriage didn't bother McDonald one bit. He was determined to have "the 18-kilowatt blonde," as the press called Dora. Big Mike ordered some of his thugs to pick up Sam Barclay and deliver him to his office. Within hours a puzzled Barclay was standing before McDonald's massive desk. Big Mike opened a desk drawer and then tossed a bundle of money in Barclay's direction.

Barclay stared down at the cash. "What's this?"

"Money, what's it look like?"

"What's it for?"

"It's for a divorce, yours and Dora's."

"How much is here?" Barclay fingered the wad of bills gently, thoughtfully.

"Thirty thousand dollars. Want to count it?"

The ballplayer smiled widely and slipped the bundle in his pocket. "Your word is good with me, Big Mike. And the divorce is okay, too."

The gambler's devotion to Dora was so deep that he agreed to give up Catholicism and convert to the Jewish faith. At first McDonald felt that he had finally found the perfect woman. Dora doted on his every whim, was slavish in his presence, and called him "daddy," which pleased him no end. Dora's posture no doubt reflected the fact that she was not only thirty-five years younger than Big Mike but had been one of his children's playmates.

The king of the gamblers proved his undying love for Dora by building her a towering limestone mansion on Drexel Boulevard, one twice as resplendent as that bought for Mary Noonan. He showered Dora with jewels and designer clothes. He opened a bank account for her from which she could draw enormous sums. Strangely enough, Dora spent little of the money Big Mike gave her; she stayed at home most of the time, refusing to indulge in the Chicago night life she had once reveled in as a burlesque queen. Her time away from McDonald was fully occupied, however, in the pursuit of a secret pleasure—the company of a sixteen-year-old boy, Webster Guerin, who lived down the street.

Guerin was spotted by Dora while he performed some summer chores in the neighborhood. She was immediately attracted to the tall, blond-haired, green-eyed youth and inveigled him into a relationship by, first, having Guerin perform useless odd jobs. Soon the youth was seeing Dora at every opportunity. When Big Mike left for his office in the morning, Guerin would sneak in the back door of the Drexel Boulevard mansion, climbing the back stairs to Dora's bedroom suite.

This tempestuous affair continued for years. At one point Guerin's mother, learning of the relationship, went to Dora, begging Mrs. McDonald to release her son from "an unhealthy union

Left: *Dora Feldman McDonald around the time she murdered Webster Guerin.* Right:
*Webster Guerin, the object of Dora McDonald's obsession and wrath.*

that keeps him in perpetual sin." Dora exploded; she grabbed a
poker and, brandishing the implement wildly, chased Mrs.
Guerin from her home as the McDonald servants stared in shock.

Guerin graduated from high school, then college, continuing to
see Dora secretly. He told his paramour that he wanted to open
up offices as a commercial artist but it would take money. Dora
volunteered a sum that was refused. It was not enough, Guerin
told her. He wanted thousands of dollars and subtly hinted that
if he did not receive what he needed, Big Mike might learn of
their sexual liaison. It was outright blackmail, but Dora gave
Guerin several thousand dollars without argument.

Opening sumptuous offices—Suite 703 of the Omaha Building
at La Salle and Van Buren streets—Guerin announced himself to
the world as a commercial artist ready for business. In return for
Dora's backing, Guerin continued to see her. Her sexual demands
were ceaseless, but Webster was up to performing; his own sex
drive must have been extraordinary. At the time, he not only was
pleasuring Mrs. McDonald but was carrying on a torrid romance
with another woman, one his own age, whom he intended to
marry.

Dora learned of Guerin's secret love from private detectives she had hired to spy on her boy-lover. She confronted the budding artist, and Guerin promptly promised to see the girl no more. The next day he ran away with his secret girl friend. Mrs. McDonald was in hot pursuit, her private detectives, like bloodhounds, running Guerin and the girl to the ground. Dora coaxed, cajoled, and threatened Guerin into returning to Chicago, which he did, promising the older woman that he would remain faithful to her.

Then a report reached Dora that Guerin had once more taken up with the girl friend. Livid, Dora went to Guerin's offices on the morning of February 21, 1907. She brushed past a secretary and closed the door to Guerin's private office. The secretary heard the couple arguing loudly. Then came the sound of two distinct shots.

Workmen from the building, summoned by the secretary, broke down Guerin's office door, which Dora had locked. They found Mrs. McDonald kneeling over the bloody form of Webster Guerin, who was quite dead, a bullet through the neck, another through the heart. There was a smoking pistol in Dora's hand. As she was led away to police headquarters Mrs. Dora McDonald said through heaving sobs: "I loved him so much."

To the police Dora readily admitted her guilt. "I killed him," she said. "I entered his office and told him I knew he was cheating on me. I took out the pistol and aimed it at him. I told him to sit in the chair in the middle of the floor. He took the seat and grinned at me. He said: 'You don't shoot. You don't know how to use that pistol.' I said: 'I know where your heart is and I will not miss by an inch.' Then he laughed at me and I fired."

When Big Mike heard of the killing, he sat at his desk in stunned silence for hours. Leaving nothing out, his minions described the sordid affair his wife and Guerin had been carrying on. With each detail McDonald's face grew more ashen. He had come to know Guerin in the last year or so, thinking that the reason for the youth's presence in the McDonald house was to court his own daughter, not to sleep with his beloved Dora. Big Mike was spared nothing. Detectives who had interrogated Dora bluntly told him that his wife had sneered at the mention of his name, telling them how much "the old man disgusts me!"

Feeling every minute of his sixty-six years, Big Mike sagged in his office chair, asking that he be taken home. Arriving at the

Drexel Boulevard mansion, Mike took to bed and stayed there for weeks, wanting to die.

To his bedside came a weeping Dora Feldman McDonald, released on a $50,000 bond that, incredibly, had been provided by Big Mike. She prayed fervently to be forgiven. McDonald turned his face to the wall, refusing to talk to her. Another visitor then arrived in Big Mike's bedchamber: Mary Noonan, who crawled on her hands and knees, wailing also for forgiveness. She knelt next to Dora, and these two faithless spouses offered up their prayers in unison. Mike McDonald could only moan in agony at the bizarre scene.

Weeks later the gambling czar was taken to a hospital. There he told newsmen that he was returning to the Catholic faith and that "Mary Noonan is my one and only wife under God." He still had not wholly forgiven his second wife, however, and refused to leave her one penny in his will. Stranger still, the woman who had most recently deceived him, Dora Feldman McDonald, received, at his expressed edict, one third of his millions, the rest going to his two children. McDonald also put aside a cash defense fund of $40,000 for Dora and assigned his lawyers, Asa Trude and James Hilton Lewis, to "get the little girl off any way you can."

Dora did "get off," early in 1908, a jury deliberating for six and a half hours before deciding that the third Mrs. McDonald "had been driven momentarily insane" by the scheming Webster Guerin. Many clamored that Big Mike's attorneys had bribed the jury and that the only reason the killer was set free was because Big Mike's influence controlled the courts as well as the rest of Chicago.

By that time, Dora's fate meant nothing to McDonald. He had died in a hospital bed on August 9, 1907, eight months before Dora was set free to spend his fortune (she would die ten years later in poverty). McDonald's last words, his deathbed cronies later insisted, summed up his bitter disillusionment with a disastrous love life. Groaned Big Mike at the end: "So I'm a sucker after all!"

# 1909

## DR. BENNETT CLARKE HYDE

### THE LETHAL INHERITANCE

No medical murderer in this century has approached his lethal goals with such zeal and ambition as did the dedicated Dr. Bennett Clarke Hyde. To inherit the vast Swope family fortune through his wife, Frances, Hyde decided in 1909 that he would kill off all of those who stood before his wife in line of inheritance. It was an incredible plan, one that only a supreme egotist would undertake, a scheme horribly identical to the films *The List of Adrian Messenger* and *Kind Hearts and Coronets,* except that Hyde was real and his victims suffered authentic and agonizing deaths at his scrubbed and delicate hands.

By age forty Hyde already had a thriving medical practice and had married the niece of Thomas Swope, one of the founders of Kansas City. His wife's share of the Swope fortune would, upon the old man's death, exceed several hundred thousand dollars but the greedy physician was not content with such "paltry amounts" when millions were to be had. As medical adviser to the Swope family, the vainglorious Dr. Hyde was convinced that he was in a position to vastly improve his fortune.

The Swope house in Kansas City was busy with life. Living with the elderly Swope was his sister-in-law, her adult children, and Swope's longtime friend and adviser, James Hunton, who had been appointed administrator of Swope's will. Upon his death, the old man had decreed, his large estate would be divided among several nephews and nieces. The will also stated that should those in line for the inheritance die, their portion of the estate would be divided by the survivors.

Dr. Hyde realized that the will would soon be put into effect in that Thomas Swope was then eighty-two years old and in poor

50

health. Yet, to make sure that he was in a position to control matters, Hyde decided that he would replace Hunton as administrator of the will.

Hunton fell ill in September 1909, and Hyde, as the family physician, quite naturally attended the old man. Swope's friend was suffering from apoplexy, diagnosed Hyde, but he knew just how to treat him. The physician applied the ancient technique of bloodletting, long since abandoned as a practical remedy. Hunton simply bled to death.

Old man Swope was devastated by the passing of his friend. He himself became ill with grief and came under the care of the ever-attentive Dr. Hyde. The nurse on duty became suspicious of the physician, however, when Hyde took her aside, telling her: "Now that Hunton is dead, Mr. Swope will require a new administrator for his estate. I think it would be a good idea if you suggested to Mr. Swope that I take over those duties."

"I'll do nothing of the kind," replied the nurse. "It's not my place."

Hyde shrugged and went on with his murder plan. He appeared in Swope's room shortly with a box of pink pills, giving one to the old man. Within twenty minutes Swope went into violent convulsions. His flesh became blue and cold to the touch. He cried out to the nurse: "I wish I had not taken that pill!" Hyde ordered the nurse to leave the room, telling her to boil some water. She returned some minutes later to see Dr. Hyde pulling a sheet over the old man's face.

"He's gone, poor soul," said the physician.

"What? Already?" The nurse checked to see if Swope was dead. He was, but she remained perplexed.

"At that age they can go quickly," said Dr. Hyde.

"How?"

"Apoplexy, same as Hunton," explained the doctor. Hyde signed the death certificate hours later, citing "apoplexy" as the cause of Thomas Swope's death.

Swope's millions were shortly allocated to relatives by the family lawyer. Hyde's wife, Frances, as one of Swope's nieces, received more than $250,000, the balance of the estate being spread throughout the family. Though he was endowed with a substantial sum, greed consumed Hyde. His success in the murders of Hunton and Swope undoubtedly bolstered his belief that

*Dr. Bennett Clarke Hyde, the murdering medico of Kansas City.*

he could go on killing without being detected. He thereby resolved to eliminate all the heirs who stood in line before his wife.

Following Swope's death by mere weeks, four of the five nephews and nieces involved in the inheritance, other than Mrs. Hyde, were taken violently ill. The family physician diagnosed typhoid. They were put to bed, the solicitous Hyde in constant attendance. When another niece arrived from Europe, Dr. Hyde met her at the train station. He somehow induced her to drink a glass of water, which she said tasted bitter. By the time she arrived at the ancestral mansion, this niece, too, was stricken with typhoid.

Christman Swope, one of the nephews, died toward the end of November 1909. The other stricken family members hung precariously close to death. As Christman Swope had died in horrible convulsions similar to those that had seized his uncle, the family nurse, suspicious of Hyde all along, went to Mrs. Frances Hyde to resign, telling her: "People are being murdered in this house."

Mrs. Hyde—who was wholly devoted to her husband and would remain so in the years to come when Hyde was accused of mass murder—unwittingly brought attention to her husband by informing the family lawyer of the nurse's strange behavior and statement. The lawyer insisted that another doctor be brought in to attend the Swope family.

The lawyer and the newly appointed physician suspected Hyde of causing the family deaths and infecting other family members with typhoid after a bacteriologist they brought in stated that no trace of typhoid germs was present in the family's water supply. Further, no one in the neighborhood of the Swope home was affected by the dreaded disease. "Typhoid has been introduced from the outside," reported the specialist.

Hyde was watched closely and, during his absence from family patients, the Swopes remarkably improved. The doctor suddenly developed the habit of taking long walks at night. On one of these evening strolls Hyde was seen by a Swope relative following him to take something out of his pocket and stamp it into a snowbank. The relative retrieved the item, a broken capsule with the instantly recognizable odor of potassium cyanide.

The suspicious family members went to authorities, who in turn ordered that the bodies of Hunton and Thomas Swope be exhumed. Several out-of-state experts, including Dr. Victor Vaughan, who had worked on several notorious murder cases in New York, were brought in to examine the remains of Hunton and Swope. Large amounts of strychnine were found in both bodies.

On February 9, 1910, Dr. Bennett Clarke Hyde was charged by a coroner's jury with the murders of Hunton and Swope. He was jailed but released on $100,000 bail. His subsequent trial was a sensation in the press, and fascination with the mass-murder plot gripped the nation. The case against Hyde was powerful and convincing. A druggist came forward to testify that Hyde had purchased cyanide from his pharmacy, using the excuse that he wanted to kill wild dogs that had been "howling near my house and causing me no end of sleepless nights."

Hyde had thought himself a master murderer, the prosecution pointed out, in that he dosed both Hunton and Swope with two poisons that would counteract each other to conceal symptoms, strychnine agitating the nerves of the heart and producing convulsions, cyanide slowing down the heart and congealing the blood. (However, the scheming physician, although he thought he had created the foolproof murder technique, completely ignored the glaring fact that he alone possessed the obvious motive for the murders.)

Dr. L. Stewart, a surprise witness for the prosecution, gave damning testimony against Hyde. The physician stated that Hyde had come to him in late October 1909, telling him that he intended to take up the study of bacteriology and that he required typhoid germs for that purpose. Stewart supplied Dr. Hyde with the cultures but had second thoughts and went to Hyde's home to retrieve the germs. Hyde told Stewart that the cultures were gone, that he had dropped the slides and had to dispose of them.

Hyde's month-long trial ended in a sixty-hour deliberation by the jury, which returned a guilty verdict of first-degree murder. Dr. Bennett Clarke Hyde was sentenced to life imprisonment. As he was leaving the courtroom en route to prison, Dr. Hyde turned to newsmen and said smugly: "This case is not closed. My dear wife Frances will not forsake me. She knows that this is a plot by certain members of the Swope family to get rid of me. They have hated me from the start—thought me an interloper. Yes, Frances will know what to do."

Mrs. Frances Hyde did know what to do, and she had the wherewithal to do it. She hired the most expensive lawyers her fortune could command. A legal barrage against the courts commenced, the likes of which had never been seen in American jurisprudence. Every conceivable motion was filed on behalf of Hyde. Mrs. Hyde spent lavishly in a publicity campaign that painted her husband a martyr to family jealousy; she had completely broken with the Swopes by then, swearing her undying allegiance to her murdering spouse.

In 1911, Mrs. Hyde's army of lawyers persuaded the Supreme Court of Kansas to order a new trial on the grounds of legal errors in Dr. Hyde's first trial. Dr. Hyde was then, in an unprecedented move, allowed to go free on bail. Due to the illness of a juror (some claimed the jury member was bribed to feign sickness), the second trial was declared a mistrial. At Hyde's third trial the jury could not agree, and again charges of bribery were registered but to no avail.

Not until January 1917 was the murdering medico again put on trial, fully seven years after his systematic and wholesale slayings. Of course, the many trials of Hyde were part of the plan to free him. The fourth trial ended abruptly when defense lawyers simply pointed out a rule of law. Their client had already faced trial three times without result and, according to existing statutes, could not be tried again. Hyde was by no means acquitted, responded the court, but the state, under the law, was compelled to set him free.

Hyde returned to his wife but not to his medical practice. He went into premature retirement, living comfortably for more than a decade on his wife's riches. No record remains to show if Frances Hyde ever came to believe that her husband had gotten away with murder. She did, however, toward the end of her husband's life, take up a separate residence from the nerveless Dr. Bennett Clarke Hyde. She decided to move out one day when the soft-spoken physician recommended some medicine for an upset stomach.

# 1910

## STANLEY KETCHEL
### MURDER OF
### A CHAMPION

He was called the "Michigan Assassin," and lived up to that awesome sobriquet with a wild will in the ring. A fierce, almost insane boxer, Stanley Ketchel knew nothing really of life except the arena that gave him fame, fortune, and violent death at an early age. He was as tough outside the ring as he was inside, a brawling, drinking, womanizing slugger. He remains, seventy-some years after his murder, a legend in hobo and cowboy songs and undoubtedly one of the greatest, if not *the* greatest, middleweight champion who ever slipped on gloves.

Born on September 14, 1886, and raised in near poverty in Michigan by Polish-German parents, Stanislaus Kaicel ran away from his Grand Rapids home when he was sixteen, intending to go west to become a cowboy, which had been his abiding boyhood dream. He worked his way west by slaving for penny wages as a railroad and mining-camp laborer, shoveling iron ore twelve hours a day. As he wandered through mining towns and hobo camps, his short temper brought about endless fights, and it was at such times that Ketchel realized that he carried knockout punches in both fists. While the bruising blond-haired Ketchel worked on and off as a bouncer in the roughest western saloons, much as Jack Dempsey did after him, he toughened his knuckles on grown men half again his size and never lost a barroom brawl. Telling his fellow "knights of the road" that he would some day make his great fortune with his fists, Ketchel kept on the move, riding the rails or hiking the horizonless western roads in search of destiny.

The search ended in the fall of 1903 and fame began, but only as a sliver of light that fell briefly but surely on a future boxing champion of the world. At the time, Ketchel drifted into the untamed town of Butte, Montana, going immediately to the huge

"Big Casino" saloon, a place he and every other boy of the road knew to be a sanctuary. Entering the cavernous saloon, the penniless, hungry Ketchel walked to the rear of the noisy hall where hobos, young and old, were sprawled on the floor close to an enormous potbellied stove, sleeping fitfully, scheming their next meals. He squatted on the bare floor, eyeing the throngs of miners and painted prostitutes jammed to the bar. A man in a bowler hat, his loud striped shirt emblazoned with red garters on the sleeves, sat at a scuffed upright piano, banging away, a one-man ragtime orchestra.

More than any other, a feature of the Big Casino that captivated Ketchel was a conspicuous regulation prize ring in the center of the hall. The ring was the answer to the empty stomachs of the derelicts huddled on the floor. Those with enough strength would battle here each night for a five-dollar purse, winner take all. (But the winners invariably bought their opponents a fifty-cent dinner, steak and trimmings, in the name of sport.) This night the stakes were ten times higher, fifty dollars to any fool impetuous enough to attempt beating the local champion, the much-feared Kid Tracey. Everyone in the Northwest knew of Tracey and his slashing fists; no one had been able to beat him, let alone stand up to his furious onslaughts. Promoters and gamblers sauntered about the hall booming out their challenge—who present had the nerve to face Tracey in four rounds of boxing?

Ketchel got up and elbowed his way to the bar. He leaned forward and said loudly to the bartender: "Who's the man to see about going with Tracey in the ring?"

"You're lookin' at him, sonny."

Ten minutes later Ketchel was climbing into the ring wearing borrowed trunks. Tracey looked over his challenger with contempt: a scrawny specimen not really worth the energy. The promoters shrugged and told the champion that he was the only opponent willing to face him. "There'll only be one round," murmured Tracey.

The champion was correct. The moment the two sluggers came together, Ketchel unleashed a furious assault that surprised Tracey, who fought back with equal savagery. It was the fiercest ring battle ever fought in Butte, Montana, and within two minutes the teen-age Ketchel stood grimly over the fallen form of Kid Tracey, winning by a knockout.

The referee ran to the victor. "What's your name, boy?"

"Stanislaus Kaicel," replied the youth, still staring down at the motionless Tracey.

"That's no good," grunted the referee as he held the boy's arm in the air and shouted above the din: "The winner—Kid Ketchel!" The youth's name would be Americanized further to Stanley Ketchel, but he did not mind; his victory purse, and those giant fortunes to come from his peerless performances in the ring, brought food, comfort, and eventual luxury into an otherwise empty existence.

Ketchel not only became the reigning champion in Butte but traveled through Montana to whip soundly any and all comers in Helena, Miles City, and Great Falls. He fought for three years, taking on all comers and not only beating them but punishing them; Ketchel had a whirlwind attack that was equaled by few others in the history of boxing. He belonged to that dedicated or fanatical few (including Ad Wolgast, Battling Nelson, Jack Dempsey, and Harry Greb) who refused ever to quit in the ring. Ketchel, who liked to be called Steve by his friends, would fight sixty-three fights in his riotous professional career as a welterweight and, later, a middleweight. He would win fifty-nine battles, forty-nine victories by knockouts. And, as his opponents knew, Ketchel was almost lethal in the ring, fighting like a man unbalanced, a slugger gone berserk. His conduct in the ring would later be termed "bestial" and "maniacal." Some called Stanley Ketchel "insane." But it was a fine madness.

What Ketchel's opponents did not know was that the slugger "psyched" himself up before each fight to the point where he genuinely hated his adversary. Writer-gambler-entrepreneur Wilson Mizner, who managed Ketchel for several years, explained Ketchel's technique. According to Mizner, Ketchel had a violent attachment to his mother, Julia Oblinski Kaicel. Although this sturdy woman had raised five powerful sons, her relationship with Stanley was the strongest; whenever troubles overpowered him, he raced home to take strength from her, actually kneeling before her and placing his head in her lap to weep like a small child.

"Now when Ketchel stepped into a ring," Mizner recalled, "he would start imagining that his opponent had insulted his mother. By the time the idea was set in his mind, and sometimes it took

*The battling middleweight champion Stanley Ketchel.*

a round or two, he would be fighting with insane fury."

The great slugger lost only four fights, two early in his career to Maurice Thompson (whom he later devastated). The third fight Ketchel lost was to Billy Papke, a fight that should have been awarded to Ketchel, who was fouled. The fourth fight Ketchel lost was to Jack Johnson, but here Ketchel was fighting out of his class, a middleweight against a heavyweight, and yet he still managed to floor the powerful Johnson. But fighting or living out of his class became Ketchel's obsession.

When he began to earn large amounts of money, Ketchel bought expensive clothes, purchasing dozens of candy-striped silk shirts and straw skimmers. He trained on wine and women, having an insatiable appetite for both. He was often brash, sometimes brutal, with his sweethearts and friends, which earned him the reputation of being a "hard man," an image Ring Lardner distilled into his biting portrait of Ketchel, "Champion." (Ketchel was nowhere near the vicious brute Lardner sketched, except in the ring.)

The good-looking Ketchel at the height of his career was literally surrounded by attractive women, from high-society admirers to sultry slatterns of the saloon world he so loved. He caroused and slept with them all. The fighter would go for some weeks drinking and whoring and yet, in the words of Dr. Irwin Ross, who knew Ketchel, he would "step into a ring looking like a college kid fresh from the training table, and ruin the opposition." Minutes after leaving the ring where his opponent still sprawled unconscious, Ketchel would demand liquor and female companionship. Yet Wilson Mizner felt he could do no harm; he was "a laugh, a pair of shoulders and a heart."

In 1908, Ketchel met with Jack Sullivan, knocking out his opponent in twenty rounds and clinching the middleweight championship. Ketchel celebrated by drinking himself into a stupor and taking a harem of courtesans to bed, a marathon debauch of several weeks. As champion he wasted no time and took on Billy Papke in Milwaukee on June 4, 1908, whipping the challenger decisively in ten rounds. Papke was given a rematch, but there was little hope of ever beating the Michigan Assassin, who was considered by all to be invincible. The pair met for the second time on September 7, 1908, in Los Angeles. Papke was prepared with a surprise move, a blatant foul that under today's rulings would have instantly forfeited the fight to Ketchel.

The two men came together in the first round, and at ring center Ketchel extended both gloved hands for the traditional shake. Papke, knowing the champion's guard was down, ignored the shake and blasted a left hook that rocked Ketchel, following this blow with a straight right that landed between the champ's eyes, sending him to the canvas. Ketchel barely managed to stagger to his feet after a nine count, and when he did stand up, he had been almost blinded by the foul punches. Papke knocked him down at will during the first round, but he hung on. In the next few rounds Ketchel's eyes were swollen shut so that, between rounds, his lids had to be lanced and drained. He staggered through twelve rounds, trying to pry his eyelids open with his thumbs, groping for and swinging wildly for Papke, until the referee stopped the fight. Ketchel, cursing Papke, was led like a blind man from the ring.

Revenge came six weeks later in San Francisco when the two middleweights met again. A solemn Ketchel approached Papke; the new champion was grinning wide. They stood staring at each other as the referee droned his instructions. Ketchel suddenly waved the referee away and gave Papke a speech that chilled his blood, a speech Papke could recite almost verbatim until the day of his death. (Papke, oddly enough, would, like Ketchel, meet a violent death, killing his wife and himself in 1936.)

Ketchel said to Papke: "You copped a sneak on me that time in Los Angeles, didn't you, Bill? Well, you're going to have the reputation of being middleweight champion a shorter time than any man in history. I'm going to murder you in the next half hour. You'll never put up a good fight again as long as you live. You needed twelve rounds to drop a blind man! I'm going to leave your eyes open so you can see the referee count you out in the eleventh. I'll show you in the first I can stop you, but I'll wait until the eleventh."

Ketchel's first-round onslaught was amazing; he knocked Papke down almost from the first bell, and he continued to knock him down every round (fourteen knockdowns in all), timing his knockdowns so that Papke was often saved by the bell, making sure Papke would linger another round, fighting in spurts, cannonading Papke and then drawing back. By the eleventh round Papke came into the ring a wreck, shaking his head in fear, his eyes darting everywhere as if looking for an avenue of escape. His nose was broken, as were several ribs; his face was bruised, cut, and running blood.

"It's the eleventh," shouted Ketchel as he rushed forward and, with whirlwind blows, smashed Papke to the canvas. Papke toppled face first, unconscious. Stanley Ketchel left the ring, once more with the middleweight crown.

That title, Stanley had boasted as a teen-ager, would be his some day and he would never lose it. He had also bragged that he would be not only middleweight champion but heavyweight champion. By 1909 no one in his division dared face Ketchel. He had beaten all comers and was considered to be the greatest fighter in the history of the sport. There was only one person left to vanquish, the heavyweight champion Jack Johnson.

Johnson was the first of the black heavyweight champions, and he had proved himself a great fighter, a defensive boxer with incredible strength. Physically he was a giant, and out of the arena he lived a life as wild and reckless as Ketchel's, drinking and wenching with savage abandonment. Johnson's penchant for white women caused him to be hated by white fight fans, and Ketchel was looked upon as "The Great White Hope" who would vanquish the interloping black fighter, despite the great physical disparity between them. The behemoth Johnson towered above Ketchel and had an enormous reach over the smaller man; he outweighed the 160-pound middleweight by at least 40 pounds.

The bout, which was to take place on October 16, 1909, in Coloma, California, and had been nagged into existence by Ketchel, was one of the most talked about events in the history of boxing. Many knew Ketchel's record and felt him to be the better fighter.

Moreover, Johnson incurred the wrath of most fans by taking the Ketchel fight lightly. He laughed about "the little man" who dared to step out and up from his middleweight division. He was casual, even cavalier, about the Michigan Assassin. This attitude, of course, reflected Johnson's fighting style; the Galveston fighter would talk in a carefree manner with friends at ringside during his fights. When an opponent landed a telling blow on Johnson,

*Ketchel (left) with Jack Johnson, after weighing-in ceremonies before their incredible battle. (UPI)*

he would laugh and then grin widely to show pridefully his full set of gold teeth.

The black fighter refused to train for the Ketchel fight, such was his contempt, he said, for having to battle a middleweight. This widely publicized attitude, of course, drove up the betting odds, the so-called smart money going to Ketchel. It was later speculated that Sam Fitzpatrick, Johnson's manager, had instructed his fighter to play the nonchalant in order to boost the odds so that he and Johnson would reap huge winnings on their own bets, winnings that would handily exceed the purse.

Johnson promised his manager he would go into serious training but it amounted to little—anemic calisthenics and some rope
skipping—and when reporters were around, he performed some
casual bag punching. It was a token gesture for eight days before
the fight.

The enormous throng assembled for the outdoor fight cheered
itself hoarse when Ketchel entered the ring. Johnson was greeted
with boos and hisses, which he ignored by smiling widely. It was
a popular belief then and after that this heavyweight-champion-
ship fight was fixed—Johnson had agreed to carry the smaller
Ketchel to make a good showing, and Ketchel had promised to
put up a good fight but allow Johnson to win. For eleven rounds
the "tank job" appeared to be a reality. Ketchel, however, if such
a story had any credibility, did not fight according to the plan but
was constantly on the attack, making the huge Johnson
backpedal. He threw powerhouse blows, only one in a dozen
landing on Johnson, who was known as a defensive boxer.
Ketchel's reach simply wasn't long enough; Johnson kept picking
off his punches.

Said Damon Runyon of Jack Johnson's boxing style: "He had
a knack of catching punches as an outfielder catches a baseball.
He reached out and grabbed most of them before they got well
started." He also countered Ketchel's onslaughts with smashes to
the kidneys, uppercuts to the body, and left jabs to the face, a
determined face that was soon cut, swollen, and running blood.
The Michigan Assassin ignored the wounds and snorted and
snarled as he continued to charge the giant, flailing away.

The flat-footed Johnson struck out four times with vicious
blows that sent Ketchel to the canvas, but the youth always got
up. "His pluck and staying power were amazing," wrote sportswriter Harvey McClellan, who was ringside. "Johnson fought on
the retreat and continued to smile." Such was the fury of
Ketchel's attacks that the middleweight toppled to the canvas by
the sheer force of his own missed swings, twice almost going
through the ropes.

Ketchel's blows began to land. In the tenth he hit the heavyweight champion so hard with a left hook to the body that
Johnson dropped his toothy smile and winced in pain, angered at
the damage to the point where he rushed Ketchel and literally
picked him up and carried him to ring center. He began to batter

the smaller man, but Ketchel stood up, trading blows.

At the opening of the eleventh round Ketchel ran to Johnson and, discarding all defensive fighting, began to throw power-house punches with both hands, most of these blows finding their mark. Johnson was stunned and appeared confused. Ketchel pounded him viciously, then landed a tremendous right cross high to Johnson's jaw that sent him reeling about the ring, and before the round was finished a huge lump had appeared on Johnson's jaw. "A few inches lower and it might have put an end to Johnson's career," wrote McClellan.

Johnson finally recovered and charged Ketchel, landing a terrific hook that almost floored Ketchel, but the Michigan Assassin kept fighting until the gong. "That man ain't human," Johnson reportedly grunted to his seconds during the break.

With the sound of the bell opening the twelfth round, Stanley Ketchel thought to do or die and ran pell-mell to Johnson's corner, throwing everything he had at the heavyweight. Backed into his own corner, Johnson desperately clinched with Ketchel, then broke free and began to back away. Ketchel sprang after him, throwing a fierce right to the head. Johnson ducked, but the blow still caught him in back of the ear. The crowd was shocked to see the heavyweight champion rocked and wobbly-legged. He staggered and stumbled toward Ketchel like a drunken man; he was going down. Johnson crashed to the canvas on his seat, head rolling, as the referee began to count him out. (The champion later admitted that Ketchel's punch was the hardest he ever took.)

Johnson was in a fog, going onto all fours, rocking wildly. Ketchel stood waiting grimly to rush forward and finish the job if need be, and in that moment the crowd believed the impossible had happened, that David had slain Goliath. Slowly, Johnson got to one knee and, at the count of eight, rose slowly, still dazed. He saw Ketchel rushing forward. Suddenly, Johnson pitched himself forward and the human cannonballs rushed toward each other. Johnson's blow landed first, a bone-crushing smash to Ketchel's mouth that staggered him, then another terrific blow to his stomach. Tottering backward, Johnson caught the Michigan Assassin with a final enormous punch to the jaw that sent Ketchel to the canvas, where he flattened face upward. Johnson leaned against the ropes, exhausted, as the referee began to count. (Motion pictures of this classic battle show Johnson, after hitting Ketchel with these decisive blows, almost doing a cartwheel in turning after his opponent, such was Johnson's momentum.)

Stanley Ketchel was still out when the referee counted ten. He had lived his finest hour in the ring as an incomparable middleweight who almost became heavyweight champion of the world. The blows Jack Johnson administered to Ketchel in the twelfth round of their fight ruined the middleweight as a fighter. He had a few more successful bouts, but by the fall of 1910, Stanley Ketchel was through with the ring. He went off to rest, to recover from a "nervous breakdown," one report had it, traveling to Conway, Missouri, where his friend Colonel R. P. "Pete" Dickerson owned a ranch.

It was here that Stanley Ketchel met Goldie Smith, the ranch cook, and fell in love for the first and last time of his young life. Goldie, a buxom blonde who had led a nomadic life, was older than Ketchel. He found her not only attractive but receptive to his advances, although she warned the fighter that Walter A. Kurtz, a ranch hand, considered himself her sweetheart and might become violent.

"I'm not worrying about that stiff," Ketchel grunted.

When Ketchel was not present, Goldie gave her affections to Kurtz. The physically ill Ketchel—some said the Johnson fight had rendered him permanently punch-drunk—slept a great deal and then went through the motions of training for his next fight. He rode horses at all hours over the sprawling Dickerson ranch. Everyone knew, except Stanley Ketchel, that his fighting days were over.

His thoughts finally turned to other activities and, on October 8, 1910, Ketchel wrote Wilson Mizner:

Dear Bill:

   More than ever before I'm stuck on this farming thing and I guess I'll be here for life. I have bought 3,300 acres and I intend to incorporate for about $300,000, put in a sawmill and lumber it off. It will be one of the finest farms in the world. If I do any more fighting, Bill, it will be for fun or for charity. This is the place for me.

Your farmer pal,
Steve

Ketchel continued to woo Goldie, who in turn played Kurtz and the boxer against each other. Ketchel, of course, with his good looks and winning ways, had the upper hand. Kurtz became insanely jealous as he watched Goldie and Ketchel stroll about the ranch, hand in hand, kissing and petting. Kurtz seethed, waited, and planned. He watched Ketchel's every movement, noting that the fighter carried a revolver almost everywhere he went.

On the morning of October 15, 1910, Ketchel walked into the Dickerson dining room to have breakfast. He found that his chair was not, as usual, against the wall. (Ketchel preferred to sit with his back against the wall so that he could see all who entered.) The fighter sat down to his usual large breakfast and began to eat, but not before he placed his revolver in his lap. He had his back to the door.

Kurtz suddenly burst through the door, holding a .22 rifle that belonged to Ketchel. "Throw up your hands!" shouted Kurtz.

Ketchel turned in his chair and gave Kurtz a contemptuous look. "Beat it," he growled.

His face turning red with anger, Kurtz waved the rifle wildly and shouted: "You may be a prizefighter but you can't come down here and insult my woman without paying for it!"

Putting down a forkful of scrambled eggs, Stanley Ketchel, who had never refused a challenge in his life, began to rise slowly, instinctively, his grim face half-turned toward his antagonist. At that moment Kurtz took careful aim at the fighter and fired. The bullet struck Ketchel in the back, under the shoulder blade. He toppled forward into his breakfast plate.

For a moment Kurtz stood motionless in the doorway, then ran to the mortally wounded Ketchel and went through his pockets, taking the two thousand-dollar bills Kurtz knew the fighter always carried. As an afterthought Kurtz slipped Ketchel's diamond ring from his finger, then fled.

Colonel Dickerson, hearing the shot, ran to the main house and found Ketchel on the floor. He lifted the dying champion in his arms. Ketchel blinked and barely managed the words, his last: "Take me home to Mom, Pete." The fighter was removed to a hospital in Springfield, Missouri, and died that night.

Kurtz was tracked down the following day. He had fled on foot and, hungry and tired, begged a room and food from a farmer, Thomas Haggard, outside of Niangua, Missouri. Haggard, learning his identity, sat all night with a shotgun pointed at the sleeping man and when he awoke, turned him in to the authorities. Kurtz, authorities soon learned, was really Colorado-born Walter Dipley, a Navy deserter with a criminal record. His only defense at his trial was to wail, "Well, I told Ketchel to throw up his hands and I had to shoot him when he did not obey." He was given a life sentence, released in 1934.

Ketchel was much mourned: everyone agreed that the sport of boxing had lost one of its great champions, if not the greatest champion who ever lived. His body was taken home to his mother and buried in the family plot in Grand Rapids.

Wilson Mizner was one of the last to learn of the prizefighter's murder. He wept, then said: "That darling kid can't be dead. Start counting over him—he'll get up!"

# 1918

## CHARLES CHAPIN
## DEBTS THAT KILLED

Murder was unthinkable in the mind of Charles Chapin in the spring of 1914. At age sixty Chapin had realized all of his lifelong ambitions and had accumulated a healthy fortune that would provide an uncomplicated retirement for him and his wife, Nellie. Leisure, comfort, security, all of these made up Chapin's future. As editor of the New York *Evening World*, Chapin earned a substantial salary. In addition he had made huge sums of money in stock speculation, which enabled him to maintain residences in New York and San Francisco; he had cars, a yacht, and employed house servants for Nellie, to whom he had been devoted for thirty years. But it was those very stock manipulations that brought Chapin to ruin, unhinging his mind to the point where he thought the only way out of his dilemma was murder and suicide.

Chapin began as a reporter for the *St. Louis Post-Dispatch* in the early 1890s before going to work for Joseph Pulitzer's New York *World*. He became one of Pulitzer's favorite newsmen. The publisher took to calling him "Pinch," a nickname earned by Chapin's obtaining scoops "in a pinch." Within a few years the hard-driving Chapin was made city editor of Pulitzer's *Evening World*, where under his control the paper's news-headline emphasis and story content was on the sensational. He was, in the words of W. A. Swanberg, writing in *Pulitzer*, "a zealot who frankly gloated over newsmaking disasters."

As an editor, Chapin was ruthless in obtaining stories that would snare New York's evening readership. He drove his reporters mercilessly. Many a cub later claimed that Chapin's methods created great journalists and accorded him respect, but many more grew to loathe the city editor. In the years Pulitzer allowed Chapin complete reign over the *Evening World* ("junior," as this paper was called to the mother paper, which appeared in the morning), the editor became a free-wheeling autocrat who would stop at nothing to topple anyone who incurred his wrath, and it was later claimed that he had personally ruined scores of newsmen who got in his way.

Once, when hearing that Chapin was ill, columnist Irvin S. Cobb, who had felt Pinch's lash, snorted: "Let's hope it's nothing trivial." Years later, when Chapin was serving time in Sing Sing, Warden Lewis E. Lawes received a letter from one of the editor's former reporters. The anonymous missive dripped the following venom:

I knew Mr. Chapin long and from a certain angle intimately in the years he was at the New York *World.* That is, I knew intimately the anguished stories of the hundreds and thousands of young writers whose lives he made a living hell. He was the worst curse our reportorial craft ever enjoyed. I used to think him a sort of devil sitting on enthroned power in the *World* office and making Park Row gutters flow red with the blood of ambitious young men. If you enjoy him I hope you keep him long and carefully.

Power was easily understood by Chapin. As a child he had watched keenly as his penny-pinching granduncle, Russell Sage, built his multimillion-dollar Wall Street empire. (Sage was a true eccentric. He refused to wear socks, had only one business suit, which he replaced every two years, walked to work each day rather than spend a nickel for the trolley, ate only an apple for lunch, and allowed his wife but one new dress a year; Mrs. Margaret Sage, upon his death, gave away his millions to charity.) Chapin's fascination for wealth never abated, and through his family connections he invested almost every penny of his $125 weekly salary in speculative stocks, which returned handsome profits to him during the early 1900s. He was able to purchase several racehorses and a yacht, and to live in style at the Plaza with his wife Nellie.

When Sage died in 1906, Chapin was shocked to learn that his granduncle had left him nothing, in spite of the years of favors, errands, and various services the editor graciously bestowed upon his superrich relative. Chapin resolved to make his own millions in the stock market and in commodities.

At first, he reaped great profits, which he used to plunge headlong into the sugar market. When the bottom fell out of sugar, Chapin lost not only his own cash reserves and securities but an $8,000 trust fund for which he was the guardian.

He thought of suicide and even made feverish plans to fake an accident so that his wife would benefit from his insurance. Before Chapin's fraudulent misuse of the trust fund was revealed, a wealthy friend (who later became a New York judge) came to his rescue, advancing him the funds to cover the losses.

Chapin had survived this near disaster with a vow to never again speculate in stocks. But, within months, his will weakened. As he said later, in *Charles Chapin's Story* (written while he was a prisoner in Sing Sing): "Unlike the burned child who dreads the fire, I didn't keep away from the flames that scorched and almost consumed me. One would naturally suppose that after all I had gone through I would have learned a lesson and would never again be drawn into the whirlpool of stock speculation. But the microbe that had fastened in my mind wasn't easily uprooted."

If Chapin had not begun with great success in the markets, if his investments had failed at the onset, he might have easily forsaken speculation; but his profits had for a great period of time been uninterrupted. He felt that he had suffered "a bad break" and that his business acumen, for the most part, was still to be trusted. A friend came to Chapin with a "sure tip." He borrowed heavily and plunged into more speculation. This time he won.

"The check that came to me was so munificent that I almost felt rich," he later wrote. "Part of it went to creditors, but the greater share into another speculative investment. Again I won and kept on winning until one day the stock market was thrown into a wild panic by news that Germany had declared war."

This time Chapin's ruination was complete. He had lost more than $100,000 and was $20,000 in debt, an enormous sum in 1914. "The next four years I was in hell," said Chapin. "Creditors harassed me day and night and there was no way of satisfying them. They got my salary as fast as I could earn it and sometimes much faster." He borrowed from every friend who would loan him money.

Chapin's nights were filled with nightmares, the words "insanity and death" looming constantly before him. Again he thought of suicide. He went to Maine, ostensibly on a fishing trip, where he planned to drown himself. Rowing onto a stormy lake, Chapin suddenly remembered that he had not paid the last two premiums on his life insurance policy. He returned to New York to discover process servers awaiting him. Chapin's creditors relentlessly pursued him. His checks bounced. He knew that he soon would be turned out of his hotel and his belongings seized. Mostly, Chapin thought of Nellie and the wretched poverty and shame she would have to endure because of his bankruptcy.

On the night of September 16, 1918, he and his wife were in bed in their suite at the Hotel Cumberland. Chapin, who had purchased a gun, planned to shoot her first, then kill himself. In agony he turned in the bed, withdrew the revolver from beneath his pillow and fired into his wife's breast. "My wife never knew that the man she loved killed her," Chapin later admitted. "She died while peacefully asleep. That is all the consolation I shall ever have and it makes easier to bear what I must face as long as I live. It would have been horrible if she had known."

Chapin did not shoot himself. His aim had been poor and Nellie Chapin did not die instantly, lingering for two hours in an unconscious state. Chapin waited for her to die, reasoning that "had I killed myself while she were yet alive and she had survived, all that I sacrificed to save her from penury and want would have been in vain."

By the time Mrs. Chapin died, the editor had lost his nerve. He got dressed, then walked through Central Park and the Manhattan streets in a daze. It was many hours later when he approached a newsstand, staring down at a headline that read:

CHARLES CHAPIN WANTED FOR MURDER!

"Then it all came back," he remembered. "I wasn't dead; I was alive and I was wanted by the police for murder! How many headlines like that I had written in my forty years as a newspaper man! And now it was me who was wanted for murder." Chapin went to the nearest police station and turned himself in. He readily confessed to killing his wife and asked that he be electrocuted. Chapin was placed in the Tombs, occupying a cell on Murderers' Row.

Even though he refused to defend himself, Abe Levy, a noted criminal lawyer, took Chapin's case for no fee, pleading Chapin not guilty by reason of insanity. He was convicted of second-degree murder, and Judge Bartow Weeks sentenced Chapin, then sixty, to twenty years to life.

Chapin went gladly to Sing Sing, knowing that he would die behind the prison walls. Almost immediately, he grew ill and was sent to the prison hospital. It was apparent to hospital physicians that he had no will to live. Warden Lewis Lawes, then newly appointed to Sing Sing, visited Chapin.

"Charlie," said Lawes, "how would you like to get out of bed?"

"No," groaned Chapin.

"I think I'll put you to work, Charlie."

"No."

"Something that I think you will like. You will be the editor of the *Bulletin.*"

Lawes had taken the correct approach in appealing to the veteran newsman. Within a week Chapin was out of the hospital and at the helm of the prison's newspaper. These duties brought new life back to Chapin, but he again sank into depression when Sing Sing's board suspended the paper's publication. Then one day Chapin approached Lawes and asked to be permitted to take care of the prison's lawn. Lawes agreed, providing him with seed, a lawn mower, a sickle, a hose, and a pair of clippers. Chapin was back months later, asking that he be allowed to turn Sing Sing's prison yard into a garden. At first Lawes stalled, then acquiesced. One of Chapin's friends sent him Luther Burbank's eight-volume work on flora and fauna, and the editor studied furiously all winter. By spring Chapin's sense of authority returned, and he commandeered thirty prisoners to work under his supervision as he landscaped the prison yard, turning a desolate area of gravel, scrap iron, and rock into a magnificent garden area.

Old friends sent Chapin flower seeds and rose bushes, which he planted, earning himself the sobriquet "The Rose Man of Sing Sing." The prison garden bloomed, almost an acre of beds and borders with flowers of all kinds, from peonies to asters. For three years Chapin obsessively slaved at his greenery.

In 1923, Chapin wrote Lawes an astounding note that read: "I would suggest that all men assigned to work in the garden be given to understand that they are not to shirk. Most of them disappear if I am not around an hour before the whistle blows. I expect them to work from 8 A.M. to 11:30, and from 1 P.M. until

3:30, except in stormy weather, and they should be given to understand that shirking will not be tolerated."

It was the hard-driving Chapin of old, unswervingly pursuing his goal. He was not popular with many inmates, but that mattered little to him. He took great pride in his gardens. On one occasion he entered Warden Lawes's office with an armful of roses, saying: "First choice, Warden. A thanksgiving offering to you for your cooperation."

Chapin's marvelous gardens were all but destroyed in the summer of 1930 when a new drainage system was installed in Sing Sing. His lawns were gouged and chopped, his rose hedges uprooted. Chapin sank into depression. His vitality vanished as quickly as had his gardens and lawns. In early December 1930, Charles Chapin caught pneumonia and was sent to the prison hospital.

Lawes visited his famous prisoner, asking: "Is there anything you want, Charlie?"

"Nothing," replied Chapin. "Nothing at all. I am tired and I want to die." He then asked that he be buried next to his wife. Lawes promised to do so. Chapin died on December 13, 1930, at age seventy-two.

A few years later Lawes wrote in *20,000 Years in Sing Sing:* "Chapin's province has been reconstructed. Rose hedges again stand guard at its borders. They are living, conscious realities. Breathing of the spirit and soul of their godfather, Charles Chapin—Sing Sing's Rose Man."

# 1924

෴

# KID MCCOY
## THE MARRYING
## MURDERER

He was a lover and a brawler, a smooth-talking Broadway type who loved the limelight and show business. Moreover, Kid McCoy, born October 17, 1873, whose real name was Norman Selby, was a terrific fighter who battled his way through the middle- and welterweight ranks from 1891 to 1900, beating such erstwhile scrappers as Peter Maher, Joe Choynski, Tom Sharkey, Jack Madden, and Jack O'Brien; he had more than 150 bouts, winning most of them. In a fifteen-round slugfest on March 2, 1896, McCoy, using his famous "corkscrew" punch, beat Tommy Ryan for the welterweight championship.

A cunning fellow, McCoy had used more than his fists on Ryan. He tricked Ryan into believing that he would be a weak contender, writing the champion a letter in which he, McCoy, admitted that his chances against Ryan were slim and went on to beg the champ to "take it easy" on him and carry him for a few rounds, so that he could pocket some money. Ryan read the pleading letter, sneered his contempt for McCoy, and then proceeded to train haphazardly for the championship fight by working out occasionally in the back room of his Syracuse, New York, saloon.

Thinking his opponent a weakling, Ryan fought McCoy recklessly and only after fifteen brutal rounds realized too late that Kid McCoy had mercilessly beaten him and taken his title through a ruse. "The bastard played possum," griped Ryan as he was led from the ring, still bleeding from severe cuts.

McCoy kept his welterweight crown for two years, abandoning the title in 1897 to open a cabaret in New York where he catered to the stars of the theater, befriending countless celebrities, from Lillian Russell to Nora Bayes. Promoters convinced McCoy to reenter the ring in 1900, at age twenty-seven, and take on onetime heavyweight champion James J. "Gentleman Jim" Corbett. He was soundly thrashed by Corbett and promptly retired for good.

The fighter, however, did not retire his strutting image. In his travels through the saloon worlds of New York and Europe, McCoy would introduce himself as "the real McCoy," the first so named to do so. (George Braidwood McCoy, character actor and radio broadcaster, later called himself "The Real McCoy," but he was second to Selby.) A loudmouthed drunk once staggered into McCoy's New York cabaret, interrupting the fighter as he was talking to an attractive woman. Annoyed, McCoy faced the drunk squarely and said: "I'm Kid McCoy, the boxer, so you'd better beat it."

"Yeah?" sneered the drunk. "Well, I'm Julius Caesar!"

McCoy lashed out with his corkscrew punch and floored the drunk. Ten minutes later the man blinked into consciousness, rubbing his welted chin. "Jesus!" he reportedly exclaimed to the fighter. "You *are* the real McCoy!"

Although McCoy was mean and vicious inside the ring, he was all charm outside, generally liked by men and women alike, especially women. But whenever McCoy had anything to do with boxing, he reverted to animal instincts. A society friend who frequented McCoy's cabaret pestered the fighter to teach him to box. McCoy shook his head. The gentleman persisted, stating: "Look, I'd be willing to pay you for your services."

McCoy's eyes narrowed. He suddenly looked beyond his friend's shoulder and said: "Who's that coming through the door?" The man turned, and in that instant McCoy slammed a vicious blow to his ear, sending him to the floor. Humorlessly, McCoy stared down at his startled friend. "The first lesson," the fighter growled, "is never trust anybody. That'll be ten bucks, pal."

The handsome McCoy—he stood five feet eleven and had dark thick hair—was a darling with the ladies, and he apparently married any woman who caught his eye, going to the altar nine times from 1894 to 1920. McCoy married Lottie Piehler in 1894 and divorced her a year later. He married Charlotte Smith in 1897 and divorced her the same year. The fighter wed Mrs. Julia Woodruff Crosselman three times—in 1897, 1901, and 1902—divorcing her in 1900, 1901, and 1902. In 1903, McCoy married In-

dianola Arnold, divorcing her the following year. In 1905 he wed
Mrs. Estelle Ellis, divorcing her in 1910. Next came Mrs. Edna
Valentine Hein, married in 1911, divorced in 1917. Three years
later Dagmar Dahlgren became the ninth Mrs. Selby, divorced
that same year, 1920. There may have been other marriages, but
they were not recorded for posterity. It would appear that Kid
McCoy stayed married to one woman until he became infatuated
with another. His many divorce settlements depleted the vast
amounts of money he had accumulated through boxing and his
cabaret, but McCoy did not seem to mind. He was a lover first
and a money-maker second. He spent his fortune, estimated once
to be more than half a million dollars ($10 million by today's
standards), on clothes, jewelry for his women and himself, luxurious living quarters, anything costly that pleased him.

During his colorful career as a boxer McCoy fought for large
purses and developed the habits of the spendthrift, causing him
to take on difficult opponents, which would mean larger prize
money. His most implausible money fight occurred in South
Africa before the turn of the century. British colonials offered
McCoy $10,000 to travel to a trading post hundreds of miles
north of Johannesburg to fight someone the natives called "King
of the Kaffirs." The fighter accepted with alacrity and departed
for the trading post.

Arriving by stagecoach, McCoy entered the area that passed
for the town square of the small community and was thunder-
struck by an awesome sight. Before him was the King, working
out with a so-called sparring partner. McCoy's intended opponent stood more than six feet six in his bare feet and weighed
almost three hundred pounds. The man "sparring" with the King
was almost as big. The boxer was really alarmed by the fact that
the King and his partner were using clubs on each other instead
of fists.

"Why the clubs?" asked McCoy of his guide.

The British colonial smiled at McCoy and replied: "They don't
seem to be able to hurt each other with their fists, old boy."

McCoy retired to a hut to think over his dilemma. The King
outweighed him by 140 pounds, and his reach was almost twice
that of McCoy's. Then there was the club. McCoy went back to
the town square to look over his opponent once more. Then he
asked his guide: "Does he always fight barefooted?"

"Oh, yes, old boy," smiled the guide. "He'll be barefoot when you meet him tomorrow, too."

Going immediately to the trading post, McCoy purchased a large box of tacks and gave the package to his second, telling him: "Stay next to that bozo's corner tomorrow. Keep your eye on me. When I tap myself twice on the head, you throw them tacks out in front of his feet." The second nodded.

The following day an anxious McCoy got into the ring. He at first thought to wait until the middle of the first round before signaling his second, but when he was handed a club while sitting in his corner, McCoy turned pale. The bell rang, and the King of the Kaffirs stood up with a roar. McCoy immediately tapped his head twice, and his second threw out the tacks in front of the King.

After a few steps the King let out a bellow of pain and grabbed one foot, balancing on the other as he attempted to dig out the tacks buried in his flesh. McCoy, tossing aside his club, raced forward and hit the King with his best corkscrew punch, sending the giant to the canvas unconscious. Without waiting for the referee to announce him the winner, Kid McCoy dashed to a waiting stagecoach, which left the trading post just ahead of a howling mob of incensed natives. McCoy later insisted that he did collect his purse, but only after reasoning with the fight promoters, saying: "If that beezock can use clubs, I can use tacks."

By 1924, McCoy's salad days were over. He had spent his money and used up his welcome in most cities, particularly in New York, where his divorces and brawls were legendary. At age fifty-one he was no longer the dandy, now gone bald and flabby. McCoy had relocated to Los Angeles, where his show business friends got him bit parts in movies. To support himself, he took a job as a guard in an airplane manufacturing plant and by virtue of this position was allowed to carry a gun.

The .32-caliber pistol McCoy carried was given to him by one of his sporting friends, Hubert Kittle, an ex-police officer, daredevil aviator, and a suspect in several robberies. The fighter carried the weapon on his person almost all of the time: for personal reasons, he confided to a few friends.

The "personal reason" was a wealthy art and antique dealer, Albert E. Mors. His wife, Theresa W. Mors, had taken up with McCoy, leaving her husband and living with the fighter as his common-law wife in the exclusive Nottingham Apartments on Leeward Avenue under the name of Shields. Mrs. Mors had filed for divorce. Her husband in turn had named McCoy as correspondent in the proceedings. McCoy had become Mrs. Mors's "protector," vowing a terrible wrath upon Mors should he bother the fighter's intended tenth bride.

Whether or not Mrs. Mors had decided to marry the ex-champ was in debate up until the night of August 12–13, 1924, when she was slain. The dark-eyed, plumpish Theresa and McCoy began to drink heavily late that night in their apartment. According to the prosecution, later demanding McCoy's execution for murder, the fighter had learned that Theresa had changed her mind about marrying him. She was a wealthy woman, possessing about $6,000 in cash, $20,000 in valuable gems, an overall estate worth $125,000, $80,000 in life insurance, and the antique store her husband had left her in the divorce settlement.

McCoy was after Theresa's money, District Attorney Asa Keyes would later insist, and, when he learned she was leaving him, approached Mrs. Mors around midnight, August 12–13 when she was drunk, placed his .32-caliber pistol behind her left ear, and blew out her brains. Intoxicated, the fighter staggered into another room, found a picture of himself that Theresa liked and placed it on her bosom, then covered the body sprawled on the dining room floor with a sheet. He left the pistol next to her body, then went out, going to his car and driving about aimlessly for some time before arriving at the Hollywood police station.

Police were puzzled by McCoy's appearance. He demanded to see the officer who had once removed him from the Mors's home before Theresa was divorced. That officer was not present, McCoy was told. The fighter snarled: "It's a lucky thing for him that he's not here."

"Why's that?" asked Officer A. T. Griffin.

"Read the papers in the morning and you'll know why," McCoy said with a half smile. Then he added: "Hell, I'll be in the can tomorrow."

Griffin and another officer named Young were amused by the fighter's conduct. Kid McCoy was always getting into scrapes, but his colorful personality and his flair for the dramatic proved to be entertaining. The officers did not take the fighter seriously but insisted that they drive him home, telling him that he was in no shape to maneuver his own car. Griffin and Young drove McCoy back to the Nottingham Apartments, seeing him to the door.

As they stood in the hallway the fighter blocked the view into the apartment with his body, but officer Griffin later testified that he saw on the dining room floor what he thought to be a pile of linen, which was later determined to be the body of Theresa Mors under a sheet.

McCoy spent the next hour, according to his later recollection, swilling whiskey from a bottle, talking to the corpse of his lover, and contemplating his suicide. He wrote out two wills, leaving his meager belongings, about $300 in old clothes, to his mother, Mary Selby. Two hours later he was standing outside the home of his sister, Jennie Thomas, scratching the screen of her bedroom window until she awoke and came to the back door to speak to him.

Mrs. Thomas, who disliked her brother for his violent ways and later became a witness for the prosecution, asked him what he was doing.

McCoy's speech was slurred as he blurted out: "I just had to kill that woman!"

Jennie replied (also according to later testimony): "Did you kill that man, too?" (She meant Albert Mors.)

"Yeah, I got him, too," McCoy reportedly replied. He then handed Jennie a box containing Theresa's jewels and turned about, lurching away into the darkness and out of sight.

At dawn the fighter, carrying his .32 pistol, was standing outside Mrs. Mors's art-antique store on Seventh Street. He entered the store and found three men present, customers William G. Ross and Sam H. Stern, and a clerk, V. C. Emden. Brandishing his pistol, McCoy ordered everyone to sit down and "stay put." He went to a counter and opened a music box, and began keeping time with the music, using the pistol as a director's baton. He suddenly slammed down the lid of the music box and said as he waved the pistol in the direction of the three terrified men: "All right now, I want you all to take off your shoes and pants, and empty out your pockets. Hurry, give me the money." The three men obeyed, but Ross made a sudden movement and McCoy squeezed off a round that smacked into Ross's leg. Ross collapsed to the floor in a scream of pain. McCoy, scooping up the money, dashed for the door.

Upon reaching the street, the fighter whirled about as he heard his name called. Moving toward him were Mr. and Mrs. Sam Schapp, owners of the next-door millinery shop and close friends of Theresa Mors. They had heard the shot from the Mors store and had come running.

McCoy scowled at the Schapps, whom he hated. They had for months, he knew, been urging Mrs. Mors to get rid of the "punch-drunk" fighter, to leave him and go east to New York where she had family and friends and could begin a new life.

"Norman," said Sam Schapp to McCoy. "My God, what are you doing?"

The fighter answered the question with a shot. As Schapp fell to the pavement, McCoy fired again, the bullet striking Mrs. Schapp. (Both later recovered from these minor wounds, as did Ross.) McCoy ran into the street, jumping onto the running board of a passing Ford; he yelled to the driver to "get going!" The panicky driver accelerated rapidly, sending the car weaving back and forth up Seventh Street in a roar.

By then a cop on the beat had responded to the sidewalk shooting. He also commandeered a car and, standing on the running board, directed the driver to follow McCoy. The driver of McCoy's car careened off Seventh Street and up Arborata, following the berserk fighter's instructions. McCoy saw the car carrying the policeman was gaining and ordered the driver to stop. He jumped to the street and ran into Westlake Park, the policeman, revolver drawn, following him at a gallop. The cop gained on the fighter; McCoy was out of shape, winded and flushed.

"I'll shoot you if you don't stop, mister!" yelled the cop as he neared his prey. McCoy stopped, turned, and, with his head on his chest, meekly offered up his pistol.

Police escorted McCoy home, where the body of Theresa Mors had been discovered hours earlier by Hiram David, janitor for the Nottingham Apartments. McCoy admitted killing his lover, saying that she was going to leave him, according to the testimony later given by several police officers. He not only admitted the murder but insisted repeatedly that he alone was responsible for the woman's death.

McCoy was taken to the city jail and locked up. In the late afternoon Detective Captain Herman Cline took McCoy from his cell and, in an unorthodox move, suggested that the two of them have a late lunch and "talk about this mess." Cline drove McCoy to a small Mexican restaurant, buying him dinner. The fighter ate ravenously, gulping down several glasses of water, sobering now, it seemed to Cline.

Between huge mouthfuls of food Kid McCoy suddenly changed his story. He had not murdered the hapless Mrs. Mors, he adamantly insisted. She had committed suicide. Yes, he was certain the poor woman killed herself. Albert Mors was responsible for it all; the ex-husband had threatened Theresa with bodily harm. He had hired thugs to beat her up and had even tried to implicate her in a charge of smuggling gems. The woman was beside herself, at wit's end, and had suddenly killed herself with McCoy's pistol before he could stop her.

"When Theresa fired that shot into her head," McCoy said, beans and rice spilling out of his mouth with his words, "all the lights in the world went out for me." He rambled on, according to Captain Cline, his narrative disjointed, sometimes incomprehensible. Toward the end of his monologue McCoy said clearly:

I love her. I never loved a woman so before. Well, she's dead now, but I still love her. I don't care what becomes of me now. I was going to marry Theresa Mors just as soon as we could get things right side up again. Now this thing has happened. I never can find happiness again, so what does it matter.

Yesterday we went for an automobile ride together and we didn't return until eight o'clock [P.M.]. Theresa was very blue and I tried hard to cheer her up. Finally she announced that she couldn't stand it any longer. She said: "I'm going to end it all." She took the pistol out of the drawer. I jumped for her but she shot herself just as I reached her.

Theresa fell into my arms. I placed her on the floor. She died with my arms about her and trying to speak to me. I placed a sheet over her. Then I put my picture in her folded arms. I was covered with blood so I washed up and got my revolver and started out to kill Albert Mors, the goddamned

*Norman Selby (right), better known as Kid McCoy, with parole officer, Ed Whyte, upon his release from San Quentin in 1932. (Wide World)*

man who caused it all. I didn't find him. If I had I would have killed him. I'll kill him yet!

The object of McCoy's wrath, Albert Mors, was later reached by newsmen. Stated Mors: "It was an act of God and a case of retribution. I told my wife to keep away from McCoy."

Captain Cline, who had returned McCoy to his cell, met with District Attorney Keyes and pointed out to the D.A. that the fighter had every opportunity to inform the Hollywood police when appearing at the station and when being returned home that his lover was dead. "If it was a case of suicide, why did he not inform the police then," Cline asked Keyes in front of newsmen. "It was murder, not suicide, that's why, and McCoy still wanted to get Mors in the morning."

The Schapps, recovering in a hospital, echoed Cline's accusation, saying that McCoy killed Mrs. Mors after she rejected his marriage proposal and realized that he would be unable to obtain her riches. Said Sam Schapp from his hospital bed:

> I talked to Mrs. Mors like a brother would. I told her she was foolish to have anything to do with Kid McCoy. I told her that he was simply after her money and that by marrying him she would make herself the laughingstock of the country. My wife talked to her in the same way. Finally, Mrs. Mors broke down and told us that she saw our point of view and promised to give up McCoy. She said that she was going to see McCoy that night and she would tell him that she could never marry him and that she was going back to New York without him. She was very sincere about it and left us with the firm determination to call everything off between McCoy and herself.

Six days later McCoy was examined by three court-appointed psychiatrists, who found the boxer sane enough to stand trial for murder. Dr. Paul Bowers commented: "McCoy was suave, diplomatic and cooperative during his tests. The accused did very well for a man whose education had been neglected."

McCoy read these remarks in his cell and, early the next morning, began to act queerly. He dismantled part of the hammock in his cell, pulling out the ironwork from the wall, exerting what guards called "superhuman" strength, and piling the debris in the middle of the cell floor. He next took out a roll of toilet paper and wove this in and out of the bars of the cell, all the while murmuring gibberish puncutated by random screaming that caused the other prisoners to create a commotion.

Guards came on the run and stared at the paper entwined about the bars of McCoy's cell. "That's pretty good, isn't it?" McCoy said to them. "That's my rat trap. I made it to catch that rat Mors when he tries to get in here and kill me. Believe me, I'm ready for him." The fighter held up a wooden club he had fashioned from a support beam for the hammock. McCoy then threw down the club and sprang to the bars, moving up and down the iron framework of the cell like a monkey, yelling and singing.

Dr. Victor Parkin was summoned, and he calmed the fighter. McCoy then told the psychiatrist in a soft voice: "You know, Theresa visited me during the night. She stayed with me more than an hour. She's as beautiful as a picture. She kissed me and comforted me. She said I soon would be out from behind the bars. And she promised to come back and visit me again. You know, doctor, that you can't separate true love. They can keep me in here locked up but they can't keep me and Theresa apart. There are things of the spirit that are too strong for iron and distance."

McCoy's overt symptoms of dementia were discussed by Dr. Parkin, who observed the fighter for four hours and then concluded that McCoy was feigning a mental breakdown. Parkin then later told the press: "Norman Selby is a shrewd person. He is carrying his old ring generalship into the cell with him."

That "generalship" was remembered by McCoy's cronies and friends. Sportsman Dick Ferris immediately began to gather a defense fund. Jim Jeffries and James J. Corbett signed their names to telegrams asking for contributions to this fund. When California reporters heard that William J. Fallon, "The Great Mouthpiece," might take on the defense, they called the attorney in New York.

"No, I can't talk about it," said Fallon on the phone. "There may be something to say later and there may not. I was asked if I took the case what my fee would probably be."

"And you said $100,000?" a reporter asked Fallon.

"Who told you that?" The line went dead. The Great Mouthpiece had hung up.

McCoy's defense was finally handled by R. D. Knickerbocker. On the first day of the trial the court clerk intoned: "Did feloniously assault and commit murder." McCoy took a step toward the clerk and roared: "I did not!" Knickerbocker entered a plea of not guilty for his client.

Newsmen snapped photos of McCoy as he sat glumly in court. Wrote one scribe: "McCoy presented a sorry figure as he entered the courtroom. His head sagged so that the glistening bald oval of his skull attracted the eye. The short clipped black curls were unkempt. Most of the glances from the famous gimlet eyes were directed sideways or were shot out during short upward jerks of his head. Jauntiness was lost by the weight of a blue denim shirt inscribed 'County Jail.'"

At his friends' urgings McCoy replaced his stodgy attorney, Knickerbocker, with Jerry Geisler, then just beginning his fabulous career as a defense attorney. Geisler saw to it that the jury comprised mostly females, nine in number, thinking that they would empathize with McCoy as a star-crossed lover. His tactic worked to some extent.

The prosecution detailed its case, using the testimony of McCoy's sister, Jennie, against him, telling the court that McCoy had murdered Mrs. Mors in cold blood after learning that she was leaving him and would not give him any money. "This man with a black heart, this brute," intoned chief prosecutor Charles W. Frick, "is a murderer." He went on to ridicule McCoy's claim that Theresa Mors committed suicide. "When this man shot this woman just back of the left ear she was facing away from him."

The position of the bullet's entry into the victim was the hardest evidence to overcome by the defense. It appeared next to impossible for Theresa Mors to have killed herself. Geisler later stated: "One of the difficulties facing me as Selby's attorney was that Mrs. Mors was not left-handed, although, if she had fired that shot, she had done it with her left hand. To make things even tougher for Selby, she must have pulled the trigger with the thumb of her left hand."

Geisler argued long and hard on the suicide claim but his position was weak. He put his client on the stand. McCoy played to the ladies on the jury, dramatically reenacting what he insisted was Mrs. Mors's suicide, showing how her left hand was contorted while holding the pistol as he struggled with her just before the gun went off. His story was, at best, confusing.

Several character witnesses were also put on the stand, including the famous sportswriter Damon Runyon, who testified on McCoy's behalf. The jury retired to spend seventy-eight hours in deliberation, taking twenty-four ballots, finally compromising on a guilty verdict, but for manslaughter, not murder. It was later said that not only were the female members of the jury enamored of the romantic McCoy but the death of the defendant's mother during his long trial earned him great sympathy as well.

McCoy was sentenced from one to ten years for the Mors killing. At later trials he also received one to fourteen years each on two counts of assault, and from six months to ten years for his attacks on the Schapps and those in the Mors shop.

Upon leaving the court after hearing his final sentences on February 20, 1925, McCoy, in chains, saw the great comedian Charlie Chaplin (who at the time was suing one Charles Amador for imitating his Little Tramp act). "Hi ya, Charlie," McCoy said, throwing his arm around Chaplin. They shook hands and then the comedian watched as McCoy was led across Temple Street to the jail.

McCoy had conducted himself with dignity throughout his several trials. Only once did he appear to break down, and that was upon hearing his conviction for manslaughter. He cried briefly, then wiped away tears and turned to reporters in the courtroom, saying: "They might as well have sentenced me to hang for first degree murder. I am innocent. This manslaughter verdict makes me appear guilty. But I am innocent. It was suicide."

Throughout his almost eight years as an inmate of San Quentin, McCoy would maintain his innocence. He was a model prisoner, never causing trouble. McCoy spent most of his time reading, even when at prison chores, which, given his celebrity status, guards ignored. He worked at the prison firehouse, where often he would put down a book to perform some quick shadowboxing. He asked the warden repeatedly if he could teach other prisoners the "manly art" of boxing but was always denied his request. Then, while McCoy was working on a prison road gang near San Simeon one day, a small plane crashed nearby and the fighter raced up the side of a hill to pull the pilot away from the burning debris, saving his life. For this act of bravery McCoy was sent a pair of boxing gloves and a punching bag. "Thanks for the gloves and the bag, warden," McCoy wrote to Warden Holohan. "They'll keep me in shape until I get back to the firehouse. If you have any second-hand paroles around, I could use those, too."

The fighter became known as San Quentin's wry quipster. "Woman was made from a rib," he once stated to a visitor, "and she's still a ticklish problem." On another occasion McCoy wagged his finger at a strutting youngster new to the prison, saying: "Remember that the bright lights go out the quickest. Kid McCoy knows."

No other prisoner during this time ever received as many gifts from the outside world as did Kid McCoy. His theatrical friends had not abandoned him. Foodstuffs of all kinds, from mayonnaise to figs, streamed into his San Quentin mailbox throughout the years of his imprisonment. McCoy shared his gifts with those who worked with him in the firehouse. He also received large amounts of mail, often cash, from friends including Lionel Barrymore, who had been a frequenter of the boxer's cabaret in New York. Show-business celebrities, such as singer Sophie Tucker, visited McCoy regularly.

In late 1931, Henry Ford, Sr., wrote to the governor of California stating that if Kid McCoy were paroled, he, Ford, would guarantee him a job training his employees in physical fitness. Further, a most remarkable petition arrived before the prison's parole board, signed by more dignitaries than ever have affixed their signatures to any such document. Heading the list was Vice-President Charles Curtis, General Douglas MacArthur, New York's Governor Al Smith, six U.S. senators, six governors, and dozens of congressmen, mayors, businessmen, sports figures, and movie stars.

McCoy was freed in 1932, going to work for Ford in Detroit. As the years passed, he became depressed when no one even remembered his fame in the ring, let alone the fact that he was "the *real* McCoy." He had once said: "It's no fun telling people you're Kid McCoy if they've never heard of you before."

Returning to his Detroit hotel room one day in April 1940, Kid McCoy swallowed a bottle of sleeping pills, committing suicide at age sixty-six. Upon hearing of his death, Jerry Geisler lamented: "I am still convinced that the shooting for which Selby drew a manslaughter penalty was accidental, that Mrs. Mors shot herself and that Selby confessed because he wanted to die." By then the details of the Mors killing were fuzzy and faded. Most people tended to agree with Geisler, although there were others intimately familiar with the case who knew that a person's fame could sometimes overshadow actual deeds, even murder.

# 1928

## ARNOLD ROTHSTEIN
### A BULLET FOR "MR. BIG"

A criminal genius, Arnold Rothstein was a man known by many names in his time—Mr. Big, The Big Bankroll, The Man to See, The Brain, The Man Uptown, Mr. A., or, as his few friends called him, A.R. At the peak of his success Rothstein's empire encompassed nationwide gambling, prostitution, drugs, labor racketeering, bootlegging, gem-smuggling, loan-sharking, just about any illegal enterprise that could return to A.R. incredible profits on his investments. He was worth untold millions upon his death at forty-six, but only he knew where his money was and the pipeline that spewed forth these millions into his coffers. Rothstein kept everything in his head, shrewdly refusing to write anything down on paper that could later be used in court against him. He could compute with astounding accuracy impossible figures in his head, from odds at the racetrack to involved interest payments on his gigantic personal loans. These mental gymnastics earned for him the sobriquet "The Brain," but it also caused lifelong migraine headaches.

Born in 1882 to middle-class Jewish parents in New York, Rothstein was given a comfortable home and a solid education as a youth. His parents, Abraham and Esther Rothstein, doted on Arnold, his father setting a strict moral code for the boy. Abraham Rothstein, a successful dry goods merchant, was so honest that residents of his community referred to him as Rothstein the Just. "Honor all men and love them as brothers" was the credo Abraham Rothstein insisted his sons, Harry and Arnold, adopt. From all reports Harry lived up to his father's expectations; Arnold did not. In fact, at age three Arnold attempted to kill his older brother with a knife. He was envious of Harry, whose good behavior regularly won him accolades from his parents.

Arnold scoffed at "idiot do-gooders" and went his own way, quitting school at sixteen and spending most of his time gambling —shooting craps or playing poker. His father persisted in trying to teach him the fine points of the Jewish faith and history. One evening Arnold got up from the dining room table and shoved away the books his father had put before him. "Aww, who cares about that stuff?" he sneered at Abraham Rothstein. "This is America, not Jerusalem. I'm an American. Let Harry be a Jew!"

Rothstein's attitude toward his family reflected his world outlook. He was hardhearted from childhood and displayed nerves of steel whenever faced with pressure. Along with his iron will Rothstein reveled in his ego, one that convinced him early that he was intellectually superior to most men. He never smoked or drank and thought those who did were spiritually weak. Never a physical man, Rothstein quickly learned how to control the street toughs he associated with; he merely bought them all the liquor they could drink in return for their protection. As a youth he was a shrewd gambler, quitting when ahead and then loaning money to others so that they could play, charging exorbitant rates. At eighteen he was a wealthy, crafty loan shark.

By the time he entered his forties, Rothstein had developed his illegal mainstay, moneylending, receiving staggering interest rates. When a client refused to pay him, A.R. simply shrugged, turning the matter over to his "enforcer," the gigantic and cretinous thug Monk Eastman, the most feared hoodlum in New York, reputed to have murdered more than fifty men, who served as Rothstein's collector.

At first Rothstein invested his early wealth in posh gambling houses, becoming a silent partner and raking in half the profits. By 1910, Rothstein secretly owned dozens of the most resplendent gambling dens across the country. His take was enormous, but he never opened a bank account, secreting suitcases full of cash in his many apartments and in bank vaults.

It was during this period that Rothstein cultivated friendships with such newsmen as Frank Ward O'Malley and Damon Runyon, who was to later portray Rothstein in a sympathetic light as Nathan Detroit in *Guys and Dolls*. A.R. wished to be known as a gentleman gambler who was intelligent and witty; he even

*The "Big Bank Roll," Arnold Rothstein, New York's super gambler.*

managed to work his wiles on the cunning Wilson Mizner, play-
wright and con man, who came to believe that Rothstein represented the civilized aspect of American crime.

Rothstein bolstered this image by becoming a Broadway habi-
tué, frequenting the celebrity restaurants along the Main Stem.
The five-feet-seven-inch gambler kept slim with a strict diet,
eating only figs as snacks. He wore conservative Wall Street suits,
shunning the garish garb of his criminal associates. Inside his
pocket he always carried a wad of crisp new thousand-dollar
bills. It was later said with some accuracy that Rothstein carried
as much as half a million dollars on his person, doling out huge
loans in cash as he made his Broadway rounds, and receiving
IOU's at stiff interest rates and on short terms.

Although he was constantly trailed by his strong-arm men,
who made sure A.R. was not relieved of his roll by thieves,

Rothstein's walkabout habits were always cautionary. He never strolled next to the curb of the street and always took a new route home each night. Before entering a restaurant, he would have one of his minions describe the number of persons present and where they were seated. His movements were amazingly quick, pantherlike, one report had it. Donald Henderson Clarke's *In the Reign of Rothstein* describes an incident when "the lights went out suddenly in the restaurant in which he was sitting late at night. They flashed on again in an instant, and disclosed Rothstein seated easily twenty feet from his original position. He moved like a ray of light, whether it was to take one of the innumerable telephone calls which poured in on him wherever he was, or whether it was merely to rise and greet a friend."

The gambler was just as quick to take advantage of any opportunity to enrich himself. When his friend and fellow gambler Herman "Beansie" Rosenthal was murdered in public view outside the Hotel Metropole in 1912 by four gangsters, Rothstein took over Rosenthal's gambling operation, which was essentially the control of every floating crap game in New York. A.R. was often in attendance at the bigger crap games, and this was twice his undoing when he and others were robbed of huge amounts of cash, Rothstein losing a $3,500 stickpin to a gunman in a 1917 raid. The thieves were later arrested and sent to prison through Rothstein's superb police connections.

The police, however, sometimes blundered in on Rothstein's big games. On January 19, 1919, three detectives heard of a wild crap game taking place in an apartment on the fourth floor of 301 West 57th Street. Pounding on the door, the detectives were greeted with three shots that smashed through the wood, grazing them. They broke down the door to find twenty well-dressed men standing with upraised hands. One detective raced to an open window to discover Arnold Rothstein standing on a fire escape. There was a revolver in his pocket. Three bullets had been fired from it. The gambler calmly explained that he had a permit to carry the weapon and he had fired through the door thinking the detectives were thieves. The entire party was taken to police headquarters, charged with "suspicion of felonious assault," each held under $1,000 bail. A.R. laughed and peeled off $21,000 from his bankroll, providing the bail for all. The matter was later lost

*Nicky Arnstein, with his wife, Fannie Brice (right), and a friend, in 1919.*

in a welter of legal maneuvering on the part of Rothstein's battery of lawyers.

One of the crap players bailed out by Rothstein was Abe Attell, former featherweight boxing champion and A.R.'s "fixer" in crooked sporting events. It was this very same Abe Attell who bribed eight players of the Chicago White Sox baseball team to throw the 1919 World Series, on orders from Rothstein, who was said to have made $5 million in bets on the "Black Sox" scandal. The fixing of the World Series brought Rothstein whispered no-toriety across the nation, although he was never indicted in the matter. Everyone *knew*, however, that he had been the master-mind, as Scott Fitzgerald was later to state in *The Great Gatsby*, fixing the blame squarely upon his character, Meyer Wolfsheim, a clear-cut profile of Rothstein.

The blame for the $5 million loss in Liberty bonds a year earlier could also have been placed at Rothstein's door. He had financed strong-arm thugs to carry out his scheme in robbing Wall Street messengers carrying negotiable bonds and then fenced the bonds for a profit of about $5 million. When police closed in, Rothstein ordered the actual thieves to tell police that A.R.'s close friend Jules W. "Nicky" Arnstein was the culprit.

With typical hypocrisy Rothstein pretended to rush to Arn-stein's aid when Nicky was finally arrested. He provided Arn-stein's wife, Follies star Fannie Brice, with $100,000 bail for her errant husband and instructed his chief lawyer, William Fallon, to defend his good friend Arnstein. Fallon managed to get a hung jury in Arnstein's first trial but then abruptly caused an argument and quit the case, leaving Arnstein to face a conviction and jail sentence following a second trial, all of which had been planned out in advance by Arnold "The Brain" Rothstein.

Fortune continued to smile on the King of the Gamblers through the 1920s. He financed young bootleggers such as Jack "Legs" Diamond, Waxey Gordon, and Dutch Schultz, all of whom later became millionaire beer barons and kicked back handsome profits from their booze empires to A.R. He backed drug and gem smuggling operations that brought him more mil-lions. In 1921, in one race, Rothstein ran his horse Sidereal, an unknown Thoroughbred, and, manipulating the odds, won $800,000. He had the proverbial Midas touch.

By the late 1920s, Rothstein had already conferred with such underworld sachems as Johnny Torrio and Frank Costello, drawing the plans for a nationwide crime cartel that was to become the national crime syndicate. Rothstein would direct this organization, along with a few other board members. At the beginning of 1928, Rothstein was one of the most powerful men in America. He was then forty-six and possessed untold millions. He had no intention of retiring. When his wife, Carolyn, begged him to quit the rackets, A.R. sent her off on a European holiday, telling her that when she returned, he would divorce her. He busied himself with his show girls and his myriad enterprises. As Leo Katcher wrote in *The Big Bankroll,* "life, to him, was a balance sheet. His mind was a computing machine. Addition for him and subtraction for others. He had always wanted money and he still wanted money. He just wanted more of it in 1928 than he had wanted in 1908 or 1918."

But the year 1928 saw the impossible happen—Arnold Rothstein started to lose. Hard luck dogged him at every turn. He dropped $130,000 at Belmont Park on Memorial Day that year. Loans that may have totaled millions to judges, political bosses, and crime czars remained outstanding. A.R. could not collect the principal amounts, let alone the interest. (Those borrowing included such prominent persons as Judge John Vitale, Jimmy Hines, and Frank Costello.) He had advanced many millions to European and Middle East contacts to purchase great stores of cocaine and heroin to feed his newly founded drug empire, but the shipments were slow in coming and he had seen little return on his investment.

Rothstein sought to make a killing in the presidential election, placing huge bets on Herbert Hoover. Meanwhile he occupied his time by playing poker for big stakes. One of these games, held in the apartment of Jimmy Meehan, lasted for two days, September 8–10, 1928. Present were out-of-town gamblers Alvin C. "Titanic" Thompson and Nate "Nigger Nate" Raymond, Meyer Boston, Martin Bowe, Joe Bernstein, George F. "Hump" McManus, and Rothstein.

Throughout the game Rothstein, normally a conservative player, bet wildly, losing hundreds of thousands of dollars hour after hour. He ran out of cash early and began signing IOU's. The big winner was Raymond, who held more than $300,000 in Rothstein's markers. At game's end a tired, disgusted, and desperate

*George "Hump" McManus, New York gambler, is shown entering court to be tried for the Rothstein murder. (Wide World)*

Rothstein offered to cut the cards with Raymond for $100,000. The West Coast gambler agreed, and won. Rothstein's face flushed with anger, and he asked for all his signed chits of paper. These were dutifully turned over to him so that he could tally his losses. He told each player what he owed them, then to their surprise he tore up the IOU's and marched out of the apartment, saying over his shoulder: "I'll pay off in a day or two. I don't carry that kind of dough under my fingernails."

Raymond and Thompson, the big winners, had never before played with Rothstein and were bewildered by his actions, especially Raymond, who berated McManus, who had set up the game and was Rothstein's contact man.

"Is this the way he always does business?" Titanic Thompson asked McManus.

George McManus shrugged and said: "That's A.R. Hell, he's good for it."

But it was not business as usual for Rothstein. Days, then weeks went by and Rothstein had not made his debts good. The word raced along Broadway that The Big Bankroll was doing the unthinkable—he was going to welsh on a bet. Rothstein was approached by Nicky Arnstein, who advised him to pay Raymond and Thompson. "I won't pay a cent," snarled A.R. "The game was rigged."

"Arnold, rigged or not," cautioned Arnstein, "you have to pay off. Even if it was crooked, no point to your advertising that you were a sucker."

Even Damon Runyon learned of Rothstein's decision not to pay. "I never thought you'd welsh on a bet, A.R." the writer told the gambler in Lindy's Restaurant one afternoon.

The gambler bristled: "I never welsh! I'm just making them sweat a little."

Later, A.R. sent word to Raymond and the others that he would buy them off, but at cut rates. A Rothstein flunkie returned with a message from the West Coast gambler, who was then on his honeymoon. "Raymond says he wants to do business," reported the runner. "He wants to go home."

Rothstein smiled and said: "The longer he waits, the more he'll want to go home."

The gamblers were running out of patience with Rothstein. They finally asked Jimmy Hines, of Tammany Hall, to intervene. Hines met with Rothstein and practically ordered him to settle the matter. "You've got to pay off, Arnold," he told A.R. "You've put George in a bind." McManus, who had a brother in the police department, would be ruined, Hines told Rothstein. Never again would any of the big-time gamblers trust him to "front" important games. He was being held responsible for Rothstein's debts to Raymond and Thompson.

Rothstein told Hines: "They'll get their money, but when I want to give it to them and not a minute before."

The gambler still had not paid the debts by November 4, 1928, the eve of the presidential election. That night Rothstein sat in Lindy's Restaurant making final bets on Hoover, placing a $60,-000 wager with Meyer Boston. (Incredibly, Boston also held one of Rothstein's markers from the big poker game, albeit for a paltry $20,000.) As was his custom, Rothstein took calls regularly from Lindy's phone, taking and making bets. At 10 P.M., Abe Scher, the cashier in the restaurant, called A.R. to the phone once again. Scher was later grilled by police concerning this last phone call, but the cashier had nothing to offer. "The way he talks," said Scher, "you could stand right beside him and not hear anything. Besides, who listens?"

Following the brief phone conversation, Rothstein walked outside the restaurant, beckoning to one of his minions, Jimmy Meehan. "McManus wants to see me," A.R. said. He withdrew a revolver from his pocket and handed it to Meehan. "Here keep this for me. I'm going over to the Park Central. I'll be right back."

Rothstein never returned to Lindy's to munch on another cheesecake or make another wager. He had left an attractive blonde sitting at his table, one Inez Norton, his current heart-throb, a bosomy show girl who departed the restaurant shortly after Rothstein left. She was later to tell police: "Arnold was very gay—his normal, natural self—and very much in love. He didn't seem to have anything on his mind. He certainly didn't fear anything. We spoke of many subjects but mostly of love and he said that he hoped soon to be free to marry me. He said everything would be mine—his property and the money—but I cared only for him."

At 10:47 P.M., Vincent J. Kelly, who operated the servants' elevator at the Park Central Hotel, found Arnold Rothstein crumpled on the floor next to the servants' entrance to the hotel on 56th Street, holding his abdomen. Kelly called Thomas Calhoun, a night watchman, and both men ran to the stricken gambler.

"I've been shot," Rothstein groaned to the two men. "Call me a taxi."

"Who shot you?" asked Calhoun.

"Never mind," said Rothstein. "Get me a taxi."

Calhoun instead called the police, and Patrolman William S. Davis came on the run. An ambulance was called. Davis leaned over Rothstein, asking who had shot him.

Rothstein shook his head. "Get me home. The address is 912 Fifth Avenue."

"Who shot you?"

"Don't ask questions—get me a cab!"

At this time Abe Bender, who was sitting in his cab across from

*Show girl Inez Norton, Rothstein's mistress. (UPI)*

the hotel waiting for a fare, heard something strike the roof of his cab. Bender was later to tell police: "I am sitting in my hack when something comes flying down from the hotel and hits my hack a whack. It bounces into the street. I jump out and go see what it is. When I see it is a gun I figure I better get it to the cops right away." Irate detectives told the cabbie that he probably destroyed any fingerprints on the weapon by handling it. Replied Bender: "At a time like this, who thinks of fingerprints? I am a hackie, not Sherlock Holmes."

Within minutes after being found wounded, Rothstein was rushed by ambulance to the Polyclinic Hospital. The bullet wound was fatal, but The Big Bankroll lingered for two days. Detectives repeatedly asked who had shot him, but Rothstein would only shake his head, rigidly maintaining the underworld code of silence. To Detective Patrick Flood, Rothstein did say, before lapsing into a coma: "I won't talk about it. I'll take care of it myself." He died in silence on November 6, 1928.

Room 349 of the Park Central Hotel had been occupied by George "Hump" McManus, and it was later concluded that the weapon used to kill Rothstein was thrown from that room through a broken screen and had been found by cab driver Abe Bender. But the weapon yielded no fingerprints. Raymond, Thompson, and the other gamblers owed money by Rothstein were picked up and questioned. All had alibis. McManus was indicted for murder, but the charges were dropped when no evidence could be mounted against him.

The murder of Arnold Rothstein was never solved. Many later claimed that the gamblers had nothing to do with A.R.'s death, that the real reason for Mr. Big's assassination was the take-over of Rothstein's criminal empire by Frank Costello and other syndicate chieftains.

Investigators did unravel some of Rothstein's shady business dealings, including a narcotics shipment worth $7 million. But the whereabouts of his real fortune, millions in cash and gems, was never determined. Oddly enough, Rothstein's streak of bad luck ended with his death. He had bet almost $2 million that Herbert Hoover would be elected and had won a posthumous fortune. But, following Rothstein's own example at the end, those who had taken his bets never paid off.

# 1930

## ALFRED "JAKE" LINGLE
### END OF A TYCOON REPORTER

The dapper little man, well dressed in a tailored $300 suit and a straw boater perched rakishly on his head, stepped from the entrance of the Stevens Hotel on Chicago's Michigan Avenue. He walked to the limousine waiting at curbside, started to get into the car, then had second thoughts as he sucked in the spring air and reveled in the sunny day and the blue sky above. He told his chauffeur that he would walk the mile and a half to work, up Michigan Avenue to the *Tribune* tower.

It was almost noon, but Alfred "Jake" Lingle was in no hurry and he strolled leisurely north. His job as a reporter for the *Chicago Tribune* was secure; he was the top crime reporter on the newspaper, so much respected that he was called Chicago's "gangologist." Lingle was not a reporter who sat in front of a typewriter and wrote. It is doubtful that he ever wrote a news story in his life, let alone knew how to work a typewriter. He was known as a "legman," a street reporter who knew every Chicago alley and byway where crime news was to be had. He was on speaking terms with every important mobster in the city, and his contacts in the police department were impeccable.

Lingle's work routine was loose. He would drop by the *Tribune* offices around noon, then make his rounds in the Loop, picking up tips and reports from his underworld contacts, chiefly at the southwest corner of Randolph and Clark streets. Here, at "The Corner," Lingle would find the most notorious gamblers, bookmakers, and racetrack touts. After picking up what news he could from these underworld types, the reporter would take the train to the racetrack, where he always bet heavily. He would later call in what news he had for rewrite men to turn into a story.

101

The evenings meant nightclubbing and attractive female company for the roving Lingle. Though married with two children, the reporter had moved out of his modest home and into the Stevens Hotel early in 1928. He continued to support his family but saw his wife Helen and children little, spending most of his time with his gambling friends and the many show girls he wined, dined, and bedded. In the late evenings, it was later revealed, Lingle received phone calls and visitors who sought his advice. The kind of counsel bestowed upon his callers was not disclosed until after his violent death.

Lingle's routine on Monday, June 9, 1930, did not vary. He arrived at the *Tribune* offices and spoke with one of the editors, saying: "I've been hearing some rumbles of a new stirring among the gangs. There's something brewing in the North Side gang, but I can't get a line on it. I've been trying to find Bugs Moran—he'd tell me, I think, what the dope is. Maybe I'll find him today."

The editor nodded. It was Lingle's usual banter, and he had been checking in with the *Tribune* in this fashion for eighteen years, having joined the newspaper staff as a legman in 1912. After exchanging small talk with reporters, Lingle was off, sauntering out of the building and strolling easily south and westward. He bought a few ties and a new pair of shoes for a Board of Trade dinner he was to attend that night. He had these items sent over to his hotel suite.

Lingle then walked to the Sherman House to have lunch in the coffee shop. This was a hangout for politicians and underworld types and he spoke briefly with a few acquaintances. As Lingle emerged from the restaurant he met Police Sergeant Thomas Alcock, of the Detective Bureau. He wore a nervous look and said: "I'm being tailed, Tom." But he did not explain his mysterious remark, moving on quickly out of the hotel foyer and eastward on Randolph Street, heading for the Illinois Central Railroad station at Michigan and Randolph where he customarily caught the 1:30 P.M. train to Washington Park racetrack in Homewood.

In front of the main building of the Public Library on Randolph Street, Lingle paused to buy a copy of the *Daily Racing Form*. A roadster pulled up to the curb, the driver honking the horn. Lingle looked up. Three men were in the car. All were dressed in dark suits and hats and were swarthy in appearance, according to cabdriver Armour Lapansee, who was parked nearby and waiting

*Alfred "Jake" Lingle,* Chicago Tribune *reporter, who once boasted: "I fix the price of beer in this town."*

for a fare. One of the men smiled at Lingle and said: "Play Hy Schneider in the third, Jake!"

Lingle waved gratefully for the tip, replying: "I've got him."

The reporter turned and walked down the stairs leading to the pedestrian subway, a hundred-feet-long, twenty-feet-wide tunnel going underneath Michigan Avenue to the IC terminal. Jake lit one of his $3.50 cigars, a giant Havana, smoking as he looked over the racing sheet and ambled along with the heavy crowds. Two men hurriedly followed Lingle into the tunnel from Randolph Street, one tall, lean, and blond, the other short and dark. Several witnesses would later claim that the blond man wore the collar of a Roman Catholic priest.

Nestled inside the coat pocket of the blond-haired man was a .38 snub-nosed Colt revolver. He held his hand over the weapon as he slowly closed in on Lingle, his companion dropping back to act as a lookout. Fred Pasley, a fellow *Tribune* reporter who had long known Jake Lingle and was later to write of the assassination in *Al Capone*, stated: "The humor or whatever it is that guides gangland in selecting its execution sites is ghastly beyond words. . . . Here [the IC tunnel] the in and outgoing currents of traffic bottleneck; surge and eddy in near confluence as they pursue their opposite courses. At high tide, in rush hours, it is a series of human whirlpools and maelstroms. It was, relatively, as if the assassins had picked Times Square subway station."

When Lingle was little more than midway in the tunnel, the blond-haired young man suddenly whipped out the revolver and rushed up behind the reporter, jamming the weapon to Lingle's head and firing once. The bullet crashed through Lingle's brain and came out his forehead. Lingle fell straight forward on his face as women screamed and people ran in all directions. Mrs. Ann Applegate, who had been walking behind the killer and Lingle, saw the blond-haired man rush down the tunnel. "Isn't somebody going to stop that man?" she yelled. Clark L. "Red" Applegate, her husband, turned and raced after the fleeing killer, who ran up the east stairway and onto Michigan Avenue, which he crossed at a run.

In the tunnel all was confusion. Dr. Joseph Springer, who had worked in the coroner's office and knew Lingle, had passed the reporter and his killer in the tunnel moments before the shooting; he had not recognized the reporter. After the single shot was fired, Springer rushed to the fallen man and, wiping away the blood gushing from his wound, identified Lingle. The cigar the reporter had been smoking was still burning, clenched tightly in the dead man's teeth. His fingers clutched the racing form in a death grip. Springer pronounced him dead.

Meanwhile, Applegate and others pursued the killer across Michigan Avenue, shouting to the traffic cop on duty, Patrolman

*Jake Lingle, dead on the Illinois Central tunnel floor, June 9, 1930.*

Anthony Ruthy, to "Get that man!" They pointed to the running blond-haired man. "He's a murderer!" Ruthy drew his revolver and raced up Randolph Street, going west, but he was unsure of his prey because terrified citizens were now running in all directions. The killer raced down the north side of Randolph Street, cut through a northbound alleyway, then a westbound alley, then south on Wabash, and then west again on Randolph, where Ruthy lost him.

Winded, Applegate rejoined his wife in the tunnel. She was standing close to Dr. Springer and the dead man. "I couldn't get him," Applegate told his wife. "The cops are after him."

"Poor man," said Ann Applegate, looking down at the body. "He never had a chance."

Her husband grabbed her firmly by the arm and led her toward the east side of the tunnel. The Applegates, who were racehorse trainers and owners, caught the interurban electric train to Washington Park without realizing that the slain man was their good friend Jake Lingle. Police began to clog the tunnel, frantically questioning those who had lingered. Harry Komen, who had seen the blond-haired man dashing up the alley off Randolph, walked down the tunnel stairs to deliver a gray left-handed glove to a policeman, saying: "Here—the guy the cop was chasing dropped this."

The killer had also dropped the murder weapon on the spot, but newsmen who had arrived en masse with the police had already handled the revolver and had obliterated any prints that might have been taken from it. Patrick Campbell had been close to the victim when the shooting occurred. He insisted that "a priest bumped into me. I asked him, 'What's the matter?' and he answered, 'I think someone has been shot and I am going to get out of here!'"

To that, Lieutenant of Detectives William Cusack snorted a resounding "No, never! He was no priest. A priest would never do that. He would have gone to the side of the stricken person."

Several others had seen a priest running in the tunnel, and this, coupled to police remarks, gave rise to the belief that the killer had cleverly disguised himself with a priest's collar, discarding the clerical garb as he raced from the tunnel. (The collar was never found.) Employing disguises in gangland murders was a device already well known to Chicago police and its citizens; the four killers who slew the seven Moran mobsters in the St. Valentine's Day Massacre a year earlier had been dressed as policemen.

As soon as Lingle's identity had been established, the top staff members of all the city's newspapers rushed to the murder scene. Right behind them was Commissioner of Police William P. Russell. Russell's presence, to the unknowing, seemed a bit strange. Chicago's top police official had never visited the scene of any of the myriad mob killings over the past two years. Yet here he stood in the train tunnel, staring down at the body of Alfred Lingle. A short time later all in Chicago learned that Russell was Lingle's best friend, a friendship that went beyond camaraderie, and into dark and sinister corners of Jake Lingle's past.

"Jake was like a son to me," Russell told reporters as he watched the news photographers capture the bloody scene for their cameras. "Who could have done such an awful thing?"

The answer to that question became, in the weeks that followed, an obsessive crusade for the *Chicago Tribune.* The newspaper's editors were incensed that gangsters would dare to shoot down their ace crime expert. *Tribune* publisher Colonel Robert McCormick quickly offered a $25,000 reward for information leading to the apprehension and conviction of the killer. William Randolph Hearst, who was then at war with the *Tribune,* showed his magnanimity by offering an equal amount. The *Evening Post* put up another $5,000. Civic groups scraped together $725. The overall reward was $55,725, a staggering amount, and the *Tribune* promised to put up more money if needed.

The *Tribune* also declared war on the gangsters who had committed the deed. "The meaning of the murder is plain," said its lead editorial the following day. "It was committed in reprisal and in an attempt at intimidation. Mr. Lingle was a police reporter and an exceptionally well-informed one. . . . What made him valuable to his newspaper marked him as dangerous to the killers. . . . The *Tribune* accepts this challenge. It is war. There will be casualties, but that is to be expected, it being war. . . . Justice will make a fight of it or will abdicate."

Justice in Lingle's case had abdicated many years before his murder, the facts later revealed. As the press dug deeper into his past it was learned that the $65-a-week reporter was enormously wealthy, that from mid-1928 to almost the day of his death, he had been depositing huge amounts of money, $750 to $1,000, in his bank account on successive days. In the last year of his life Lingle spent more than $60,000 on high living, and he never dropped less than $500 a day at the racetrack.

Also uncovered was a diamond-studded belt, given to him by his good friend Al Capone, the crime czar of Chicago. Further, the reporter had an expensive West Side home where his family lived and a $18,000 summer home in Long Beach, Indiana. He had explained his newfound riches by claiming that a relative had died and left him a small family fortune.

There was no rich relative, but there was Police Commissioner Russell, who served as Lingle's passport to wealth. Jake had known Russell since the officer had been a beat cop in 1910. He had followed Russell about on his beat and continued a close association with him as Russell rose through the ranks. Russell had at first served as Lingle's pipeline to mob activity and later, when Russell became police commissioner, as the necessary clout Lingle wielded against the mobs as an extortionist for favors, chiefly the approval for gambling and liquor operations.

It was Lingle himself who was instrumental in having Russell appointed to the top cop position. The reporter was asked by his

*Police Commissioner William Russell, Lingle's best friend and always flowing pipeline.*

editors in the summer of 1928 who he thought would make a good police commissioner, the position having been recently vacated. Lingle urged the *Tribune* editors to support Russell, and they did. Russell was appointed on August 1, 1928, and afterward Lingle was known in certain circles as the "unofficial Chief of Police."

Those wanting to open a gambling den or a speakeasy in Chicago saw Lingle first, and through his connection with Russell the reporter made sure the new den went unmolested by police. In truth, Jake Lingle, lowly *Tribune* legman, was one of the most powerful men in Chicago. He once boasted: "I fix the price of beer in this town," and he meant it.

During the massive investigation into Lingle's background, employees of the Stevens Hotel were interviewed. The house detective stated that Lingle received phone calls at all hours of the night. When asked who would be calling the reporter, the detective replied: "Why, policemen calling up to have Jake get them transferred or promoted, or politicians wanting the fix put in for somebody. Jake could do it. He had a lot of power. I've known him twenty years. He was up there among the big boys and had a lot of responsibilities."

One of the "big boys" Lingle frequently visited—in his posh South Side offices and even at his palatial Palm Island, Florida, estate—was Al Capone. In addition to political favors Lingle bestowed upon Scarface, he fed him valuable information on police activity and reported on the doings of Capone's deadly rivals, the North Side gang headed by George "Bugs" Moran. In return, Capone lavished money on the unscrupulous reporter and was the real source of Lingle's large income. In his dealings with Lingle the only prerequisite Scarface insisted upon was loyalty. Lingle betrayed that loyalty early in 1930, an act that caused his death.

With Capone out of town for several weeks, Lingle was approached by Bugs Moran, who knew that Lingle was more than $100,000 in debt over gambling losses. Moran had bought up Lingle's IOU's. He offered these to Lingle, plus an additional $50,000 in return for information Lingle could provide him on police activities and Capone's shady empire. The reporter switched sides, becoming a vassal to Moran. When Capone discovered this treason, he ordered the newsman murdered. A breach of loyalty to Scarface was a capital sin.

When these facts surfaced, Commissioner Russell, along with several of his top aides, immediately resigned and went into hasty retirement. Colonel Robert McCormick of the *Tribune,* for all of his wrathful indignation over Lingle's murder, was forced to admit publicly that his martyred newsman had been a crook. Said one *Tribune* editorial: "Alfred Lingle now takes on a different character, one in which he was unknown to the management of the *Tribune* when he was alive. . . . The reasonable appearance against Lingle now is that he was accepted in the world of politics and crime for something undreamed of in his office and that he used this in undertakings which made him money and brought him to his death."

The enormous reward, however, still stood for the apprehension of his killer. Crooked or not, Jake Lingle had been murdered in such a publicly shocking fashion that his death demanded a solution. (Lingle had not been the only newsman ever killed up to that time by gangsters; Julius Rosenheim, a crime tipster for the Chicago *Daily News,* had been shot to death, along with eighteen assorted gangsters, in February 1930.)

As the hunt for Lingle's killer went on, police traced the weapon used in the murder to Peter von Frantzius, who was the armorer to the Chicago gangs. There was no law prohibiting the sale of automatic firearms, including submachine guns, to anyone in Illinois at the time. Von Frantzius was shown the murder weapon and said that he had sold it and two other revolvers to Ted Newbury, a onetime Moran gunsel who had gone over to Scarface. That put the killing in Capone's camp.

An undercover detective, John Hagan, at the request of the police and the *Tribune* then joined the Moran gang as a bootlegger in July 1930. For months he dangerously investigated the Lingle killing, even traveling to St. Louis on a tip to work briefly for mobster Pat Hogan. It was Hogan who finally revealed the fact that Lingle had been killed by an out-of-town murderer-for-hire, a man known as "Buster." Hagan later learned that "Buster" was Leo Bader, a burglar, bootlegger, extortionist, and killer who had been used by Al Capone to eliminate many Chicago rivals. Bader's real name was Leo Vincent Brothers, and he had employed many disguises while "on the job," several times posing as a priest.

Through Hagan, Brothers was apprehended in Chicago and put on trial on March 16, 1931, for Lingle's killing. Eight eyewitnesses to the killing in the IC tunnel bravely came forward and identified Brothers as the murderer. The defense in the case was weak, with Louis Piquett (who would later become John Dillinger's lawyer and front man) unsuccessfully trying to shake the testimony of the eyewitnesses. Brothers was convicted of first-degree murder

*Leo Vincent Brothers, Jake Lingle's killer.*

on April 2, 1931, following a twenty-seven-hour deliberation. Though his client was convicted, Piquett, through Capone's influence and money, did manage to bring about a shocking sentence.

The jury itself set a minimum sentence for Brothers; in that era juries could legally fix sentences. The sentence was fourteen years in prison, making Brothers eligible for parole in eight years. (He was released eight years later to the day.) The press raved against the jury's decision, labeling the act a "Capone sentence," in that several of Scarface's top gunmen—Jack "Three-Fingered" White, and Albert Anselmi and John Scalise—had received fourteen-year sentences for committing clear-cut murders. But nothing the press did altered Brothers's prison term.

The handsome, blond-haired gangster rose in court to hear his sentence, smiled, then turned to the reporters' gallery and smugly stated: "I can do that standing on my head," coining a new underworld cliché.

Two months later undercover man John Hagan was given the *Tribune* reward of $25,000. It was considerably more than Leo Brothers had earned for the murder of Chicago's gangologist; when apprehended, Brothers was living in a $5-a-week room and had less than $10 in his pocket. His reason for being in Chicago at the time was to collect the "hit money" due him from Capone. In the end Scarface refused to pay the hired gun, carping that Brothers had brought down too much pressure on him through the spectacular slaying of Lingle. It was the kind of penny-pinching on the part of a multimillionaire beer baron that would induce other underpaid hirelings to begin talking to authorities, talk that eventually led to Capone's conviction on charges of tax evasion.

Capone did spend lavishly on Lingle at the end, sending huge floral wreaths to his funeral, all marked "From Al." The crime kingpin told a reporter a year after Lingle's death: "Why, Jake was my pal up to the day he died. There was only one thing wrong with him—horse races."

# 1930

## JERRY BUCKLEY
### CRUSADE OF DEATH

It was common knowledge across the country by 1930 that Detroit was a thoroughly corrupt city, as mob-ridden and as dangerous as Capone's Chicago. Its political machinery and police department burgeoned with grafters, kickback artists, and boondogglers on the hefty payroll of the underworld. The most notorious criminal element was the Purple Gang, whose members controlled most of the illegal liquor distribution and sales and were responsible for countless murders.

Crime-ridden Detroit, however, did have a champion for law and order, a powerful and charismatic individual who spoke daily over the airways from radio station WMBC, Jerry Buckley. The broadcaster was a native Detroiter whose father had been successful in real estate. Buckley had once worked as a private investigator, numbering Henry Ford among his clients.

Even though the public had taken pains to elect a so-called reform mayor, Charles Bowles, who had installed ex-FBI chief Thomas Wilcox as police commissioner (ousting the ineffectual Harold Emmons) and announced an all-out campaign against the criminal element, Detroit remained a murder capital for the mobs, and the situation promised to worsen. Buckley, who was thought of as Detroit's civic conscience, mounted a crusade against Bowles and other city officials, demanding that they clean up the city. He was just as dogged in lambasting the criminal element, raging against the transgressions of the Purple Gang and other mobs.

Such open defiance against Detroit's ruthless powerhouses proved more than dangerous. "I get twenty threats a day," Buckley casually told a reporter. "There is always someone who says I'll be killed." To protect himself Buckley took a room in the La Salle Hotel, which also housed the WMBC studio. When the threats mounted, Buckley sometimes stayed in his room for several days. He appeared resigned to his fate, once remarking: "When the time comes I'll be killed."

Murder was nothing new to Detroit, and at the beginning of July 1930, the city was fairly dotted with the bodies of the slain. On July 4 two dope peddlers were gunned down just outside the entrance of the La Salle Hotel. Eight more men, all victims of gangland reprisals, were shot to death in downtown streets in the following two weeks. In his broadcasts Buckley dubbed the awful month of carnage "Bloody July."

Public indignation, whipped up by Buckley and the newspapers, reached fever pitch. Suddenly there were widespread demands that Mayor Bowles be recalled. At first Buckley held back his endorsement from this movement, saying that he thought a recall undemocratic. But two days before the recall balloting Buckley joined the movement and urged all Detroiters to vote Bowles out of office.

The broadcaster was on hand at City Hall, reporting over the airways on the night of July 21–22, 1930, as the recall vote was counted. At 1 A.M., Buckley went on the air from the WMBC studio to inform his myriad listeners that the citizens of Detroit had won a great battle; Mayor Bowles had been recalled.

Minutes later Buckley received a phone call in his studio from a woman who asked that he meet her in the lobby. "Okay, it's a date," he was heard to say. A short time later the broadcaster went to the lobby and sat facing the Adelaide Street entranceway, reading a paper. The normally busy lobby was oddly deserted.

Buckley never saw the three men come through the lobby entrance and walk the thirty feet to his chair. All three suddenly drew revolvers and aimed them almost point-blank at the broadcaster, firing shot after shot into Buckley, blowing him off his chair.

There was only one other person sitting in the lobby at the time: Jack Klein, a projectionist, who promptly dove behind a couch. Hotel employees were nowhere to be seen. Calmly the three killers looked down at the fallen Buckley, then emptied their pistols into his already dead body. They sauntered from the lobby, stepped into a car, and drove off down Woodward Avenue.

The blatant murder of Jerry Buckley had Detroit up in arms.

*The three men suspected of murdering Jerry Buckley (left to right), Ted Pizzino, Angelo Livecchi, and Joseph Bommarito. (Wide World)*

Everyone was convinced that city officials, enraged at his endorsement of the Bowles recall, had brought about the broadcaster's murder. "Who killed Buckley?" became the shrill and insistent public outcry.

Police Commissioner Wilcox announced that he would personally handle the investigation and would not rest until the killers had been apprehended. He then disappeared and was finally run to ground in Duluth, where he had gone to attend a four-day police convention. Two young patrolmen next uncovered evidence linked to the Buckley slaying in a Grosse Pointe residence owned by a member of the Purple Gang; but their report was inexplicably "misplaced" and the evidence they had uncovered vanished. Moreover, the two young cops were separated and put on beat patrol.

Wilbur M. Bruckner, attorney general, and later governor of the state, had had enough. He convened a grand jury to look into the matter, carefully selecting members including the poet Edgar Guest and wealthy manufacturer Christopher F. Coda. Those high-ranking cops thought to be honest were assigned to follow up any clues or tips in the murder. Lieutenant J. H. Hoffman did exactly that, trailing a gunman called Ted Pizzino to New York and arresting him as Pizzino was about to close a bank account. Pizzino was returned to Detroit and charged with the murder of Jerry Buckley, along with mobster Joseph Bommarito and Angelo Livecchi, a mysterious figure who lived in the La Salle Hotel and had been seen hanging about the lobby a short time before Buckley had been assassinated.

All three were tried before Judge Edward Jeffries, a severe critic of city officials who was thought to be "unreachable" by the criminal element. The prosecution produced several eyewitnesses to the slaying, its star witness being cabdriver Gus Reno, who identified Pizzino, Bommarito, and Livecchi as the three men who ran from the hotel lobby and jumped in a getaway car immediately after the shooting. He had been sitting in his cab only a few feet away at the time, he said, waiting for a fare.

Projectionist Jack Klein also identified the trio of killers, as did Robert Jackson, a hotel porter. Another man, Fred Tara, made the same identification, although he constantly cried to the judge that the news photographers taking his picture would seal his doom. "It's my death sentence," screamed Tara, and he later recanted his testimony, then changed it back to his original accusation.

The case for the prosecution seemed to indicate a clear-cut conviction. The entire city was stunned when the jury returned a verdict of "not guilty as charged." Shameful, said the prosecutors of the decision. The press echoed this sentiment, but the killers nevertheless walked sneeringly from the courtroom as free men. It was generally concluded that the power of the corrupt city administration and the mobs that controlled the politicians had reached into the hall of justice to "convince" jury members that a "not guilty" verdict was preferable to being killed one by one.

Pizzino and Livecchi did not, however, escape eventual justice.

They were arrested for the murder of the two dope peddlers killed almost two weeks before Buckley. Following a quick trial they were convicted and sentenced to life imprisonment. Only Bommarito remained free.

The mysterious woman who called Buckley on the murder night was never found, and, moreover, the reason for Buckley's killing was never determined, a question that still nags Detroit historians to this day.

About a month after the murder trial thousands of mournful Detroiters gathered in a memorial service for Jerry Buckley, who at the time was proclaimed to be "a champion of human life." Ex-mayor Charles Bowles, along with his minions, did not attend the ceremonies.

# 1935

## THELMA TODD
### A SILVER SCREEN
### MYSTERY

Hollywood in the 1920s was a sinful and wayward place, its acting community and some of the moguls who ran the studios indulging in every known vice under a carefully designed protective screen provided by public relations people. This army of PR types deftly covered up suicides, drug addiction, alcoholism, sex perversions, manslaughter, and, perhaps in the case of the ravishing blond actress Thelma Todd, murder.

Born in 1905 to a prominent politician, John Shaw Todd of Lawrence, Massachusetts, Thelma was raised in a safe and comfortable environment. Though a lovely girl at an early age, Thelma had no aspirations to act, and only on a whim did she enter a beauty contest while still a teen-ager, winning the title of Miss Massachusetts. Thelma went on to earn her degree in education, supplementing her income with modeling jobs. She became a sixth-grade teacher and might have remained in that position had it not been for a friend of her father's, a theater manager who sent off her picture to film producer Jesse Lasky without Thelma's knowledge, urging the producer to hire the beautiful blonde for his studio, Paramount.

In one of those odd quirks of fate Lasky received the photo, and instead of discarding it as was his habit with all unsolicited job requests, he was utterly enchanted with Thelma's beauty. The producer wrote to Thelma, offering her a place in Paramount's acting school in Astoria, Queens, a school that was designed to be a talent pool for the West Coast studio.

After some deliberation Thelma accepted and moved to Astoria, where she underwent a rigorous routine, not only learning how to act but acquiring the finer points of etiquette, makeup, fencing, swimming, driving an auto, dancing, all the abilities that might be required of someone acting in motion pictures. She

*Thelma Todd, wearing a dark wig for her role in* **Kismet**.

excelled in these pursuits, and after six months she and fifteen others in the school were rewarded with one-year contracts, following a sumptuous dinner party at the Ritz-Carlton Hotel on March 2, 1926.

Some Paramount producer had the bright idea of putting all sixteen apprentices into one film, *Fascinating Youth,* each acting out parts especially written for him or her. The picture was a box-office success, chiefly due to Thelma Todd, who displayed a natural flair for comedy, and to a strikingly handsome young man with blond wavy hair, one Charles "Buddy" Rogers, who would later marry one of the greatest stars of the silent film era, "America's Sweetheart," Mary Pickford.

The film career of Thelma Todd was mercurial, the shapely, wholesome blonde appearing in one smash hit after another, playing in all manner of films—westerns, comedies, dramas, musicals, mysteries. She displayed an amazing ability to adapt to any role, although Thelma was best remembered as a delightful comedienne whose timing was all but perfect. The public and critics alike heaped praise upon Thelma year after year, one reviewer calling her "the loveliest blonde ever seen on the screen."

Thelma played opposite Gary Cooper in *Nevada* in 1927 for Paramount, firmly establishing herself as a leading lady. (It was Cooper's fourth major film by that time.) She went on to star in many other Paramount productions, so excelling in comedy that she was loaned out to Hal Roach, who made her a sensation by putting her into seventeen two-reelers with ZaSu Pitts and another twenty-one two-reelers with Patsy Kelly, hilarious comedies that brought Thelma her greatest popularity. ZaSu and Patsy also became Thelma's closest friends in Hollywood.

By the beginning of the 1930s, Thelma was one of the most sought-after comediennes in filmdom, appearing with Hollywood's top comedy stars—Buster Keaton in *Speak Easily,* Joe E. Brown in *Son of a Sailor,* Laurel and Hardy in *The Bohemian Girl.* She went on to star with the zany Marx Brothers in *Horse Feathers* and *Monkey Business.* One of the reasons Thelma was so much in demand for these early talkies was that she had a beautiful speaking voice. Unlike many silent screen stars, Thelma made the transition to talking pictures easily whereas matinee idols such as John Gilbert, Nita Naldi, and others having unconvincing voices fell by the wayside.

Left: *Thelma Todd just before her mysterious death in 1935.* Right: *Pat DiCicco, Thelma's former husband and onetime suspect in her death.*

Thelma's acting range was wide, and she knew it. In an effort to change her screen image from a star of comedy to one of serious drama, she even changed her name to Alison Loyd to appear in the gangster drama *Corsair* in 1931. It was an immense hit that proved Thelma could handle any kind of role.

Popular, famous, and rich, Thelma was also prudent with her money. She correctly reasoned that her career could not go on forever, that there was perhaps only a ten-year span in which she could command leading roles. (By 1935 she had completed seventy films, sixty of which were talkies, a staggering record for a thirty-year-old actress.) Thelma began investing her money in real estate and later, with loans from ZaSu Pitts, opened up a popular cafe, Thelma Todd's Roadside Rest, on the Pacific Highway between Santa Monica and Malibu, beneath the Palisades.

Thelma's partner in the restaurant was director Roland West, who was also her lover. Thelma had had many lovers up to 1935. Where she was cautious with her money, she had been reckless in her love life, having short-lived affairs and many one-night encounters. It was also rumored that she was addicted to drugs, specifically heroin, but this was never proven.

The actress's only experience with matrimony ended in divorce. Thelma married Pasquale "Pat" DiCicco, a talent agent, in July 1932, eloping to Prescott, Arizona, and later going through an elaborate marriage ceremony in Los Angeles. Thelma filed for divorce on March 3, 1934, charging incompatibility and cruelty, but continued to see the handsome DiCicco on and off almost to the time of her violent end.

DiCicco's last meeting with Thelma was a stormy one. Comedian Stanley Lupino and his daughter, Ida, than an unknown actress who was to become one of Hollywood's most dynamic stars and an exceptional director, decided to give Thelma a party at the posh Hollywood nightclub, the Trocadero, on December 14, 1935, a Saturday night. DiCicco had invited himself when he ran into Ida Lupino a few days before the party and demanded to be put on the invitation list. A place was reserved for him next to Thelma, but when the talent agent appeared at the Trocadero on the night of the party, he was accompanied by two attractive starlets. He ignored the banquet table where he was to sit, going to another table. Thelma later approached her ex-husband and upbraided him for his conduct. Ida Lupino witnessed the confrontation and later stated that Thelma "was very indignant. She berated him bitterly for slighting me and herself." Another guest said the two had "a terrific argument." A few hours later Thelma Todd made a grand exit from the nightclub, guests escorting her outside to her waiting limousine. The fur-wrapped "Ice Cream Blonde" turned and gave her admirers an exaggerated wave and said only one word: "Good-bye!" She had uttered this farewell, many later claimed, in a voice prophetic with doom, but then such dramatic descriptions in the aftermath of Hollywood tragedies are to be expected.

Ernest O. Peters, Thelma's chauffeur that night, drove the actress to her restaurant on the Pacific Highway where Thelma maintained an apartment above the cafe. En route the actress told Peters to drive faster, stating that she feared that "gangsters are following us." She added that she might be kidnapped or even killed by gangsters, Peters later claimed. He drove at 70 mph.

Arriving at the Roadside Rest, Thelma got out of the rented limousine and told Peters to go home.

"Don't you want me to walk you up to your apartment?" the chauffeur asked. This was his usual custom.

"That won't be necessary," Thelma told him. "Go home, Ernest."

With that Peters drove off. He was the last person to see Thelma Todd alive, or so authorities later insisted, despite the later testimony of some startling witnesses. It was 2 A.M., Sunday morning, December 15.

On Monday, Thelma's maid arrived for work. She could not find her employer anywhere inside the spacious apartment above the Roadside Rest. Looking out a rear window, she peered up the hill to where Thelma's business partner and sometime lover, Roland West, had a two-car garage and a bungalow. Thelma kept her own car in the garage. The doors to the garage were partly open, and the maid guessed that her mistress was visiting West. At 10:30 A.M. the maid climbed the 270 stairs leading to the top of the hill and entered the garage. There she found her employer slumped over the steering wheel of her open Packard convertible. The key was in the ignition and the gas tank, investigators later discovered, was empty. Thelma Todd still wore the evening gown and fur coat she had worn at the Trocadero party.

Police responded quickly to the maid's frantic summons and noted that though there were no apparent signs of a struggle, the actress's face had blood on it and there was blood splattered on the seat and on the running board. Yet Thelma's body revealed no open wounds, only a few bruises. The bruises were later explained away by investigators as having been received when Thelma apparently fell forward on the steering wheel of the car. (An autopsy later disclosed that the *inside* of the actress's throat "was bruised" with the kind of marks a bottle might make if jammed down her throat.)

To the officers originally investigating the death, Thelma's lawyer, and her mother, the actress's end was a clear-cut case of murder. Then Hollywood executives moved in and silence descended, the matter quietly turned over to a coroner's jury. Quickly the jury decided that Thelma's death was accidental. She

*Thelma Todd dead in her car, as police captain Bert Wallis checks for signs of murder. (UPI)*

had, members concluded, decided to drive somewhere after her chauffeur had dropped her off. In an alcoholic state, she had started her car in the closed garage, passed out, and then perished from asphyxiation. "Death due to carbon monoxide poisoning," was the jury's verdict. The case was officially closed by the police.

Thelma's mother, who at first had been convinced that her daughter had been killed, suddenly agreed with the coroner's jury. The actress's lawyer, however, persisted in stating that she had been murdered and that there was a cover-up going on. The police refused to discuss the case.

If the coroner's jury had been correct, there was still no explanation for the blood covering the actress or her car. Her clothes were in a rumpled disarray when the body was found, and this suggested some sort of struggle. Then there were the evening slippers the actress was wearing when found. If she had trudged up the 270 stairs from her restaurant to the garage, experts later proved, the delicate shoes would have been scuffed. There was not a mark on them. This led many to conclude that Thelma had been carried to the garage and placed in the car after having been knocked unconscious.

The findings of the coroner's jury were replete with errors. Jury members supported the claim that Thelma Todd had died in the early hours of Sunday morning, December 15, yet the autopsy performed on the actress showed that her stomach contained food that had to have been consumed only a few hours before her body was discovered by the maid on December 16. Then several Hollywood dignitaries came forth to state emphatically that Thelma had indeed been alive Sunday, that they had seen and spoken with her.

One of these was Mrs. Wallace Ford, who insisted that she had spoken with Thelma at 4 P.M. on Sunday, that the actress had called her to tell her she would be attending Mrs. Ford's cocktail party that night, saying: "And when you see who's coming with me, you'll drop dead."

A druggist came forward to support Mrs. Ford's statements, saying that a woman answering Thelma Todd's description came into his pharmacy to make a phone call at approximately 4 P.M. on Sunday, the time when Mrs. Ford received Thelma's call. Although she obviously did not attend the Ford party, Thelma was seen again seven hours later at 11 P.M. on Sunday night, when she entered a tobacco store and asked the owner to dial a phone number ending in 7771 before suddenly running to the street, where she joined a handsome man who was holding her fur coat.

Then Jewel Carmen, estranged wife of Roland West, Thelma's business partner, stated that she had seen Thelma, whom she knew well, pass her on a street in a car driven by a well-dressed male companion she had never seen before. The companion might well have been a new lover Thelma had taken, a man from San Francisco she had not identified by name but had mentioned to friends at the Trocadero party. He was never found.

Against the wishes of studio heads a police spokesman attempted to end the controversy once and for all. He stated that it was the conclusion of investigators that Thelma Todd had lost the key to her apartment and had climbed the stairs behind her restaurant to start her car to keep warm, that she either fell asleep with the motor running or passed out from intoxication. This had caused her death. Period. End of investigation.

Deputy District Attorney George Johnson laughed at this explanation. Said Johnson: "It seems too difficult to believe Miss Todd went to that garage and started the motor of her car to keep warm." Johnson added that he believed Thelma had killed herself. She had made cryptic remarks in recent months that indicated despondency and depression, he said. On one occasion Thelma had stated: "Life isn't worth the candle. While we're here we should laugh, be gay and have fun."

Almost all who knew the actress objected to the suicide theory. There was absolutely no reason for Thelma to kill herself, retorted Patsy Kelly, her costar in many Hal Roach comedies. ZaSu Pitts and others echoed Miss Kelly's statements, pointing out that the golden-haired actress had everything to live for—she was wealthy, successful, and attractive, and her future was full of promise.

Murder was the only answer according to many. Suspicions and whispered accusations abounded. Pat DiCicco had a motive, it was claimed, in that he had argued with Thelma violently on the night of her last public appearance. DiCicco, one report had it, wanted her back and was incensed by the many lovers Thelma had taken on since their divorce.

Then there were the reports of gangsters who had intimidated the actress. She herself had mentioned her fear of mobsters lurking in the shadows. Thelma's lawyer claimed that gangsters representing New York mob kingpin Lucky Luciano, who had already expanded his syndicate interests to the West Coast, approached Thelma, demanding that she turn over to them space above her restaurant where they could establish a crooked gambling casino. When she refused, they threatened to kill her. The attorney demanded a second inquest at which time, he said, he could prove his claims. Producer Hal Roach, who was terrified of Luciano, it was said, went to the attorney and convinced him to drop the matter.

The primary suspect in the murder theory remained Roland West. He had been discarded as a lover by Thelma for the affections of the unnamed San Francisco businessman. The onetime director was reportedly livid with rage at Thelma and had had a violent argument with her when she returned from the Trocadero party, one in which the actress's screamed obscenities were heard by neighbors late Sunday morning. West had really staged this fight, some said later, using a girl friend as a stand-in for Thelma, whom he had already killed and dragged up the stairs to the garage, where he also staged her suicide. West, who died obscurely in 1952, had directed a number of involved murder mysteries, including *Alibi*, *The Monster*, and *The Bat Whispers*. It was reported that he was obsessed with committing the perfect crime. His hatred for his ex-lover, Thelma, provided the motive. Despite widespread suspicions of West, he was never seriously questioned about Thelma's death.

The final chapter of this unusual death unfolded when the Los Angeles Police Department received a telegram from Ogden, Utah. The sender, a woman later described as middle-aged, black-haired and well-dressed, but who was not named, claimed that she had evidence against the man who had "killed Thelma Todd," that he was living in Ogden and had resided in Ogden since the actress's death.

Ogden police were informed of the telegram and conducted their own investigation. A short time later Ogden's Mayor Harmon Peery and the city police chief, Rial Moore, sent a report to the Los Angeles Police Department stating: "Someone should question the man who has been located."

But the Los Angeles police did not follow up the Ogden report, replying to Peery that the Todd case was closed. They did not intend to spend another minute investigating what to them was an accidental death. That was the end of the matter, at least along official lines.

A bizarre footnote to the Todd case is a scene from *Monkey Business*, still seen on late-night TV, in which Groucho Marx holds on to the milky arm of a bubbling Thelma Todd and tells her: "Now be a good girlie, or I'll lock you up in the garage!"

A month following Thelma's death her will was filed. She left all her worldly goods to her mother except for one dollar, which she bequeathed to her former husband, Pat DiCicco.

# 1943

## HENRY C. HEINZ
### ONE BURGLARY
### TOO MANY

Henry C. Heinz was the epitome of the successful American businessman and the sterling civic leader. Though he was born in New Haven, Connecticut, Heinz's family were natives of Atlanta, Georgia, where he began his career with the Central Bank and Trust Company, founded by the millionaire druggist and creator of Coca-Cola, Asa G. Candler. When this bank merged with the Citizens and Southern Bank in 1922, Heinz became a vice-president and member of the board of that institution.

Aggressive and intelligent, Heinz came into great wealth through his marriage to Candler's only daughter, Lucy. The couple moved into an enormous mansion at 1610 Ponce de Leon Avenue in Atlanta's exclusive Druid Hills. The Mediterranean-style home became an Atlanta showplace, especially during the spring, when estate grounds were opened to thousands of spectators who came to marvel at the Heinz gardens.

The couple spent a great deal of time in civic and social activities. Heinz at one time served as president of Kiwanis International and as Potentate of the Atlanta Shrine, and he became the director and president of the Atlanta Athletic Club. Further, he founded the Atlanta Boys' Club, an organization that consumed endless hours of his time. During the early years of World War II, Heinz was the city chairman of the banking division of the Third War Loan Drive. The banker's private life was unspectacular.

It was inconceivable that Henry Heinz, civic pillar of Atlanta, would be a likely prospect for murder. Yet, as the police knew, there had been warning signs that the banker was in a dangerous position. By spring in 1942, Heinz's elegant home had been burglarized twice. Someone had entered the mansion one night and made his way through the darkened, cavernous building to the bedroom where Henry and Lucy Heinz slept, daringly taking $210 from the banker's wallet, which was on a nightstand, and then quietly leaving. He was not apprehended. On another occasion a smaller amount was taken from a downstairs den, but the burglar had made a noise that awakened the banker. Heinz had rushed downstairs, to glimpse the burglar escaping into the night. He later described the intruder to police as "a large Negro man."

Police officers Bill Miller and Marion Blackwell had responded to each home-invasion report made by Heinz. After the second burglary Heinz told Miller and Blackwell that, as much as he appreciated their efforts, he did not intend to sit idly by and wait for the police to catch the intruder. He had purchased a pistol and begun target practice on the estate grounds at the rear of the mansion. When Blackwell and Miller arrived on a follow-up visit, the banker told them with a determined voice: "If that man comes back here again I'll shoot him." They knew he meant it.

Blackwell and Miller made a habit of regularly checking the Heinz estate each night, sometimes twice each night, driving slowly through the Heinz grounds without lights. One night Heinz stopped the police car and warned them: "When you drive through here, keep your spotlight on or I might mistake you for the burglar and shoot you." The officers kept their spotlight on after that but grew apprehensive every time they returned to the Heinz estate.

So it was with considerable trepidation on the night of September 29, 1943, that the two officers approached the Heinz mansion after receiving at 10 P.M. a Signal Four alarm (a burglar in the house) on their police radio. Miller and Blackwell not only feared the home invader, who apparently had had enough nerve to return to the Heinz home for a third time, but were edgy about running into Heinz and his ever-present pistol.

The officers raced their squad car through the Atlanta streets at 70 mph. Since it was wartime and gas rationing was in effect, few cars were on the streets at that time, and Blackwell and Miller covered the several miles to the Heinz estate in a few minutes. They roared into the driveway from Ponce de Leon Avenue, and Miller jumped from the squad car and raced to the front of the mansion, pounding on the locked front door. He heard a woman scream and ran to the tall windows next to the entranceway, finding them also locked. There was another scream, and Miller groped his way to the library window, also at the front of the mansion. The mansion was almost completely dark except for a light in the library. There were no outside lights burning, and the night was moonless and pitch-black.

Finding that window open, Miller crawled inside, falling forward and almost colliding with a terrified Lucy Heinz, who again screamed and pointed a trembling hand to the couch where her husband's body lay.

While Miller was trying to get into the mansion at the front, Officer Blackwell drove to the rear, wheeling the squad car about so that its lights played upon the mansion. He got out cautiously, gun drawn, and made his way to the side entrance, where he entered the house, going to the library to join Miller and Mrs. Heinz. He took one look at the banker sprawled on the couch and realized that Henry Heinz was dead.

Leaving Miller on duty inside, Blackwell returned to the squad car and called for an ambulance and more detectives. He was asked over the radio to describe the intruder. "Probably a large Negro man," the officer replied, giving the description he had gotten from Heinz at the time of the last burglary.

Blackwell started back toward the mansion. As he neared the house a shot rang out, smashing into a stucco abutment close to the driveway, sending slivers of the wall into the officer's face. He spun about to see a burst of flame coming from some thick shrubbery on the grounds near the driveway. A second bullet whizzed past the officer as he dove for the cover of a tree. He pulled out his own revolver and blindly returned fire, yelling: "Miller! Miller, he's out here, shooting!"

Miller raced from the side entranceway, standing on a porch beneath the driveway light and in full view, his weapon drawn as he squinted into the darkness.

"Get the hell down!" Blackwell yelled to Miller, but at that moment another shot exploded from the bushes. Blackwell saw his partner fall off the porch; he thought Miller was dead. Cursing, Blackwell started toward the shrubbery, blazing away at the point where he had last seen the flashing gunfire. He could hear the gunman moving behind the bushes in the direction of Ponce de Leon Avenue as he advanced upon him. At that moment Miller, who had broken his ankle when he had dived from the porch to get out of the line of fire, made his way down the driveway and was at the other end of the bushes, also firing at the assailant. He and Blackwell now had the intruder in an almost perfect cross fire.

Blackwell ran forward as he saw a large, dark figure emerge from the shrubbery. He fired the last bullet from his revolver, hitting the intruder while the latter, facing Miller, got off another round, missing his mark. Miller came toward him on the run, and when only two feet away held his weapon to the head of the assailant, but the revolver misfired.

Knocking the weapon from the intruder's hand, Blackwell jumped on his back, using the butt of his empty gun to beat the man on the head. Miller also attempted to bring the large man down. Just then several detectives arrived, rushing forward in the driveway. The assailant, incredibly, fought five officers almost to a standstill, flailing out with heavy fists, knocking down one after another, until finally, the policemen, employing every bit of strength at their command, wrestled him to earth.

His face bloody, more blood seeping from gunshot wounds in the right wrist and chest, the assailant, a large white man, continued to struggle until one officer sat on his chest and another on his stomach. A detective breathlessly told him that he was "under arrest for murder."

"I'm not the damned burglar!" roared the man indignantly. He identified himself as Dr. Bryant K. Vann, of 761 Lullwater Road, whose house backed up upon the Heinz estate. "I'm Mrs. Heinz's son-in-law, dammit—let me up!"

As the shocked detectives backed away, speechless, Dr. Vann staggered to his feet to gasp that Mrs. Heinz had called him when she heard her husband struggling with the burglar. The wounded man was placed on a stretcher, and as he was taken to a waiting ambulance he explained that he had been preparing for bed when he received Mrs. Heinz's frantic phone call.

Vann had thrown on a pair of khaki trousers and, in his pajama tops and wearing only slippers, had raced out the back of his house with his army .45, inserting a full clip as he ran. He realized that the estate grounds were too dark to make his way to the Heinz mansion quickly, so he had run around the block and had entered the Heinz driveway from Ponce de Leon Avenue, just minutes after officers Blackwell and Miller had arrived. Spotting

Blackwell moving behind the house and thinking he was a burglar, Dr. Vann dived into the bushes and started shooting at him.
He thought Miller was an accomplice and had shot at him, too.
It was later concluded that had Dr. Vann gone up the narrow path
connecting his backyard to the Heinz estate, he would undoubtedly have run right into the burglar-killer, who was then fleeing
in that direction. It was a wonder that, in the confused gun battle
waged in the dark, no one had been killed. Dr. Vann admitted
that one of Blackwell's bullets had struck him in the wrist and
he had to switch his automatic to his left hand to return fire.

"You're awfully lucky to be alive," Miller told the hospital-
bound Dr. Vann, who would recover from his wounds.

"So are you," replied Vann in a weak voice.

"What a nightmare," sighed Blackwell.

The nightmare turned into the most perplexing murder Atlanta
police had experienced up to that time. Henry Heinz had been
shot five times, and not a clue to the killer's identity could be
found. The police were hampered in their work by the scores of
people drawn to the scene by the terrific gun battle between the
officers and the well-intentioned dentist. A trolley car was passing the Heinz residence just at the time Dr. Vann was subdued,
and a curious driver stopped the trolley and ran onto the Heinz
estate to investigate. All his passengers followed him. Then, in
cars and on foot, Heinz's neighbors and relatives in Druid Hills
flocked to the site. It was impossible to use bloodhounds to pick
up the killer's scent.

Mrs. Heinz, traumatized by events, was of little help. When
she calmed down, she informed police that she and her husband
had been alone in the house. She had been sewing some items for
the Red Cross and shortly before 10 P.M. grew tired and went
upstairs to take a shower, leaving Heinz alone in the library,
listening to a radio broadcast reporting the results of the Third
War Loan Drive of which he was a director.

As Mrs. Heinz stepped from the shower she heard her husband
shout from the library: "Lucy, quick, get the gun! Somebody's in
the house!" Lucy Heinz threw on a robe and rushed downstairs.
She could hear the sounds of a wild struggle coming from the
library. Then she heard two shots. From the library door she saw
her husband struggling with a large black man. She raced into

another room to search for the gun, then, not finding it, started back for the library. She heard more shots.

By the time Mrs. Heinz reached the library, the intruder had disappeared; she found her mortally wounded husband on the couch. Tables and chairs were overturned and a large stand-up lamp next to the window had been upset. She called the police, Grady Hospital, and then her son-in-law, Dr. Vann, begging him to hurry over, telling the dentist that her husband had been attacked and that the burglar was probably still in or about the house.

A few minutes later, when Mrs. Heinz started to go out into the hallway, which was in almost total darkness, she thought she felt someone brush past her. She screamed, then ran back into the library and over to the open window where she almost collided with Officer Miller, climbing into the room. Mrs. Heinz screamed again, thinking Miller was another burglar. She could remember nothing else of the frantic events.

Police found parts of the inside workings of a watch scattered on the floor of the library and the prints of a man's index and little fingers on the venetian blinds; but they could not match the prints to any known felon in Atlanta at the time, and the watch workings led nowhere. Police were stymied. The Heinz murder case might have remained unsolved to this day had it not been for a routine roundup of suspected burglars by the Atlanta police early in 1945. The home of Hughes Spaulding, a distinguished Atlanta lawyer, had been burglarized. In the dragnet, on January 14, police snared a 220-pound, 6-foot black named Horace Blalock, who held a $200-a-month railroad job.

After it was established that Blalock had made a specialty out of burglarizing fashionable homes on the northside of Atlanta, detectives decided on a hunch to match his fingerprints with the two prints taken from the home of Henry Heinz. B. W. Seabrook, later a police captain, was the fingerprint expert at the time, and he reported that Blalock's fingerprints and those taken from the venetian blinds "were identical by 18 points on the index finger and 10 points on the little finger . . . when you can find as many as 10 points identical, chances are 64 billion to one they are made by the same finger."

The odds were enough to convince Blalock to make a full

confession. He admitted to burglarizing the Heinz home twice before the night of September 29. When he crawled through the window into the library, no one was in the room at the time, and he had rummaged through Mrs. Heinz's sewing bag, thinking it a purse. Heinz then returned to the library at that moment and leaped at him, shouting for his wife to bring the gun. In the fierce struggle the lamp was knocked down, along with tables and chairs. Blalock admitted that he drew a revolver and shot the banker several times before he was able to break free, Heinz collapsing on the couch.

Blalock ran out of the library and promptly got lost in the cavernous mansion. Doubling back toward the library, he almost knocked Mrs. Heinz down. As she screamed for help Blalock ran out the side entranceway, diving into the bushes just ahead of the police car roaring into the driveway. He made his way through the shrubbery and crossed Dr. Vann's backyard at the same time the dentist, gun in hand, was circling the block and following the path of the police.

Further, Harold Jacobson, a jeweler, came forth after reading of Blalock's confession and stated that the killer had asked him to repair his watch, which had been smashed and was missing many parts. Complacent and resigned, Blalock led detectives to a bridge spanning the Chattahoochee River (the very same waterway that more than three decades later would be the depository for many victims of the Atlanta strangler) and pointed to the spot where he had thrown the gun he had used to murder Heinz.

The Heinz murder case grew even more macabre. A grand jury was asked to return to the Heinz mansion on Ponce de Leon Avenue in February 1945 to watch the killer reenact his entry into the home and to hear him describe in detail how he had struggled with and killed Henry Heinz. Mrs. Lucy Heinz was on hand at the time but refused to enter the library. She had not lived in the mansion since the night of the murder, and after describing her experiences at the time of the murder, she departed, never to return to the house again.

Blalock gave as a motive for the killing his obsession with playing the numbers, a $15-a-week gambling addiction he could not break. He had taken to robbery, he said, so that he could go on gambling. He was quickly convicted and sent to prison for life. After serving ten years, Blalock was paroled on May 18, 1955.

Some weeks later he moved to Vidalia, Georgia, where he took a job as a porter in an auto agency.

Mrs. Heinz was remarried some years later to Enrico Leide, the conductor of the Atlanta Symphony Orchestra. She died in 1962. The Heinz mansion was purchased by a woman who kept a pack of dogs and rented out the second-story rooms. Her boarders never stayed very long; they complained of seeing a ghostly man walking the grounds late at night, and vowed they could hear shots. By the early 1970s the house was utterly deserted, waiting to be demolished.

Herbert Jenkins, who had been one of the investigating officers on the night of the Heinz murder and who later became Atlanta's chief of police, watched over the years the once elegant house and grounds deteriorate under the onslaught of vandals until, in his words, it stood "forlorn, nearly hidden from the street by weeds and undergrowth. A walk around the grounds in the dead of night has nothing to recommend it."

# 1958

# THE
# TURNER-STOMPANATO
# KILLING
## A FAMILY AFFAIR

Abandonment, sadism, and murder made up the legacy of Lana Turner's childhood. The auburn-haired girl was born February 8, 1920, into poverty in Wallace, Idaho, a small mining town where her father, John Virgil Turner, labored as an itinerant copper miner but spent most of his time gambling away his meager salary. Julia Jean Mildred Frances Turner was seven when her mother, Mildred, left her father. Destitute, Mrs. Turner sent her child to Modesto, California, to a foster home where, according to Lana's later statements, she was "treated like a scullery maid," making the family's breakfast before leaving for school, and washing and ironing. For household chores she was too tired to complete, she was beaten with a stick until "my back was bruised and bleeding." When the child was ten, her father, on December 15, 1930, left a crap game in San Francisco a heavy winner, and one of the other players, police later guessed, followed him and blackjacked him to death in a dark alley. Police were unable to solve the murder.

Following the death of her father Lana was reunited with her mother, moving to San Francisco, where Mildred Turner found work as a hairdresser. Their income was so scant in those Depression years that Mrs. Turner pawned most of the family's possessions merely to stay alive. By 1936, Mrs. Turner and her blossoming teen-age daughter were living in Los Angeles, where Lana attended Hollywood High. One day in January of that year the girl skipped her classes and spent some time in a drugstore, sipping a strawberry malt. And on that day, in that hour, fate in the form of a dapper man with a black mustache stepped forth to "discover" a Hollywood sex goddess.

*A typical Lana Turner cheesecake photo, 1946.*

   William Wilkerson, editor and publisher of the powerful *Hollywood Reporter,* was having coffee in the drugstore. (The exact store,
still in debate, was either the Top Hat Malt Shop at Sunset
Boulevard and Highland Avenue, or Schwab's.) Wilkerson could
not take his eyes off the curvaceous, large-eyed girl. He finally
put down his coffee cup and walked up to her uttering a line that

would later become the most often used cliché in Hollywood: "How would you like to be in pictures?" She nodded a vacant yes, and Wilkerson handed her his card, telling her to call him.

A short time later, after Wilkerson established contacts for her, the teen-ager was led by agent Henry Wilson to director Mervyn LeRoy at Warner Bros. LeRoy was about to begin filming an antilynching movie entitled *They Won't Forget;* he took one look at the well-developed Turner girl and signed her to a $50-a-week contract, changing her name to Lana. She appeared briefly in the 1937 film's first reel almost as Wilkerson had discovered her: sipping a soda in a drugstore, wearing a tight sweater and an even tighter skirt that sharply outlined her sensual figure. She then sauntered down the street and across the town square to be raped and murdered. Her brief appearance electrified audiences nation-wide, particularly males. Lana Turner was on her way to stardom, even though she recoiled in embarrassment when she first viewed herself in the film, crying: "I look so *cheap!*" (This was not actually her first motion picture appearance; she had been a crowd extra in *A Star Is Born,* released earlier that year.) Later, the woman who would be among the ten top female film stars in the nation would look back upon her first solo appearance and remark: "I was one of those photogenic accidents. I was a fifteen-year-old kid [she had just turned seventeen] with a bosom and a backside strolling across the screen for less than a minute." It was a minute no one ever forgot, except, of course, Jack Warner, the dictatorial head of Warner Bros., who was never known for his commercial or artistic vision. After Lana appeared in a few more small roles, Warner took LeRoy aside, scolding him: "She hasn't got it! She's just a kid." LeRoy felt otherwise, and when he left Warners to go to Metro-Goldwyn-Mayer, the director took his "discovery" with him. For the next eighteen years Lana Turner would call MGM (the "family" studio, as that benevolent monarch Louis B. Mayer was fond of saying) not only her home but the source of fabulous wealth, prestige, power, and more glamour than it was possible for any one human being to bear.

"The Sweater Girl," as Lana Turner was first aptly known, appeared in several B pictures, including *Love Finds Andy Hardy* opposite Mickey Rooney and Judy Garland; Lana was the love that found Andy. In 1941, MGM decided to make luscious Lana a superstar, casting her in a lead role in *Ziegfeld Girl* opposite Hedy

Lamarr and Judy Garland. She played the role of a girl who became a theatrical success but whose life was ruined by personal tragedy, a role Lana again played effectively eleven years later in *The Bad and the Beautiful;* her real life reflected these roles with devastating accuracy.

MGM lavished upon Lana big-budget pictures and a $4,000-a-week salary by the mid-1940s. Her male leads were Hollywood superstars John Garfield, Spencer Tracy, Robert Taylor, and Clark Gable. She made four movies with Gable: *Honky Tonk, Somewhere I'll Find You, Homecoming,* and *Betrayed.* That Lana was attracted to Gable there was no doubt in anyone's mind, especially in the mind of Gable's fiery wife, comedienne Carole Lombard. Knowing her husband was attracted to blondes—Lana was by then a platinum bombshell—before the first Turner-Gable film was shot, Lombard went to MGM studio boss Louis B. Mayer. She told the mogul in her usual blunt manner that if there was any hanky-panky between Lana and Gable, she would make sure her husband would never appear again on the set. As a result the Gable-Turner relationship was cordial but cool.

Lombard's apprehensions about Lana were normal. Lana Turner at the time had the reputation of seducing her leading men. Her love life, on and off the screen, was rampant and wide-ranging. Her life, like her screen image, was devoted to romance, to men. Groomed and cultured as a Hollywood hothouse plant, Lana Turner was, in the estimate of one observer, the "most complete studio product." And as such she pursued men created for fame and glamour—Robert Hutton, Rory Calhoun, Turhan Bey, Frank Sinatra, Howard Hughes, John Dall, Fernando Lamas, Tommy Dorsey, Tyrone Power, and others.

Immature, naive, and flagrantly fickle, Lana married almost on whim, selecting and discarding husbands with alarming alacrity. She blamed it on curiosity, once saying: "Let's be honest, the physical attracts me first. Then, if you get to know the man's mind and soul and heart, that's icing on the cake."

Artie Shaw was the first "cake," baked and served in record time. Lana had been dating Hollywood attorney Gregson Bautzer. The lawyer made the mistake of breaking an appointment with his fiancée one night. Angrily, Lana took her revenge as only she could. "I had a date with Greg," the star later gushed to gossip columnist Louella Parsons, "and he called to say that he couldn't keep it. Some kind of legal business. I got mad and decided that I'd go out anyway, and I thought of someone who'd make Greg mad and jealous." She phoned the much-marrying bandleader Artie Shaw. Before midnight on their first date, "Artie said it would be nice if we got married. I said it would be nice, too. The next thing I knew we were on our way to Las Vegas." The marriage lasted four months.

Stephen Crane, an unknown actor, dated Lana for less than a month in 1943 before wedding her. An annulment quickly followed when Lana learned that Crane's divorce from a previous spouse was not final. Discovering herself pregnant, Lana married Crane again. In 1944, Cheryl Crane, Lana's only child, was born. A year after that Lana divorced Crane.

Next came Henry J. "Bob" Topping, millionaire playboy, a two-fisted drinker and fighter who shared his love of pornographic films with Lana and guests attending parties at their luxurious mansion. The Turner-Topping marriage, which ended after four and a half years in Nevada, was regularly puncuated with accusations, drunken revels, and violence. On one occasion Lana brought home singer Billy Daniels whose private warbling to her was interrupted by a drunken, indignant Topping, who slugged Lana and ordered Daniels from his home.

Lana, forever being marked up by her lovers, employed dark glasses to hide black eyes. "I find men terribly exciting," Lana was quoted at this time, "and any girl who says she doesn't is an anemic old maid, a streetwalker or a saint."

The star, who continued to appear in box-office if not critical successes, such as *The Postman Always Rings Twice* (which many consider Lana's best performance in a wholly lackluster career), realized that her marital adventures were impulsive at best. "How does it happen," she inquired of Louella Parsons, "that something that makes so much sense in the moonlight doesn't make any sense in the sunlight?" Later she would muse: "Whenever I do something, it seems so right. And turns out so wrong."

More wrong turns in marriage were made with actor Lex Barker, Fred May, and Robert Eaton; her seventh marriage was to Ronald Dante. Throughout her shaky unions Lana lived like an empress, spending her enormous salary on a huge Beverly Hills home, servants, jewels, furs, cars, a wardrobe, spending at a rate that alarmed at least one of her husbands, Lex Barker.

When Barker pointed out that she was throwing money away, Lana agreed to curb her spendthrift ways, promising to limit her weekly purchases. Some weeks later Barker accused her of going on a shopping spree. Lana admitted that she had purchased hundreds of dollars' worth of items but that she hadn't "spent a dime." How was that possible, Barker wanted to know. "I charged it," replied Lana.

The marriage to Barker, some later claimed, was broken up by Lana's daughter, Cheryl; in fact the girl was charged with destroying three marriages altogether, whispering her suspicions of her mother's mates into Lana's ear, accusing the husbands of being unfaithful and, in one instance, too attentive to Cheryl herself. "Possibly it was a case of jealousy," wrote Charles Nuetzel in *Whodunit? Hollywood Style.* "Possibly Cheryl felt that her mother was away too much on motion picture locations and she didn't want to share any of her mother's time with strange men." That both Lana and her daughter were overly possessive of each other became evident with the surfacing of the shady Hollywood gigolo and sometime mobster, Johnny Stompanato.

Stompanato was a rugged-looking ex-Marine born in Woodstock, Illinois, in 1925. He attended Kemper Military School in Boonville, Missouri, graduating in 1943 and entering Notre Dame for a brief period until joining the Marine Corps in 1944, being discharged three years later. By 1948, Stompanato had been married and divorced twice, and was in Hollywood. The darkly handsome drifter was taken under his wing by gangster Mickey Cohen, successor to West Coast rackets king, Benjamin "Bugsy" Siegel. Cohen used Stompanato as his bodyguard and chauffeur, later promoting him to his bagman, collecting money extorted from movie officials. Soon Stompanato sidelined in blackmail, a racket that became so lucrative it made him independent. His prey consisted of wealthy females, usually divorced or separated from Hollywood husbands.

Stompanato's technique followed traditional blackmail methods. He would ingratiate himself with a victim, romancing her into a bedchamber where hidden cameras recorded their sexual encounter. The photos were then sold, along with the negatives, to the victim for large amounts. Years after Stompanato's violent end a wooden box belonging to the gigolo was delivered to Beverly Hills Police Chief Clinton H. Anderson, who later reported:

"Inside the box, along with a revolver [.32-caliber snub-nosed], bankbooks and personal papers, officers found a roll [of] film negatives. Printed and enlarged, the negatives revealed pictures of nude women in compromising situations. Some of the pictures had apparently been taken while the victims were unaware they were being photographed, and they were recognizable. The pictures would have been a gold mine for a blackmailer." Writing in *Beverly Hills Is My Beat,* Anderson added: "Stompanato's unusual picture collection verified information we already had, but we made no serious attempt to pursue our investigation further. It would have been a cruel embarrassment to the victims, and would have served no legal purpose since the principal was now dead." It was no secret to the police, Anderson also insisted, that Stompanato "had accepted money from a number of his women friends," ostensibly in the role of a gigolo, but more likely as a lover-turned-blackmailer.

How this unsavory fellow came to know and woo superstar Lana Turner is not clear. Some reports had it that Stompanato, who kept close checks on available Hollywood women of means, learned of Lana's break-up with Lex Barker (in 1957) and, only a few days after the dissolution of that marriage, boldly called the lovesick woman, asking for a date, his smooth request answered with a desperate yes. Yet others claim that Lana met Stompanato through mobster Mickey Cohen. "Movie stars have long been suckers for gangsters," wrote William H. A. Carr in *Hollywood Tragedy,* "and Lana appears to have been attracted to them, like so many others."

Johnny Stompanato, with his short dark curly hair, sharp jaw and profile, projected little more than the predictable beach athlete. Addicted to shiny shirts that he wore open almost to the navel to exhibit his chest, ostentatious, gauche, even crude, he was completely unlike the male stars with whom Lana had acted, and just the opposite of most of her husbands. Yet Stompanato held for her a fatal charm, captivating her, almost enslaving her. Lana undoubtedly had the mean-streaked, passionate, almost lethal Stompanato in mind when she later complained that she "usually wound up with delinquent adults." She also told journalist Jim Bacon: "I really am stupid about men."

At first it was all charm, with Stompanato playing the perfect gentleman. He paid a great deal of attention to Cheryl, swimming and horseback riding with the teen-ager, writing her long letters when she was traveling with Lana. Mickey Cohen, when later asked about the relationship between his underworld protégé and Lana's daughter, held up crossed fingers, commenting in his usual snarl: "Johnny and the kid was like that. She was crazy about him."

Lana's dependency upon Stompanato, which had grown to an obsession, may have been caused by her recent release from MGM after eighteen years of stardom. The thirty-five-year-old actress, suddenly adrift, became desperate not only for work in films but for a continuation of the kind of attention showered upon her during her MGM heyday. Her handsome Johnny filled that need. Even when Lana finally landed another leading part, opposite Sean Connery, in *Another Time, Another Place,* which was filmed on location in England, she begged for Stompanato's understanding, support, and, slavishly, his love, writing him imploring letters that gushed schoolgirl devotion.

Some samples:

My Beloved Love, just this morning your precious exciting letter arrived. . . . Every line warms me and makes me ache and miss you each tiny moment—it's true—it's beautiful, yet terrible. But, just so, is deep love . . .

I'm your woman and I need you, my man! To love and be loved by—don't ever doubt or forget that. . . .

Sweetheart, please keep well, because I need you so—and so you will always be strong and able to caress me, hold me, tenderly at first, and crush me into your very own being. . . .

There's so much to say—but it's easier when you're holding me all through the night. And we can either whisper, or shout, or scream our love for each other to each other. . . . And oh, so many, many kisses—so fierce that they hurt me.

The "aches" apparently overwhelmed Lana to the point where she asked Johnny to join her and Cheryl in London. The actress generously paid for his plane fare and covered his expenses, a gesture that had developed by this time into an unthinking habit.

Lana set up Stompanato in a luxurious London house, and during the early stages of the filming the couple seemed rapturously happy. Then Stompanato began making increasing financial demands upon the actress; she had already given him $10,000, a "loan" that of course was never repaid. Johnny told his blond paramour that he required an additional $50,000. He explained that the funds were needed to buy a screenplay for a movie in which he, Johnny Stompanato, would star. Stunned, Lana explained that she did not have that kind of money. What may have been most shocking to the actress was Stompanato's sudden and desperate desire to become an actor, a secret ambition the gigolo had nurtured since he began to drift in the Hollywood backwaters. Stompanato insisted she advance the money. Lana said that her financial advisers would not tolerate the expenditure. All right, soothed Johnny, and asked for only $1,000, which would be enough "earnest money" to secure the rights to the story. Again, Lana turned him down.

Stompanato had overplayed his hand. He knew it. His blatant trading on love in return for hard cash had been obvious even to the emotionally muddled actress. Instead of developing another ploy, Stompanato erupted, first with indignation, then seething anger, opting for intimidation, threats, and outright violence. He appeared without warning on the set of *Another Time, Another Place*, marching up to the actress's costar, Sean Connery, and bellowing: "Stay away from Lana!" When Connery appeared to ignore him, Stompanato yanked out a pistol, waving it in the actor's face. With a single punch Connery sent the mobster to the floor. Despite this blow to his tough-guy image, Johnny still treated Lana as his gun moll: "When I say hop, you'll hop!" he once yelled at her. "When I say jump, you'll jump!"

He also persisted in his money demands. Lana continued to refuse until one night Stompanato exploded in a rage. "I'll mutilate you!" he screamed. "I'll hurt you so you'll be so repulsive you'll have to hide forever!" He leaped for her throat.

The terrorized actress would never forget the scene:

> After he had choked me and thrown me down, he went into the bathroom and he got a razor and he came and grabbed my head, all the time screaming at me violent things. Then

he said that it may only start with a little one now, just give me a taste of it, and even so, he would do worse.

I pleaded. I said I would do anything, anything, just please don't hurt me. "If you claim to love me, how can you hurt me? Please don't." As he let go of me, he said: "That's just to let you know I am not kidding. Don't think you can ever get away!"

Lana did manage to escape, but only after going to her director, who contacted Scotland Yard. Police quietly escorted Johnny Stompanato to the airport and sent him back to America. Many believed that the actress had successfully removed the hustler from her life, yet Lana Turner's dependency upon Stompanato was deeper than she would admit. No sooner did she finish shooting her picture and return to her California home than she contacted the man who had threatened to mutilate her for life. Before long, Stompanato was once again enjoying Lana's pleasure palace, an imposing mansion with twenty-some rooms, including a private beauty parlor, soda fountain (in honor, no doubt, of the site of her discovery and the scene in her first important film appearance), and private projection room where she watched not only the latest Hollywood releases but films of a racier nature. The gigolo swam in Lana's king-size pool and lounged next to a cabana the size of a small apartment house, where hot and cold showers and sunray rooms and massage rooms were made available to Johnny and guests. Completely air-conditioned, the entire estate, down to the last guest room, was wired with a loudspeaker system. Dozens of phones were available to guests who, along with lover-boy Stompanato, ate off a $25,000 silver service (for sixty guests). Stompanato sank easily and unashamedly into such luxury, thinking Lana's comforts to be his right.

The actress never let him think otherwise as she continued to lavish gifts upon Johnny. To strengthen their relationship, or perhaps to obviate hidden bitterness over their London horrors, Lana and Johnny decided in the spring of 1958 to take a seven-week vacation in Acapulco. They stayed at the Vía Vera Hotel, where guests in adjacent rooms "complained of their noisy love-making," according to Kenneth Anger writing in *Hollywood Baby-lon*. The couple spent half of their vacation aboard the yacht *Rose*

*Cheryl Crane, Lana's daughter (right), joined reporters to greet her mother and Johnny Stompanato upon their return from Mexico. (UPI)*

*Maria,* and whether the ship was sailing or at anchor, Lana was observed by the crew to be constantly at Stompanato's side. "I couldn't understand," the captain later commented, "why a movie queen would keep on chasing after him. But no matter what he was doing on board, she was at his side. He would sit in a deck chair and she would come along and all of a sudden sit right down in his lap without being asked."

The Mexican fling ended at the Los Angeles airport, where news photographers and Cheryl Crane had assembled to greet the returning movie star. Cheryl, by now a tall girl who almost towered over Johnny, exchanged happy smiles with her mother's boyfriend. Two weeks later she became his killer.

The couple began battling again, Stompanato coming close to violence again and again over Lana's refusal to allow him to escort her to the Academy Awards. (She was nominated for an Oscar for her role in *Peyton Place,* that great and, for that era, scandalous soaper. She did not win.) It was obvious to Stompanato that Lana did not wish to be seen in his company. A further source of argument were the large gambling debts Johnny had run up through his friend Mickey Cohen. Stompanato demanded that Lana cover these IOU's. When she refused, he went berserk.

As the two argued in an upstairs bedroom of the mansion in the early evening of April 4, 1958, Stompanato's voice rose to a roar. Cheryl ran upstairs and listened at the door to his obscenities and threats. The teen-ager heard Stompanato (as was later claimed at the coroner's inquest) tell her mother that he would beat her up, disfigure her for life with a razor. "If a man makes a living with his hands, I would destroy his hands. You make your living with your face, so I will destroy your face. I'll get you where it hurts the most. . . . I'll cut you up and I'll get your mother and your daughter, too . . . that's my business!"

Stompanato grabbed Lana by the arms. She broke away, opening the bedroom door and seeing her daughter. "Please Cheryl, please don't listen to any of this," Lana said, according to her later testimony. "I beg you to go back to your room." She closed the door and turned to Johnny. "That's just great, my child had to hear all that. . . . I can't go through this anymore."

Stompanato went to a closet, took out a jacket on a hanger, and then stood facing Lana, swearing at her. "[He] was holding the jacket on the hanger in a way that he was going to strike me with it."

Lana stood up to him. "Don't—don't ever touch me again. I am —I am absolutely finished. This is the end. And I want you to get out!" She walked to the bedroom door, Stompanato moving fast behind her. As Lana again threw open the door Cheryl rushed forward. Lana later claimed that she never saw the butcher knife with a nine-inch blade that Cheryl had retrieved from the kitchen. "I swear it was so fast, I—I truthfully thought she had hit him in the stomach. The best I can remember, they came together and they parted. I still never saw a blade."

Stompanato grabbed his abdomen, wordlessly gasping, taking a few wobbly steps forward. Then he turned slightly and fell backward onto the thick pink carpet, his arms clutching his stomach, then flying outward. Lana, at first petrified in shock, suddenly ran to her stricken lover, bending over him, lifting his sweater. "I saw the blood. . . . He made a horrible noise in his throat. . . . It's like a great nightmare. I can't believe it happened."

The actress next ran to her bathroom to snatch a towel and return to the fallen Stompanato, pressing the towel to the bloody

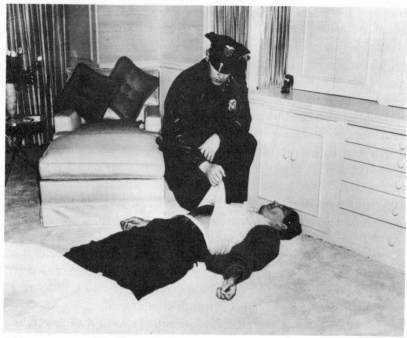

*A police officer examines the mortal wound on the body of Stompanato as his body sprawls in Lana Turner's bedroom. (Wide World)*

wound. Cheryl stood nearby, sobbing. Lana's efforts to save her paramour were useless. She knelt next to Stompanato, listening to the "very dreadful sounds in his throat of gasping—terrible sounds. I tried to breathe air into his semi-open lips . . . my mouth against his. . . . He was dying." There was nothing more to do. Lana went to the phone and called her mother, "because I had been out of the country so long and I could not remember my doctor's number." Next, Lana called the famous Hollywood lawyer Jerry Geisler, who picked up his phone a few minutes before 9 P.M. that Good Friday. "This is Lana Turner," he heard the actress say. "Could you please come to my house? Something terrible has happened." Geisler was on his way within minutes.

Cheryl was also on the phone, calling her father, Stephen Crane, at his restaurant, the Luau. "Daddy, Daddy, come quick!" the girl shouted. "Something terrible has happened."

"What's the matter?"

"Don't ask questions, Daddy. Just hurry, please!"

Crane, who was without a car, asked one of his patrons to drive him to Lana's mansion in Beverly Hills. He arrived before anyone else, leaping from the car and sprinting up the walkway. Cheryl was at the door, shouting: "Daddy, Daddy!"

"I'm coming." Half-running, he followed his daughter into the house and up the stairs, two at a time, to the second floor.

Lana met her ex-husband in the hall and said in a calm voice: "Something terrible has happened."

Crane peered into the bedroom, to see Stompanato lying on the carpet, bleeding. He turned to his daughter: "What happened, Cherie?"

"I did it, Daddy," sobbed Cheryl, "but I didn't mean to. He was going to hurt Mommy." She wept uncontrollably. "I didn't mean to, I didn't mean to."

Lana pulled the girl close to her. "I know you didn't."

"I just wanted to protect you."

In response to phone calls, two physicians arrived to work over the fatally wounded Stompanato. An ambulance was called. A beat cop, eyes wide with wonder, answered a "disturbance" call. He phoned his boss, Clinton H. Anderson, chief of the Beverly Hills Police Department. Jerry Geisler appeared, assuring Lana Turner that she would receive all his legal expertise. (This was the first meeting between the criminal lawyer and the movie queen.) Reporter Jim Bacon showed up and gained entrance to the mansion by telling policemen—by then cops were all over the estate—that he was from the "coroner's office." The house was filling up fast. By the time Chief Anderson arrived, Lana and Cheryl were weeping hysterically.

Lana pleaded with Anderson to put the blame on her. "Cheryl has killed Johnny," she sobbed. "He threatened to kill me and poor Cherie got frightened. My poor baby. Please say that I did it. I don't want her involved. Poor baby. Please say that I did it."

Geisler put his arm gently and protectively about the actress's shoulders, telling her: "Your daughter has done a courageous thing. It's too bad that a man's life is gone [Stompanato by this time had been pronounced dead] but under the circumstances the child did the only thing she could do to protect her mother from harm." He looked at Anderson and then, obviously more for the policeman's benefit and his client's strange position, said: "I understand your concern for the child's welfare. But you won't get anyplace by hiding the truth. Will she, Chief?" Anderson gave the lawyer a solemn nod.

Lana began to recite to Anderson the abuses Stompanato had heaped upon her in recent months, describing in detail how he had almost choked her to death in London. But the sympathetic police chief already knew of Johnny's unsavory past and his violent ways with women. Anderson was later to remark: "We had considerable information on him [Stompanato]. We knew he had obtained large sums of money from individuals who were afraid to complain to the police, and we were aware that he had accepted money from a number of his women friends."

As Anderson watched medical aides cover the gigolo's body and move it slowly from the Beverly Hills mansion—Lana, Cheryl, Crane, Geisler, and a host of others staring after the stretcher —the policeman remembered the last time he had seen Johnny Stompanato. "I had assisted him out the rear door of a prominent Beverly Hills hotel," he later recalled, "holding him by the collar and the seat of his well tailored slacks, after he had become abusive during a police investigation. Had we known positively that he was there for the purpose of extorting money from a hotel guest, we could have saved his victim thousands of dollars, and Stompanato might have been alive today—and in prison."

Gently, Anderson interrogated Cheryl. She was "still shocked and unable to believe that Johnny Stompanato was dead."

"I didn't mean to kill him," Cheryl told Anderson woodenly. "I just meant to frighten him."

Anderson patiently listened to the girl's story, then informed Lana that her daughter would be locked up in the Juvenile Section of the city jail. The actress broke into tears once again, begging Anderson to take her, not Cheryl.

"Can't you arrest me instead?" pleaded Lana. "It was my fault. Poor baby's not to blame for all this mess."

Hours later the fourteen-year-old was locked up, charged with murder. A short time later the press had the story and the storm broke. It was wildly speculated that Lana had really committed the killing after finding Stompanato in bed with her daughter. The columnists and gossip hounds enjoyed a field day of rumors and conjectures. Some, while appearing to be sympathetic to Lana's dilemma, used the killing as a way of indicting the actress's life-style. Wrote George Sokolsky in the *New York Journal-American:* "Cheryl Crane, the little girl of too many fathers, is a sad girl who could have had everything but who had nothing; a girl who spent her childhood and girlhood watching a procession of lovers and husbands wander in and out of her mother's bedroom and to whom the sight of her mother being physically abused by men became an everyday occurrence. She is a girl who learned about life long before she understood what she was learning." Louella Parsons dredged up every interview she had had with Lana, selected the juiciest parts, those that applied to the actress's tempestuous love life, and put the material to work again in print. Hedda Hopper, Louella's rival Hollywood sob sister, wrote: "My heart bleeds for Cheryl."

Another bombshell exploded after Mickey Cohen suddenly appeared in the editorial offices of the *Los Angeles Herald Examiner,* a Hearst newspaper, where he released the torrid love letters from Lana to Johnny. He had obtained them by sending some of his goons to Stompanato's lodgings as soon as he heard of the killing. (His thick-fingered thugs overlooked the box that contained Stompanato's blackmail photos, later given to the police.) It was Cohen who paid for Stompanato's funeral. He had expected Lana Turner to pay, and when he got the bill he became enraged and turned over her letters to the press in revenge.

The publication of the letters caused the newspaper opinion-shapers to turn against the actress. Only Walter Winchell, king of the gossipmongers, thought to champion Lana Turner, a move he knew would create controversy and sell newspapers carrying his syndicated column. "She is made of rays of the sun," waxed Winchell about Lana,

> woven of blue eyes, honey-colored hair and flowing curves. She is Lana Turner, goddess of the screen. . . . She is lashed by vicious reporting, flogged by editorials, and threatened with being deprived of her child. And of course, it is outraged virtue which screams the loudest. It seems sadistic to me to subject Lana to any more torment. No punishment that could be imagined could hurt her more than the memory of this nightmarish event. And she is condemned to live with this memory to the end of her days. In short, give your heart to the girl with a broken heart.

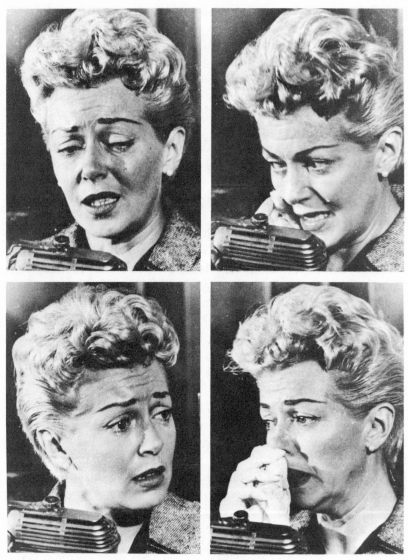

*Lana Turner testifying at a coroner's jury investigating the murder of Stompanato by her daughter. (Wide World)*

For the most part the Hollywood community, which has always carried its heart in its pocketbook, remained silent, fearing that the industry would be hurt if Lana was shown any sort of public support from members. Feisty Gloria Swanson did speak up, however, but not in support of Lana Turner. She attacked the actress *and* Winchell for coming to Lana's aid, telling the columnist that what he had written was "disgusting . . . you are trying to whitewash Lana. You are not a loyal American. . . . As far as that poor Lana Turner is concerned, the only true thing you said is that she sleeps in a woolen nightgown . . . she is not even an actress . . . she is only a trollop."

Cheryl was brought before the Juvenile Court, the charge against her reduced to manslaughter. Jerry Geisler, in a deft move, put Lana on the witness stand. She told the story of the killing with tearful passion and choking words, defending her daughter's actions. It was, as Geisler knew it would be, the finest performance the actress ever gave. Photographers ran out of film as they snapped Lana weeping and mopping her brow, appearing close to a faint as she struggled through her testimony. Cheryl repeated the story her mother gave, and the coroner's jury, having only the identical testimony of the two females upon which to base its conclusion, ruled that Cheryl committed justifiable homicide in defense of her mother.

Another emotion-packed scene took place a short time later in the courtroom of Superior Court Judge Allen T. Lynch of Santa Monica, where Cheryl was made a ward of the state and placed in the custody of her grandmother, Mildred Turner. Photographers were again rewarded with weepy scenes of Lana kneeling before her mother, eyes closed, hands clutching her mother's, a thoroughly penitent pose.

The police and courts were inundated with mail, the public accusing the police of "covering up" the real facts in the case. Oddly, syndicate gangsters like Mickey Cohen grumbled openly about the court decision. This attitude Chief Anderson found "most ironic," in that "the underworld [refused] to believe that this 'tough' ex-Marine could have been killed so easily by a fourteen-year-old girl. [Stompanato] had been considered one of their best bodyguards, and it was a damaging blow to their ego."

The case did not end with the freeing of Cheryl Crane. Mildred Turner found it too difficult to care for her granddaughter, and Cheryl was sent by court order to the El Retiro School for Girls in the San Fernando Valley. After running away twice from the school, Cheryl was allowed by the court to reunite with her mother. The girl later went to work as a hostess in the restaurant owned by her father, Stephen Crane.

Lana Turner weathered this fiercest storm of her life without loss of money or prestige. In fact, the killing and its scandalous aftermath seemed to strengthen her career; eventually the American public, as it is generally wont to do, supported the highly publicized underdog. The Stompanato affair worked favorably not only for Lana but for Hollywood. A movie based on the killing, *Where Love Has Gone,* proved to be a box-office success, as was Lana's next movie, *Imitation of Life.*

Many more films followed, including *Madame X.* Lana's appearance in this film moved critic Pauline Kael to write: "She's not *Madame X;* she's brand X; she's not an actress, she's a commodity." Countered Hollywood historian Adela Rogers St. Johns: "Look, let's not get mixed up about the *real* Lana Turner. The *real* Lana Turner is Lana Turner. She was always a movie star and loved it. Her personal life and her movie life *are one.*"

And as an actress and a person Lana Turner went on meeting and marrying men who made her unhappy. In 1976, Lana Turner vowed to live alone. "I have matured with the realization that I can live without a man!" she then exclaimed. "I can get through a day without being emotionally involved with another human being." The fifty-six-year-old star was exuberant about her decision to cut men out of her life: "Oh, how I treasure this freedom. I really do. It's a glorious, wonderful experience. I am off marriage —for life!"

# 1964

*✦*

# CANDACE MOSSLER
## MILLIONS AND
## MURDER

C urvaceous, blue-eyed, and platinum-blond, Candy Mossler acted more like an irresponsible swinger in her early twenties than a forty-five-year-old married mother of six children. Her dress, manners, and conversation exuded sex. Candy told one and all in her honey-voiced Southern accent that she was in her late thirties and that she had married banking tycoon Jacques Mossler when only a child.

Mossler was indeed twenty-four years Candy's senior and played the indulgent father to her capricious role of child bride. Having made millions in oil, the Texas tycoon invested most of his fortune in a group of banks and finance company holdings. These interests kept Mossler and Candy much on the move between their homes in Houston, Miami, and Chicago.

Candace Grace Weatherby Mossler enjoyed the hectic life. Since her teens she had proven herself to be a tough and shrewd survivor, running away from her impoverished home in Buchanan, Georgia, at fifteen and becoming a model for shoes and toothpaste. By her midtwenties the aggressive Candy owned her own modeling agency in New Orleans, and in 1948 she met and married millionaire Mossler.

Though Candy had two children, Rita and William, by a previous marriage to Norman Johnson, in 1956 she and Mossler adopted four more children, Daniel, Christopher, Eddie, and Martha; they were the offspring of a onetime Chicago mental patient who had murdered his wife. Murder and mayhem seemed to plague Candy's stormy life. In 1956 her brother, DeWitt Weatherby, a bartender in Georgia, killed a man during a heated poker game and was sent to prison for life. Candy hired Carl Sanders, who later became governor of Georgia, to aid her brother in getting his parole.

**155**

Shortly before adopting the four Chicago children, Candy took an auto trip from Atlanta to Houston. She failed to arrive and was reported missing. Search parties combed several counties for her. The rented auto that Candy had been driving was found smashed against a tree. Three days later, bruised and barefoot, a dazed Candy Mossler staggered out of a central Georgia woods. She stumbled to a farmhouse, where she called authorities, later explaining that she could remember nothing of recent events, guessing that the accident had caused her to have temporary amnesia.

The car wreck and alleged amnesia were, like many of Candy Mossler's actions, inexplicable and, to some, more than suspicious. At 1 A.M. on June 30, 1964, in Key Biscayne, Florida, Candy Mossler took her children for a car ride. She drove aimlessly about in her red Pontiac convertible, her four children, ranging in ages from eleven to twenty, sitting with her in silence. She later claimed that she developed a migraine headache so severe that she was compelled to drive to a hospital for treatment. She returned to her apartment with the children at 4:30 A.M., there to find the mutilated body of her husband, Jacques Mossler.

Mossler had been stabbed thirty-nine times and had apparently been struck over the head by a large ceramic swan that lay broken near his corpse. Some claimed it was the murder instrument, although prosecutors would later insist that a giant Coke bottle was used to heave in the financier's skull, even though the bottle was never found. Chained to a kitchen doorknob was the family's boxer dog. He had been barking furiously for more than two hours.

Police interviewed neighbors quickly as Mossler's body was removed. Mrs. Peggy Fletcher, a model living in the same apartment building, said at about 2 A.M. she had heard someone in Mossler's apartment shout the words: "Don't—don't do that to me!" The dog began to bark at that time. "The barking and the cries aroused me," Mrs. Fletcher later said. "I put on a negligee and went to the door. Just before I opened it, I heard someone else close the door across the hall and walk down the hall. Then I heard him run down the concrete outdoor stairway." She and other neighbors were sure the intruder had been a man because of the heavy footfalls they had heard.

One report had it that a man and woman had left the apartment

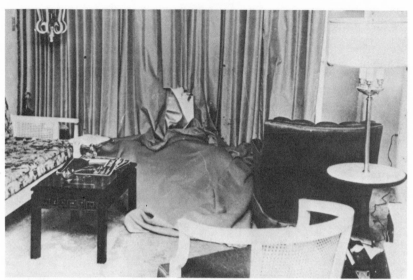

*Death scene—the body of millionaire Jacques Mossler lies under a blanket in his Miami apartment, June 30, 1964. (Wide World)*

parking area in a 1959 yellow Dodge. Another claimed that a man alone drove away in a white auto with a Dade County (Miami) tag at the same time. Several suspects were picked up within twenty-four hours, but all proved to have unbreakable alibis. A bloody palm print had been found on a kitchen counter in the Mossler apartment, and a man was picked up near Key Biscayne wearing bloody clothing. He stated that he had been beaten up by a gang of teen-age boys. His lawyer obtained a court order preventing police from questioning him further.

Then, on July 4, 1964, Houston police arrested twenty-four-year-old Melvin Lane Powers at a trailer sales lot, a concern which had been financed by Mossler. Powers, who also used the name Mossler, was the natural nephew of Candy Mossler.

Powers, police announced, had flown to Florida, killed Mossler, then flown back to Houston, all within a forty-eight-hour period. He had repeatedly stabbed his victim, then crushed his head with a giant Coke bottle. They said that the bloody palm print left by the killer matched that of Powers. Further, investigators stated that they had found a note written by Mossler that stated: "If Mel and Candace don't kill me first, I'll kill them."

*Candace Mossler consults with her lawyer Percy Foreman while standing trial for murdering her husband. (UPI)*

Candy, who hurriedly returned to her lavish Houston home following Powers's arrest, lost little time in going to her nephew's aid, hiring the flamboyant Percy Foreman to defend him, giving Foreman $46,500 in jewels as a down payment against his fee. She, too, however, was indicted for murder along with Powers only a few weeks later. Her response to the charges was typical of her: "Oh, pooh!" she drawled. She would later lash out with stronger words: "This is Russia!" and "They would convict Jesus Christ!"

Powers successfully fought extradition from Texas to Florida for more than a year but finally yielded and appeared with Candy before Florida Circuit Court Judge Harvie DuVal to deny any guilt in the killing of Jacques Mossler. Judge DuVal freed both on $50,000 bonds. As jury members were being selected in January 1966, the rugged-looking, lantern-jawed Powers went to Atlanta to await trial while Candace gave endless interviews to the press. She claimed that "the real killer" was a man named "Ted" who would admit the killing if "things get bad." To those who alleged her relationship with Powers was incestuous, she denied that her nephew was her lover. Some of her supposed love letters to Powers had been unearthed, and confronted with these, Candy only smiled widely, explaining: "I write to everyone, 'Darlin' I love you. I want you in my arms.' I say the same thing to my lawyer. It doesn't mean I really love him." Reporters could only imagine what Candy might say to a real lover.

Percy Foreman and five other lawyers represented Powers and Candy. The Texas attorney did not sidestep the incest issue as he pointedly asked prospective jurors whether evidence of adultery and incest would prejudice them. All said no.

Candy attempted to court the favor of the scores of reporters, representing more than fifty newspapers, who covered her sensational seven-week trial. The five-feet-one-inch blonde sent copies of a photo showing herself and her children mourning at her husband's grave to dozens of newspapers. She would grant an interview to any reporter who might give her a sympathetic inch of space. Dr. Joyce Brothers, popular psychologist and a Hearst minion at the time, was told by Candy that Mossler had invited his own murder through his association with homosexual weirdos.

"Who do you think killed your husband?" asked the psychologist.

"I think it was one of those strange people he used to pick up on the street all the time," replied Candy. "He would waltz into the house with strangers by the half dozen. He would tell people that we were very wealthy and important and owned a chain of banks and then say, 'Come on over and have a drink any time!'"

Another Hearst writer, Jim Bishop, saw through Candy Mossler's sweet-as-pie pose. "The lady is sixty inches of wrought iron," wrote Bishop. "It is blonde and pale and unyielding. It isn't something that God wrought. Candace did it. From the day long ago when the little Georgia belle found out females have an earthy attraction for males, Candace has coated that little body with so many veneers of honey and passion that if the real Candace stood up, Mrs. Mossler would probably disown her."

The words adultery, fornication, and incest were coupled to murder with such regularity that the trial of Candy Mossler became an obsessive ongoing story for the American reading public. The lurid details of Candy's wild love life were set down minutely. "Some claim to have seen photos of Candace embracing her Negro chauffeur," came one report. "Other photos show the swinging grandma almost nude on a bed."

Candace was all confidence and love when entering the court-room. She blew kisses to the reporters and jurors. Her hulking six-foot nephew showed no emotion during the trial. He and Candy did not testify on their own behalf, a tactic specifically dictated by Foreman.

The prosecution announced that Powers had murdered Mossler at Candy's behest so that she would inherit more than $7 million and be free to marry him. It was that simple. Prosecutor Richard Gerstein insisted that Mossler had found out about the affair between his wife and Powers and had planned to divorce Candy and cut her out of his will. To eliminate such dire possibilities, Powers, Gerstein said, flew to Miami, drove a white car provided by Candy to a Key Biscayne bar, the Stuffed Shirt Lounge, where he asked the bartender to give him a giant Coke bottle, and then went on to kill Mossler while Candy was driving about in the middle of the night with her children. Powers then drove back to the airport and took a return flight to Houston. Powers's fingerprints were in the car, said the prosecution.

Next came state's witnesses to damn Candy and Powers. William Frank Mulvey swore that Candace Mossler had given him $7,500 to murder her husband but that he spent the money on his family and was sent back to prison for another offense, having no intention of killing Mossler. Mulvey went on to say that he later met Powers in prison and that the nephew had bragged of killing the tycoon.

Gerstein, to show the sexual liaison between Candy and Powers, provided hotel clerks who testified that they had registered Mrs. Mossler and Powers as man and wife. One of them stated how he witnessed the couple "a-huggin' and a-kissin'."

Percy Foreman went to work on the prosecution's case with a vengeance, attacking the circumstantial evidence it had put before the jury and repeatedly pointing out that there was not a single eyewitness to Mossler's murder. The bloody handprint found on the countertop of the Mossler kitchen that matched Powers's print, Foreman insisted, could have been days old. And it was not unusual for Powers to have been on the premises, since he was a business associate of Mossler's.

Witness Mulvey, sneered the defense counsel, was a known

drug addict with twenty-one convictions and he would do or say anything that might get him out of prison. Next, Foreman put Mulvey's wife on the stand; she denied that her husband ever spent a dime on the family. A prison guard testified for the defense, saying that Mulvey's cell was four cells from Powers's and that the two never spoke to each other.

The powerfully built six-feet-four-inch Foreman mesmerized the jury with his dramatic presence. Members were well aware of the lawyer's reputation. In seven hundred capital cases he had lost only one client to the electric chair. He was immensely wealthy, having taken more than forty houses and an office building in Houston plus hundreds of acres of land as payment from grateful clients, in addition to $200,000 fees for high-society divorces. Foreman's wife wore a pair of slippers about the house studded with diamond engagement rings given to her husband by clients.

As was his custom, Foreman did not really try his clients but tried the victim, as the prosecution was quick to point out. The defense counsel indicted Jacques Mossler as a social misfit and pervert who regularly practiced every known sexual deviation except "the foot fetish." Foreman said that the multimillionaire could have easily been killed by any of the homosexuals he had picked up. There was, however, little substantiation for this charge. Foreman produced only one witness, who testified that he saw the victim with three men in a trailer once, and that they had "talked fancy."

Gerald Kogan, a member of the prosecuting team, told the court that Foreman's technique was "the oldest in the world—placing everybody in the world on trial but the defendants. They've tried the witnesses, the states attorney's office, the sheriff's officers of Miami and Houston, even the prison officials of the State of Texas. They have done everything in an effort to get your minds off the defendants, Candace Mossler and Melvin Lane Powers. And these are the only two people to have been shown by the evidence to have motive, reason, access and desire to kill Jacques Mossler."

Undaunted, Foreman delivered an eloquent and exhausting five-hour summation, thundering that the prosecution represented "a cabal" that had mounted a conspiracy to punish his clients for a crime they did not commit, claiming that police were

*Candy and Melvin Lane Powers jubilantly wave to supporters as they drive away from a Miami courthouse with their lawyers following their 1966 acquittal. (Wide World)*

shielding Fred Weissel, an interior decorator, alleged homosexual, and owner of a white car, who had been found bloodied six miles from the scene of the murder. The lawyer characterized the prosecution as a lynch-happy lot who were saying to the jury, in effect: "Come join us! On to the tree with the rope!"

With that, the defense rested. Foreman drove off to wait for the jury's verdict. On March 6, 1966, one of the longest criminal trials in Florida history came to an end. The jury deliberated for sixteen hours and thirty-three minutes. Members were first deadlocked, three being for conviction, nine for acquittal. After several more ballots the jury finally agreed that the circumstantial evidence against Candy and Powers was insufficient to warrant a conviction.

A "not guilty" verdict freed Mrs. Mossler and Powers. Candy went to the jury box and began kissing the members, all of whom were men. "Thank you for my little children," she said through great tears. "It is like a horrible nightmare has ended, not only for myself but for my poor little children back home. I left them crying."

As she emerged from court with Powers, Candy suddenly kissed her codefendant passionately. Then she kissed Foreman, who had not even been present to hear the verdict, having been delayed by a flat tire.

Candy Mossler was now entitled to inherit her husband's $33 million banking business. She was, at trial's end, left with little cash. Candy later claimed that Winthrop Rockefeller, an old friend—her children called him "Uncle Win"—encountered her and said: "Oh, my God, Candace. You're penniless. let me get you some money immediately." And gave her $150,000 as a loan. She admitted that she had given Powers something like $20,000 at one time or other, but was hazy on the details. It didn't matter because, as Candy said, her nephew was "a genius. . . . He is a young walking Jacques Mossler. And no wonder. He was taught by the master."

The personal trials and tribulations of Candy Mossler continued to make headlines. She married for a third time, a brawny electrician named Barnett Wade Garrison. On the night of August 13, 1972, Garrison, who was eighteen years younger than Candy, returned to the Mossler mansion in Houston to find the doors locked. He attempted to climb to a third-floor window he knew to be unlocked. Because he was using only one hand, holding on to a 9-mm automatic pistol in the other, he lost his grip and fell. He never explained why he was carrying the weapon. The fall put Garrison into a two-week coma; his mental faculties were permanently damaged. Garrison's parents took him home to Sugarland, Texas. Crying that her husband was being kidnapped, Candy followed, appearing at the Garrison home wearing a mink coat over a nightgown, hammering the front door so hard with her shoe that she dented it. The Garrisons would not respond, and Candy slipped a note under the door that read: "Barnett, I love you, but your mother won't let me see you."

A bitter divorce ended the union in 1975. Percy Foreman did not handle this bit of legal work for Candy. He had had a hard enough time collecting the fee for his defense in the murder trial, finally suing millionairess Candy to collect $585,000.

Also in 1975, Candy viciously cut three of her children—Christopher, Daniel, and Martha—out of her will since "they have not demonstrated the care, love, and affection I deserve as their mother." She added that all these errant children did was guzzle beer, walk about barefoot, hang out at a drugstore, run up enormous bills on credit cards, and use dirty language.

The notorious blonde died at age sixty-two on October 26, 1976, after arriving at the Fontainebleau Hotel in Miami. An autopsy revealed that Candace Grace Weatherby Johnson Mossler Garrison was a physical wreck at the time death claimed her. She had for years been addicted to drugs, taking Placidyl, a sleeping tablet, "like jelly beans," according to a relative. She had received thousands of injections of Demerol and Phenergan, so that her buttocks had turned as hard as rock. She had overdosed on sedatives. Pathologists performing an autopsy on Candy's body removed 475 and 500 grams of silicone from her breasts, deposited by injection, not implant. Such injections were illegal.

Melvin Powers went on to become a successful real estate developer in Houston, Texas, his worth recently set at $7 million. He did not attend the burial services for Candy, held at Arlington National Cemetery, where the remains of the incendiary blonde were put to rest next to the husband she was once accused of murdering.

# 1965

## TOM NEAL
## THE SELF-DESTRUCTIVE
## ACTOR

E veryone in Hollywood agreed that Tom Neal was a he-man who took no abuse from anyone. In fact, he proved to a suave and sophisticated Hollywood society that he was more than able to hand out abuse to any who displeased him.

The ex-boxer began in films during the mid-1940s, appearing in small parts in such war epics as *Flying Tigers* with John Wayne. Most of his roles, however, were leads in such low-budget productions as *The Unknowns* and *First Yank Into Tokyo.* A hulking figure with a permanently sullen look, Neal would have drifted into back-lot obscurity had it not been for his tempestuous affair with blond and buxom Barbara Payton, a second-rate actress who appeared in mostly third-rate films. (Before her death, Miss Payton would be repeatedly arrested for drunkenness, passing bad checks, and prostitution.)

The actor was extremely possessive when it came to women. His first wife, actress Vicky Lane, whom he married in 1944, divorced him in 1949, accusing Neal of unreasonable jealousy. About a year later Neal began seeing Barbara Payton, a casting-couch cutie whose biggest role was that of James Cagney's gun moll in *Kiss Tomorrow Goodbye* in 1950. Payton's role in the film, one of Cagney's worst, was awash with violence. Cagney literally used her as a punching bag.

*The New York Times,* reviewing this film, remarked: "As the moll, a superbly curved young lady named Barbara Payton performs as though she's trying to spit a tooth—one of the few Mr. Cagney leaves her." *Time* magazine took special note of how Cagney "viciously swats a blonde doll [Payton] with a rolled up towel." The mayhem wreaked upon Barbara in the movie positively enthralled certain film historians. Homer Dickens was to write in

*Actor Tom Neal when he was "King of the B Pictures" in Hollywood.*

*The Films of James Cagney:* "Cagney was still fascinating to watch, especially when he beat the hell out of Barbara Payton."

Instead of making Barbara Payton a star, the Cagney flop consigned her to cliché roles of dumb blondes who enjoyed violence. Such, too, was her bent in her private life, particularly when she encouraged the brutish affections of brawler Tom Neal. Barbara wanted Neal to marry her, but he was disinclined. The actress then began a tempestuous love affair with the distinguished actor Franchot Tone, mostly to arouse Neal's jealousy.

Hearing that Tone was dating Barbara, Neal on September 14, 1951, went to Payton's home and found the couple just going out. The actor rushed Tone, who was barely able to put up his hands in defense of himself. The ex-boxer landed ten or more powerful blows to Tone's face and head, breaking Tone's nose. In fact, Neal beat Franchot Tone bloody, rendering Tone so senseless that he was treated for a brain concussion. Franchot Tone was never again the same man, as his twitching eyes, slurred voice, and dazed manner suggest in later films.

Barbara Payton's reaction to all this was to fly to Tone's side. The actress told sensation-hungry reporters that her decision to be with Franchot was a result of the bestial attack he had endured for loving her. They were married in Barbara's hometown in Minnesota, but the union lasted only seven weeks. Following Payton's divorce from Tone, Barbara went back briefly to Neal, but that romance also faded and the actress drifted into a netherworld of drugs and prostitution. She was a physical wreck when she died in San Diego on May 8, 1967, at age thirty-nine.

By then Tom Neal had married twice; his second wife, Patricia, bore him a son and died of cancer in 1958 after a two-year marriage. Neal's third wife, Gail, an attractive brunette who worked as a receptionist at the swanky Palm Springs Tennis Club, married Neal on June 8, 1961, in Palm Springs, where the ex-boxer had moved. His career had collapsed after the Franchot Tone beating and, after having made 180 films, Neal had become a landscape architect in Palm Springs. (No studio would give Neal a job after nationwide publicity portrayed him as an inhuman monster.) The fallen actor had learned landscaping from two Japanese gardeners who had cared for his two-acre estate during his movie heyday. He had become extremely successful at the trade, caring for the lawns and gardens of Palm Springs' high society.

It had been more than a decade since Neal had shown Hollywood the bestial side of his nature, and most thought he had forsaken violence, that he had finally settled down to a tranquil domestic life. Yet, early Friday morning, April 2, 1965, Palm Springs police received a call from Neal's Beverly Hills attorney, James P. Cantillon. The lawyer instructed police to go to Neal's house; the ex-actor's twenty-nine-year-old wife was dead of violent causes.

Police raced to the Neal home, to find Neal waiting for them on the lawn wearing brown slacks, a white sports shirt, and a topcoat draped over his shoulders. The actor wordlessly led them inside to show them the petite form of Gail Neal. She lay on a large red couch clad in green pedal pushers and a green sweater. A blanket had been thrown over her. Pulling this back, officers saw that she was dead, a bullet wound behind her right ear. The

.45-caliber bullet had emerged from Mrs. Neal's left temple. Police found it embedded in a soft pillow.

On advice from his lawyer, Cantillon, who was present, Neal would say nothing. The attorney, however, did not protest when police booked Neal on charges of murder and hustled him off to jail. He was held without bail and four days later was officially charged with murdering his wife.

The ex-actor said that his wife had been accidentally shot, that she had been emotionally disturbed in recent weeks, that she thought someone "was following her" and had obtained the weapon that killed her for her own protection. He later claimed that while he was making love to Gail, his wife suddenly withdrew the automatic from beneath a pillow and held it to his head. Neal had, moments before, accused her of sleeping with other men. They had struggled for the weapon and it had accidentally gone off, killing her.

Neal's later testimony at his murder trial contradicted this statement. Confusedly, the ex-actor told several versions of his struggle with his wife. The prosecution doggedly persisted that Neal had murdered Gail because of his insane jealousy. Witnesses stepped forward to support the prosecution's claim. Robert Lawrence Balzer, a friend of Neal's and part owner of the Tyrol Restaurant in nearby Pine Grove, testified that Neal had visited him at his restaurant only hours after the shooting, admitting to Balzer that he had shot his wife because "she had become my whole life and I could not live without her."

Balzer, a Buddhist monk from whom Neal had often sought spiritual advice, said Neal had also come to him, troubled, at 6 P.M. on April 1, only hours before shooting his wife. They had discussed Buddhist philosophy, with Balzer remarking: "The problems of life are as a tiger at the door."

To that, Tom Neal suddenly snarled: "I am the tiger, and the walls are all around me." Seven hours later Neal was back in the restaurant telling Balzer that he had murdered his wife, that he had shot her as she lay napping on the couch.

Other witnesses came forward to support Balzer's statements, including Balzer's partner, James Willett, who also said Neal admitted the killing to him. David Gartwaite, a restaurant waiter, who knew the couple well, said Mrs. Neal was not emotionally distraught as the defense claimed. He had waited on the Neals,

Left: *Actress Barbara Payton and Tom Neal. (Wide World)* Right: *Actor Franchot Tone, hiding scars about his eyes from the beating he took from Neal, leaves a California hospital.*

who were dining in a Palm Springs steak house on the afternoon of the killing and that they appeared calm and content: "Neither had any drinks nor had they raised their voices while eating lunch."

The prosecution was hampered in its case by not being able to produce the murder weapon. Neal said nothing of its whereabouts. The weapon was never found. The statements of Police Lieutenant Richard Harries of Palm Springs, who testified for the prosecution, only served to add more mystery to the killing. As one of the investigating officers first on the scene, Harries stated that he had found both bedrooms in the Neal house in wild disarray. Men's clothing belonging to one Steven Peck was found on the premises. Peck's address was listed in the local telephone directory as 2481 Cardillo Street, the address of the Neal home. Peck was not brought into the case. Further, Harries discovered that all the windows in an apartment adjoining the Neal residence had been broken and could offer no explanation for this strange vandalism.

Even more mysterious was the sudden conduct of the prosecution, which abruptly rested its case against Neal, even though it had presented only eight of its thirty prospective witnesses. The jury of three men and nine women took a day to deliberate; then, on November 18, 1965, they surprisingly returned a verdict of

*After six years in prison, Tom Neal, at age fifty-eight, meets the press. (UPI)*

involuntary manslaughter, not murder. Tom Neal stood up in court and smiled broadly, minutes later telling newsmen: "It's been a long, tough road."

The ex-prizefighter-actor was sentenced to one to fifteen years at the California Institution for Men at Chino, a medium-security facility. The minimum sentence would normally call for a parole within a few years, but the courts doggedly denied Neal's appeals. He served seven years, being paroled in December 1971 and emerging from prison at age fifty-eight, his face lined and creased so deeply that he appeared to be a man in his eighties.

Neal went back into show business briefly, becoming an associate producer of a morning television show entitled *Apartment Hunters.* He envisioned a new career as an actor, one "who had really lived." He seldom spoke of his dark and sordid past, and when he did, he always gave different versions of his one-sided battle with Franchot Tone and the brutal slaying of his third wife. He died in Hollywood, where he had once been "king of the B pictures" on August 7, 1972, a forgotten gardener looking for lawns to mow.

# 1968

## RAMON NOVARRO
### A PERVERSION
### THAT KILLED

M ost murder cases, police will reluctantly admit, are not solved unless informants or eyewitnesses come forward to pinpoint the killer. In the case of Ramon Novarro, one of Hollywood's greatest silent film stars, his murderers unexpectedly were apprehended through normal police procedures, which often yield valuable clues but seldom the killers at large.

Ramon Novarro was an institution in Hollywood, hailed at the dawn of the 1920s as a great Latin Lover, his handsome dark features and foreign manners causing legions of flappers to swoon whenever he appeared on screen. (He was one of the "Big Three" Latin Lovers, the other two being Rudolph Valentino and Antonio Moreno.) This surefire Svengali of the box office, who was to become extremely wealthy, began his career without much hope of ever owning more than one suit before his death.

Novarro was born in Durango, Mexico, in 1899 as José Ramon Gil Samaniegos (Novarro was the name the actor later took when his film career accelerated). Originally, Novarro's family was well-to-do, his father being a successful dentist. When the family moved to California in 1913 to escape the bloodbaths of the ongoing Mexican revolution, poverty overcame them and fourteen-year-old Ramon went to work as a grocery clerk. He later took on the job of a theater usher, then worked as a piano teacher —his father had insisted that he study music as a child—and wound up doing bit parts in the infant movie industry.

But most of Novarro's income in these early days came from singing performances given in Los Angeles restaurants. His clear and convincing tenor voice attracted the attention of a dance impresario who booked him into a traveling vaudeville show. Arriving in New York with this show, Novarro found that his salary was not enough to support even a meager standard of

*Novarro as the great Latin lover with Greta Garbo in* Mata Hari.

living. To augment his income, the youth worked as a busboy in the Horn and Hardart Automat in Times Square.

A talent agent spotted Novarro on stage and signed him to a short-term Hollywood contract. The youth starred in a low-budget film entitled *Omar,* based upon the life of the Persian poet. His type of exotic good looks, then becoming the rage, immediately brought him to the attention of director Rex Ingram, who put the apprentice actor into important roles in such large-budget films as *The Prisoner of Zenda*—he played the evil-minded Rupert of Hentzau—which was a box-office smash in 1922. He went on to imitate the popular Valentino's sheik epics in *The Arab* with Alice Terry and played swashbucklers in *Scaramouche* and *The Student Prince.*

Novarro's all-time hit was *Ben-Hur* in 1927. He appeared half naked in the film, which drove his fans to near-pathological devotion. *Ben-Hur* cost MGM more than $5 million to produce, a then unheard-of sum, but returned many times that to the studio's coffers. Novarro was one of Louis B. Mayer's most important assets, and the mogul husbanded the actor, allowing him to make only one picture every two years so that he would not wear out his welcome with fans.

This arrangement, endorsed by the actor himself, gave Novarro plenty of leisure time to indulge in his various pursuits, backing and acting in locally produced plays and training his voice for a possible operatic career. The studio publicity department gave out reports that Novarro spent most of his spare time studying philosophy and that MGM had everything it could do to prevent their superstar from entering a monastery. It was all grand hokum, of course. Novarro was something of a drinker and his penchant for young men was not unknown to the Hollywood community.

He was, however, never blatant in his social transgressions, keeping his "amusements" for the most part private. In the rampantly dissolute and perverted community that was Hollywood during the 1920s, Novarro was a harmless creature, a reserved gentleman who never made scandalous headlines.

One of his best friends during this heady period of fame and wealth was Rudolph Valentino. The Great Lover confided in Ramon and showered gifts upon him, his sense of the ridiculous no doubt prompting him to give Novarro an expensive lead Art Deco dildo in 1923. Novarro cherished this gift and kept it among his special belongings, an objet d'art, as events proved, he would have been better off without.

The actor's enormous popularity kept him working in major films when movies made the transition from silent to sound. Novarro appeared in another smash hit with Greta Garbo in *Mata Hari,* a talkie made in 1932. Yet Novarro knew his days were numbered; the Latin Lovers were being phased out as the more rugged types—Clark Gable, James Cagney, Spencer Tracy—took over. Following the success of *Mata Hari,* Novarro stated: "I am

*The last photo taken of Ramon Novarro before he was murdered at age sixty-nine.*

selling personality. When I have lost my vogue, I have lost everything. Before it is too late, I want to stop." He did stop in the
mid-1930s, and, except for an occasional cameo appearance in a
film or, later, on TV, he concentrated on the real estate business,
purchasing huge lots in the San Fernando Valley.

Novarro moved into a $150,000 hillside home in remote Laurel
Canyon and entertained regularly, closely associating with his
brothers and sisters who lived in Los Angeles. He never lost his
love of the theater. In 1935 the actor backed and starred in a Los
Angeles play called *Royal Exchange,* which received scathing attacks from the press. He stayed out of the professional theater

after that, but continued to perform marionette shows for his houseguests in the full-sized theater he had built in his home.

As the years passed, Novarro's drinking increased. He continued his nocturnal liaisons with young men, but maintained discretion, having them come to his home. Two such hustlers arrived at Novarro's house, at the actor's request, on the evening of October 30, 1968. On the following morning Novarro's forty-two-year-old secretary, Edward J. Weber, let himself into the actor's home, as had been his habit for nine years. Weber was shocked to see the house in disarray. Chairs were ripped, tables turned over, pictures were torn from the walls, souvenirs and mementoes that Novarro had cherished for forty-some years lay in smashed ruins on the floors. The secretary stepped cautiously into Novarro's bedroom after calling out to him and getting no response. He found his employer near the bed, naked, his body a bloody mess. Ramon Novarro was dead, suffocated, the Art Deco dildo Valentino had given him stuffed down his throat.

Police were called and began to question neighbors and relatives, learning little. Then an officer routinely checked Novarro's phone, obtaining a record of all the calls placed from his number on the night of October 30. One of these was a long-distance call made to Chicago, to an attractive twenty-year-old brunette named Brenda Lee Metcalf.

Police called Miss Metcalf and learned that she had indeed talked to someone from Los Angeles on the night of the murder. She stated that her friend Thomas Ferguson, seventeen, had phoned her and had told her that he was calling from Novarro's house. She also stated that Tom had told her that his twenty-two-year-old brother, Paul, was with him at the time. The brothers were soon picked up by police and charged with Novarro's brutal slaying.

Paul Robert Ferguson, the older brother, had been in Los Angeles for five months. Thomas Scott Ferguson had run away from his Chicago home and had joined his older brother, who had already met Novarro, and introduced him to the actor. At first Paul admitted his guilt, saying that he had killed the actor, then he recanted and stated that his brother, Tom, had murdered Novarro. It was later revealed that, to avoid the gas chamber, Paul had told Tom to admit complete guilt because, as a juvenile, he would draw no more than a six-month term and he, Paul, would go free. Tom at first agreed to the plan, telling police that he indeed had battered the actor to death. Then Julius Libow, a Juvenile Court referee, ordered that Tom Ferguson stand trial as an adult. Tom Ferguson quickly denied his confession. It was Paul who had done the murder, he said. No, said Paul, it was Tom.

According to Brenda Lee Metcalf, who was flown in from Chicago to give testimony for the prosecution, both brothers had a hand in the killing. At least that was what she opined after her forty-eight-minute conversation with the Fergusons on the phone. From what was said, she had the impression that both were abusing Novarro. (The call was made 8:15 P.M., Los Angeles time.)

Tom had actually told her that he and his brother had gone to Novarro's home to "hustle" the actor, their visit made strictly for "sex," and that they were tearing up Novarro's home, looking for the $5,000 in cash he reportedly kept on hand at all times. The young hustler then calmly went on to tell Miss Metcalf that there were about seven hundred framed pictures on the walls of the house and they had been busy tearing these down because Paul believed the cash was hidden behind one of them. He casually told her that Paul was "up with Ramon" (in the actor's bedroom), attempting to force the actor into revealing where he had secreted the cash.

Brenda Metcalf stated that she had repeatedly warned Tom over the phone not to do "anything wrong." The youth denied any wrongdoing. It was Paul who was working on Ramon, not he. Yet when Tom put down the phone to look for cigarettes, Brenda said in court, she could hear loud screams, as if someone were in agonizing pain. When Tom returned to the phone, Brenda asked him several times what the screaming meant. It was only Paul, the youth told her lamely, trying to force the actor to tell where the money was. After almost an hour on the phone Tom told her: "I have to go now before Paul really hurts Ramon. . . . I want to find out what's going on."

During the seven-week trial, which opened in August 1969, both brothers took the stand, placing the blame squarely on each other. Paul said that Novarro had promised to make him a star, that he, Paul, was, in Novarro's words, "a young Burt Lancaster, a superstar . . . another Clint Eastwood." It was his younger

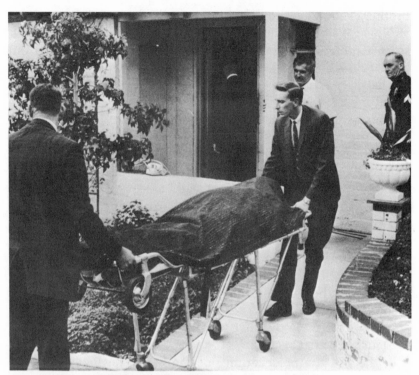

Top: *Novarro's body is removed from his Hollywood Hills home following his brutal death.* Bottom: *Two youthful male hustlers, shown in short sleeves, Tom (left) and Paul Ferguson, were convicted of beating Ramon Novarro to death. (Wide World)*

brother, Tom, who did the killing, not he, he said. After an hour at Novarro's home, Paul insisted, he had consumed many beers, some tequila, and a fifth of vodka. He claimed he passed out dead-drunk on the couch and that his brother woke him up. Paul quoted Tom as saying: " 'This guy is dead' just like he might say, 'hand me a pencil.' "

Tom had a different story. He had gone into Novarro's bedroom after getting off the phone, to see Paul standing over the actor, who was naked and bleeding. "Mostly in the face—it looked like he had a bloody nose . . . his lips were beat up . . . there was blood on his forehead."

Paul had ordered him to take Novarro into the shower and clean him up, Tom said. He stood inside the shower with the actor, washing his face and telling him not to talk to his brother, that Paul "might become violent." He claimed he took the actor back into the bedroom, putting him on the bed and then leaving the room. When he returned, he found Novarro in a pool of blood. "He looked dead," testified Tom Ferguson.

"How did you know that he was dead?"

"I just had that feeling."

In the end the prosecution put the blame on Paul Ferguson, District Attorney James Ideman describing to the jury in gruesome detail how Novarro had been "trussed up like an animal" by Ferguson. "It was done for money, by torture. . . . Done cruelly by a man who has no respect for himself or others . . . who has no remorse, no compassion, no regrets . . . and who got his brother to perjure himself."

Medical witnesses reported how Paul Ferguson had been a practicing homosexual since age nine and that he was, after consuming liquor, subject to uncontrollable outbursts of violence. He was a dangerous man with homicidal tendencies.

The jury brought in a verdict of "guilty of murder in the first degree." The torture killers were both given life sentences. Superior Court Judge Mark Brandler, who sentenced the pair, recommended that they never be paroled.

The senseless murder of Ramon Novarro produced no fortune for the hustling brothers. They went away from the murder site without ever finding anything but a few dollars Novarro had in his pockets. The actor left more than $500,000 to his four sisters, three brothers, and his secretary, Edward J. Weber.

# 1975

## JOHN S. KNIGHT III
### DEATH FROM PLEASURE

The Knight family has been an institution in American newspapers since Charles London Knight, a onetime schoolteacher, became advertising manager of the Akron *Beacon Journal.* Knight bought the paper in 1915, and his son, John S. Knight, Sr., worked briefly as a reporter for his father before going off to World War I, returning in 1919 as a much-decorated second lieutenant. Young Knight had fought in the campaigns of the Argonne and Alsace-Lorraine.

In 1920, Knight became a sportswriter for his father's newspaper but the aggressive newsman used pseudonyms for his columns because, as he later stated, "I was ashamed of the stuff— I didn't write well enough." By 1925, Knight had become the chief editorial writer and managing editor for the *Beacon Journal.* Seven years later he inherited the paper, along with the Massillon *Independent,* following his father's death. He proceeded to build a newspaper empire, buying up *The Miami Herald* in 1927 for $2 million. Knight's particular way of consolidating his assets was demonstrated shortly after he acquired the *Herald.* He traded his Massillon paper for *The Miami Tribune,* then killed the *Tribune* so that the *Herald* would have no opposition. The publisher did the same thing in Akron, buying the leading competitor to the *Beacon Journal* and folding it. Ruthless, some said of Knight's tactics. Good business, said others.

Throughout his long and energetic life Knight continued to gobble up major newspapers—the *Detroit Free Press* in 1940, the Chicago *Daily News* in 1944 (sold to the late Marshall Field IV in 1959 in a super hush-hush move), *The Charlotte Observer* in 1959, *The Philadelphia Inquirer* in 1969, the Lexington *Herald-Leader* in 1973. By the time of his death on June 16, 1981, John S. Knight, Sr., owned thirty-five newspapers and was considered to be one of

America's most powerful publishers, "a giant among his peers," according to one Knight-Ridder executive, "who had done it all. . . . He had been accorded almost all the honors that any newspaperman could receive."

The Knight patriarch also received, five years before his death, devastating news that brought shock and, later, disgrace to the family. His cherished grandson, John S. Knight III, had been brutally murdered in his luxurious $1,050-a-month penthouse in Philadelphia's exclusive Rittenhouse Square. The elder Knight had raised the boy following the death of John Knight, Jr., an army officer. Young John was apparently deeply affected by the death of his father, whose photo he carried at all times. Like his grandfather, Knight came early to the newspaper profession, filing reports at age fifteen to a Knight-Ridder newspaper from the convention floor that nominated John F. Kennedy in 1960.

A bright boy, Knight studied at Lawrenceville School in New Jersey before going on to take a BA cum laude at Harvard in 1968. Young John displayed a bit of a wild streak in college as a member of the Hasty Pudding and Phoenix clubs. He kept his grades high but spent a great deal of time playing high-stakes poker. He went on to Oxford to concentrate on philosophy, economics, and politics, finding enough time to become a member of a rowing crew and give splashy parties.

Upon his return to the United States, Knight went to work for the Knight-owned *Detroit Free Press* and proved himself an aggressive reporter, winning two prizes for his writing. He did not ignore his lofty station in life, mixing with the social elite, including "Henry Ford's crowd," as *Newsweek* once put it, frequenting the ultra-exclusive Detroit Club.

The youth also walked the seamy side of the street, enjoying Detroit's honky-tonks and, increasingly, gay bars. "His homosexual connections were known," a fellow reporter later claimed. After some years Knight moved on to become special projects editor for the Philadelphia *Daily News,* another property owned by America's largest newspaper chain. He moved into a sumptuous penthouse and indulged his fancies for Savile Row clothes and art treasures, spending $100,000 on paintings and sculpture. He spent hours weight lifting and hunting and even took up gourmet cooking.

Kept secret from his society friends was Knight's abiding passion for young men. When leaving his duties at the *Daily News* or social functions with uppercrust cronies, Knight would slum through Spruce Street, picking up young hustlers and taking them back to his palatial penthouse; he was seen in gay bars and sex boutiques. The newsman's generosity was well known, which made his subsequent murder puzzling, in that he lavished cash and gifts upon those marbled youths who favored him with sex. Said one sex-shop owner following the newspaper heir's slaying: "I can't understand why they had to kill him. From what I've heard all you had to do was ask the guy for money."

One of those to whom Knight gave money was Isaias Felix Melendez, a twenty-year-old blue-eyed hustler from a Puerto Rican family in South Philadelphia. Melendez was a lisping homosexual with an infantile body, if not mind, the type Knight liked most. He took Melendez often to his penthouse to admire the exotic weapons on the walls, the paintings and the books. Here he would prepare exquisite meals for the youth, as he had for many others, then take him to bed, later photographing him and recording their lovemaking.

All of this Knight kept from his social friends. It was later stated that he was beginning to like women more after psychiatric treatment. The newsman's transformation, however, did not take place soon enough. Unknown to him, Melendez was a member of a lethal gang that strong-armed homosexuals for money, and his chief intended victim was John S. Knight III.

On the night of December 7, 1975, Knight entertained Dr. John McKinnon, a twenty-nine-year-old psychiatrist from New Haven, and his wife, Rosemary, age twenty-seven. McKinnon had been Knight's roommate at Harvard. Ellen Roche, an assistant bank manager, was Knight's date for the evening. Another couple, managing editor for the *News* Paul Janensch and his wife, also joined the party, having dinner at a French restaurant where they were served pheasant that Knight himself had recently shot.

The party adjourned to Knight's penthouse, with Ellen Roche and the Janensches leaving shortly after midnight. The McKinnons and Knight stayed up drinking until 3 A.M. Mrs. McKinnon had fallen asleep on her husband's lap when Knight received a phone call. After he hung up, he suggested that the McKinnons retire to the guest room. The psychiatrist and his wife went into the bedroom; McKinnon, who had drunk heavily, fell quickly into a deep sleep. An hour later there were loud noises in the penthouse, sufficient to cause neighbors to call the front desk of the Dorchester and complain. A half hour later three men roughly woke Rosemary McKinnon from her slumber, pulling her from the bed, naked. They attempted to wake Dr. McKinnon but could not. One of the intruders, a mustachioed bug-eyed man with unkempt long hair, looked over the woman and asked for money and jewelry. The other two busied themselves with looking for Dr. McKinnon's wallet.

"Can I get dressed?" Mrs. McKinnon asked.

The mustachioed man, who clutched a handgun, ripped a blanket from the bed and threw this to Mrs. McKinnon. She draped it about herself as he motioned her into the study. He pointed to a desk that was locked. "Which keys open the desk drawers?" he demanded.

"I don't know," replied the terrified woman.

"Where does John keep his money?"

"I don't know." Mrs. McKinnon murmured something about being a guest.

There was a noise in the outer hallway. Mrs. McKinnon thought—hoped—it might be the building's security guard.

The mustachioed intruder pointed the gun in his hand toward the hallway door. "Be quiet," he ordered the woman.

In a minute the intruder shoved the woman down a hall to Knight's bedroom. She could see that her host was bound and gagged, tied into a ball in the corner of the room. He was moaning. "We came to settle a grudge," the mustachioed man told her by way of explaining Knight's condition. Some time later he turned to the woman, saying, "Are you freaky?"

"No."

"Does your husband satisfy you?"

"Yes."

Some minutes later Mrs. McKinnon was taken back to the study, where her hands were tied with plastic bandages. She watched the intruders systematically ransack the penthouse as they searched for Knight's money. She watched them pile up fur coats, briefcases, shirts and other items in the hallway. The mustachioed man looked in her direction and said: "I need the money. I've got a daughter sick with a blood disease and I got to take care of her." Then the man placed Mrs. McKinnon under the sofa "so

*The posh apartment of newspaper heir John S. Knight III that was ransacked by his murderers in 1975. (Wide World)*

I was in a fetal position," she later testified. He put a pillow in front of her face so that she could see little of what was happening.

One of the other intruders, a handsome youth, checked the woman. Mrs. McKinnon guessed that this man spent at least an hour walking dazedly between the guest bedroom and Knight's bedroom. He paused now and then to tell the bound woman: "I'm scared . . . I'm all doped up. . . . They made me do it." He showed her a wrist with needle punctures. "My father's a minister," he volunteered inexplicably.

The young man's companions were suddenly gone, but he stayed behind. He sat down next to Mrs. McKinnon and cut her loose from her bonds, telling her: "I've got to wait for my friends to return."

Carrying a knife, a long-barreled gun, and a harpoon gun, an ornament he had taken from Knight's wall, the young man asked Mrs. McKinnon to go into Knight's bedroom. She walked slowly into the room. There was another noise in the outer hallway, which distracted the young man for a moment. Mrs. McKinnon seized this opportunity to lunge for the long-barreled gun, which she snatched from his grasp. Before the intruder could respond, she ran to the guest room, shouting for her husband to get up. This time the psychiatrist awakened; he was startled to see his wife standing over him, clutching a rifle.

"Honey, you've got to wake up," Mrs. McKinnon begged. "Something terrible is happening. There's been a robbery. The apartment's been ransacked. John may be hurt."

McKinnon sprang up to see the young man in the hallway pointing a spear gun at his chest. "Put that down!" McKinnon yelled at him. "You don't need that, you idiot!" He raced to the bedroom door and slammed it, locking it. Turning to his wife he said: "We must get dressed. I'll take care of that fellow in the hallway while you go for help."

After the couple hurriedly threw on their clothes, McKinnon grabbed the rifle and opened the door. The young man was still there, menacing with the spear gun. "You don't need that weapon," the psychiatrist told him. "No one needs to get hurt around here." As he advanced upon the youth, holding the rifle at guard, the intruder retreated slowly before him down the hall. He darted into Knight's bedroom and leaped upon the bed, pointing the spear gun at McKinnon when he entered.

"I didn't do it to him!" shouted the intruder. He waved the gun frantically, and his body shook in apparent fear. Still holding the rifle, McKinnon stepped out of the doorway. The youth leaped forward, scuffling with the psychiatrist, then rushed past him, diving into the hallway, McKinnon on his back, knocking him to the floor and shouting: "Stay there, you son-of-a-bitch!" McKinnon then ran back into the bedroom to check on his friend Knight, who was lying under a pile of debris. He knelt beside him, tearing away at least fifteen neckties that had been tied tightly around the newsman's nose, eyes, mouth, and throat, a veritable mask covering his entire head. Knight's eyes were closed and bruised. Blood had hardened about his mouth. He was not breathing, and McKinnon, after untying his hands, checked to feel a pulse that was not there.

As McKinnon later testified, he "breathed a couple of deep breaths into his mouth. Then I smashed my fist into his chest to start his heart going. My hand was splashed with blood—there was blood all over my fingers. I tore his shirt open and saw a massive chest wound about two inches long. I stuck my fingers into the chest cavity. Then I tried mouth-to-mouth resuscitation.

I prodded open his eyes, but knew that he was dead. It was over. There was nothing for me to do."

Rosemary McKinnon had not been idle. She had dashed into the kitchen when her husband first confronted the youth holding the spear gun. There she tried to call police but there was no dial tone; the phone in the den was also dead. She ran down the hallway, glancing to see her husband scuffling with the youth, throwing open the outer hallway door and shouting: "I'll get help outside!" She ran down the hallway to the elevator and pushed the button, waiting breathlessly. As the elevator door opened she jumped inside, but the youth had already escaped the Knight penthouse and jumped into the elevator behind her. "I tried to keep his knife away by holding on to its blade," Mrs. McKinnon later stated, describing how she fought the youth as the elevator rumbled down seventeen stories. "I held him off, but cut myself on the index finger and the third finger of the right hand and also received a small wound under my left breast." The elevator stopped abruptly at the third floor and Mrs. McKinnon leaped out, running down the hallway to the fire escape. She climbed down it, then ran around to the lobby, where she called police.

When police arrived they found none of the invaders, only the badly shaken McKinnons and John S. Knight III, who was dead, stabbed to death, five knife-wounds in his back and chest. Detectives had little to go on. McKinnon stated that the phone call Knight had received, one that prompted his host to suggest he and his wife retire, was of a decidedly homosexual nature. "That kind of conversation embarrasses Rosemary and me," he was later to say.

But it was that kind of conversation that gave the police the idea to conduct a blitzkrieg hunt through Philadelphia's gay community. They scoured bars and sex shops, showing to possible informers hundreds of mug shots of convicted felons who preyed upon rich homosexuals. During this intensive manhunt Knight's sordid background came to full light. Responding to publicity about Knight's death was Billy Sage, a tall, muscular youth with shoulder-length blond hair who came forward to tell police that he had been one of Knight's homosexual lovers. The twenty-year-old Michigan man said that Knight had supported him and his wife over an extensive period. The payments followed each visit Sage made to the tycoon newsman, he said.

*They preyed on homosexuals with money; shown are (left to right) Knight's slayers Steven Maleno, Felix Melendez, and Salvatore Soli. (Wide World)*

Sage did more than merely claim his affection for Knight. He led police to a footlocker in Knight's apartment, and inside this was a trove of Polaroid photos of nude young boys and some young women, too, and scores of recordings of homosexual love-making, including Knight's own voice. Detectives also unearthed a detailed diary in Knight's handwriting, which listed dozens of male and female prostitutes in and about Philadelphia. Police began to run down this list in their hunt for Knight's killers.

Four days later Chief Inspector Joseph Golden publicly announced that warrants had been issued for Isaias Felix Melendez, Steven Maleno—a twenty-five-year-old homosexual who had a record of robbing his lovers—and thirty-eight-year-old Salvatore Soli, a known drug-peddler, car thief, and armed robber. The heavily mustachioed and tattooed Soli had once faced a charge of attempted murder.

Maleno turned himself in within twenty-four hours of Golden's announcement. He offered little information. Melendez's body was found on the morning of December 11, 1975, close to the entranceway of the Pine Valley Golf Club near Camden, New Jersey. He had been shot three times, once, it appeared, at point-blank range in the face. A few days later Linda Mary Wells, a dancer, walked up to a park ranger in Miami and said: "I know something about those murders in Philadelphia." The ranger, well aware of the great amount of publicity that had been spread in the Knight case, took her to homicide detectives. She told them everything they wanted to know, including the whereabouts of the much-wanted Salvatore Soli; he was picked up hours later in Miami's South Winds Motel, surrendering without a flicker of resistance.

Linda Wells served as the chief informant against Maleno and Soli during their trials, describing how Soli and Maleno, thinking Melendez would inform on them, drove to the New Jersey golf course with John Knight's onetime lover. Soli, said Linda, gave Maleno a handgun and told him to take Melendez into the woods. Maleno then executed Felix Melendez.

Maleno returned to Philadelphia after the killing, and Soli and Linda Wells fled south to Miami. Their car broke down and they were forced to take a Greyhound bus the rest of the way. The robbery-murder had netted the trio practically nothing, Maleno and Soli taking only about $190 in cash and some rare gold coins and leaving everything else. They had been looking for drugs the playboy was known to have had on hand, and large sums of cash. They had been misinformed about the money. Knight never kept more than $200 in cash on hand, though he did have more than $1.5 million in banks. In the end the killing was merely the result of a badly botched robbery.

At first Maleno and Soli attempted to shift the blame for Knight's murder onto the dead Melendez, but a jury convicted both of them for the killing. Maleno later confessed to the killings of Knight and Melendez and received two consecutive life terms. Soli, the mastermind of the lethal raid, fought against conviction, appealing the case, but he again lost and was sent to prison for life.

Before being led away to begin serving his term, Soli stood up in court and smirked at the judge, saying: "If it's death, give it to me now."

# 1976

## SAL MINEO
# THE MURDER
# OF A REBEL

S al Mineo had died on the screen several times as a juvenile delinquent and an apprentice thug. As Plato, the neurotic rich kid in *Rebel Without a Cause,* Mineo died uselessly, wastefully, gunned down by police as he brandished an empty gun. He went on playing homicidal, self-destructive roles, typecast into the man-child that never grew up, born for a star-crossed and violent end. In real life the actor met that very same fate, although he was anything but the type of character he portrayed on screen.

On the night of February 13, 1976, Mineo was returning from a play rehearsal of James Kirkwood's *P.S. Your Cat Is Dead,* which he was directing and which was scheduled to open shortly at the Westwood Playhouse. Mineo had appeared in the play during its San Francisco run, portraying the part of a comic bisexual burglar.

Mineo had left his blue Chevelle and was walking through the carport at the rear of his West Hollywood apartment, just below the notorious Sunset Strip, when he was confronted by a long-haired man in dark clothes.

Neighbors suddenly heard the thirty-seven-year-old actor shout: "Oh God, no! Help! Someone help!" Ray Evans, a neighbor and friend of Mineo's, ran to the carport to find the actor lying on his back, his feet in the air and a stream of blood several yards long stemming from several wounds in Mineo's chest. He had been stabbed by a "heavy type knife," as the coroner's office later explained. The wounds penetrated Mineo's heart and caused massive hemorrhaging, yet he did not die instantly.

Evans, seeing that the actor was still breathing, desperately tried to keep him alive through mouth-to-mouth resuscitation. "He kept gasping," Evans later told police, "and after about five or six minutes his last breath went into me and that was the end of it."

It was just the beginning for the Los Angeles police, who were baffled by the attack. Mineo's wallet had not been taken, and robbery as a motive for the slaying was ruled out. Acquaintances speculated wildly as to the reason for the murder. One mentioned "the drug angle." Another anonymous person sneeringly pointed to kinky Sunset Strip, notorious for its queues of male hustlers waiting at curbside to be picked up, and brought up the "long-whispered reports of the actor's alleged bisexuality and fondness for sadomasochistic ritual." Another callously snickered that "it was a new boyfriend or something. They *do* have their quarrels."

None of these posthumous slurs helped the police in finding the killer. Some witnesses claimed to have seen a white man with dark clothes flee from the scene, but descriptions were fuzzy. After weeks of tracking down "easily hundreds of tips," Lieutenant Stanley Backman of the Los Angeles Sheriff's Department reported that the Homicide Bureau had "reached a dead end."

As Mineo's body was being shipped back to Mamaroneck, New York, for burial in a family plot at the Gate of Heaven Cemetery on February 17, 1976, police fruitlessly followed trails of tired gossip and rampant rumor. Critics and friends of the actor went to their typewriters and eulogized Mineo in profiles that saw him as a "born-to-lose" character. Wrote friend Peter Bogdanovich in *Esquire*:

> That Sal was stabbed to death in an alley was so horribly in keeping with so many of the movie deaths he died that its bitter irony might have amused him. After all, he had a black sense of humor and firm grasp of the absurd—a teenage symbol in his late thirties who never had a childhood. To know that newspapers plastered his murder in banner headlines across the country . . . would probably have made him drop his head to his side and snore: "A lot of good that does me."

Roger Rosenblatt, writing in *The New Republic* less than a month after Mineo's death, saw the actor's end as a fate preordained by his movie roles and as a bloody, cathartic escape from typecasting: ". . . Sal Mineo died again, stabbed outside his West Hollywood apartment house. This time there were no searchlights hailing the American teenager gone berserk—only one man cut-

*Sal Mineo as the terrorist Dov Landau in* Exodus, *which earned him an Academy Award nomination. (Wide World)*

*Stabbed to death, Mineo's body lies beneath a sheet in the carport of his West Hollywood apartment on the night of February 13, 1976. (Wide World)*

ting up another in a grown-up world that deals with such realities calmly."

Movie critics and savants kept hammering at the grim parallel between Mineo's movie deaths and his own very real end. They portrayed Sal Mineo as the confused and violent victim of synthetic and wicked Hollywood, the birthplace of his mercurial career.

Actually, the actor, a gentle and talented man, began without a hope of ever becoming a world celebrity. Born Salvatore Mineo, Jr., on January 10, 1939, the son of a Sicilian-born coffin maker (another easy parallel to his macabre end), he came from a large family that struggled for survival in The Bronx. He lived on 217th Street, a tough neighborhood, and was recruited as a gang member at age eight, when he was dismissed from a parochial school as a troublemaker (again, much like the juvenile delinquent he was to play in *Somebody Up There Likes Me*). He managed to become reinstated and went on to attend Christopher Columbus High School, but he never received a diploma.

To keep young Sal out of trouble, his mother, Josephine, put him into a dancing class, and quite by accident two years later he was spotted by Cheryl Crawford, a Broadway producer looking for two Italian-American children to appear in Tennessee Williams's play *The Rose Tattoo.* At eleven Mineo found himself leading a goat across the stage of the Martin Beck Theatre, prattling a single line: "The goat is in the yard." He later understudied for the role of the prince in *The King and I,* and subsequently took over the role.

During these years the doe-eyed youth with the sensitive lips and thick black hair took the subway home, often alone, to The Bronx after his performances. He was a prime target for perverts, but he knew it and took precautions, especially after seeing a John Garfield film, *Castle on the Hudson,* in which Garfield as a youth begins to carry a weapon to defend himself against street toughs. He bought a blank pistol that looked enough like the real thing to make one man who approached him on the subway cower in fear until Mineo jumped from the train at the next stop, leaving his would-be molester cringing and begging for mercy on the train floor.

Mineo struck out for Hollywood in the mid-1950s while still a teen-ager and in 1955 landed a part in a movie entitled *Six Bridges to Cross,* in which he played Tony Curtis as a youth, a delinquent who grew up to rob Brink's (the story was based upon the 1950 Brink's robbery in Boston). His next movie, *Rebel Without a Cause,* shot him to fame and teen-age idolatry. In the movie Mineo portrayed a psychotic juvenile delinquent named Plato. From a wealthy family, he is morbidly fascinated with violence and death and impulsively wields a switchblade at every opportunity. Mineo died violently in the film as an aimless youth desperately looking for purpose and reason where there was none. In this role alone Sal Mineo came to typify the youth of the 1950s, and as such he was typecast in many successive movies, which included *The Young Don't Cry, Dino* (another juvenile delinquent), *Exodus*—in which he played the self-destructive terrorist Dov Landau—as well as *The Gene Krupa Story, Crime in the Streets,* and *Giant.* By the 1960s, Mineo's career had gone into a sharp decline. In 1971 he was reduced to playing a simian in an ape costume in *Escape from the Planet of the Apes.*

By then Mineo had concentrated on theater to support himself. In 1969 the actor directed *Fortune and Men's Eyes,* which had long runs in Los Angeles and New York and which portrayed prison life in homosexual terms, including a graphic homosexual rape scene. Clive Barnes of *The New York Times* scathingly reviewed the play, commenting: "If this does sound like the kind of play you'd like, you need a psychiatrist a lot more than you need a theater ticket."

During the early 1970s, Mineo busied himself with dinner theater, but his fortunes diminished with each year. His family eventually sold the $200,000 home he had purchased in 1956 for them in the exclusive Edgewater Point section of Mamaroneck, New York, with his first big film success. He himself moved from a luxurious Hollywood home to one inexpensive apartment after another until he was living on the fringe of the West Coast's seamiest district, the Sunset Strip, an area swarming with dopesters, male and female prostitutes, muggers, rapists, transvestites, sadists, masochists—every conceivable kind of degenerate and pervert. Inside this insidious phalanx strolled the man who finally killed Sal Mineo—not for sex or dope, but for money.

Following the actor's death friends tried to raise $10,000 as a reward for information leading to the arrest of the killer. Sal Mineo's name at that time—despite the fact that he had been nominated for the Academy Award twice (for his roles in *Rebel* and *Exodus*)—commanded little attention. Only a few hundred dollars trickled in. As Peter Bogdanovich aptly put it: "In this racket when you're not hot anymore, or when you're cold, you're dead anyway, so a lot of folks turned the page on Sal's murder and shrugged. He wasn't up for any picture."

One person who did not turn the page was Los Angeles housewife Mrs. Theresa Williams. In May 1977, more than a year after the killing, Mrs. Williams went to the police, telling them that her husband had admitted murdering Mineo, returning home on the night of the slaying covered with blood and casually saying: "I just killed this dude in Hollywood." (It was never disclosed why Mrs. Williams took so long in deciding to report her lethal spouse.)

*Mineo at the time of his murder in 1976. (Wide World)*

Mrs. Williams went on to state that her husband, twenty-two-year-old Lionel Ray Williams, had used a hunting knife to stab Mineo to death, a weapon he had purchased for $5.28. At first police disbelieved the woman. Williams, they remembered, had been arrested for robbery shortly after the actor had been murdered, and in a move for leniency he had offered to provide information on the Mineo killing. The black onetime pizza deliveryman told officers that Mineo had been murdered in an argument over dope, but the actor's background suggested no drug connections, so police dismissed Williams's tale. They did not dismiss his wife's information. Detectives bought a knife identical to the one Theresa Williams described and inserted it in the wound that had been made in Sal Mineo's chest; pathologists had preserved that part of the actor's anatomy for evidence. The knife fit perfectly. Williams, however, could not be arrested in Los Angeles just then. He was serving time in a Michigan jail for bouncing phony checks.

Authorities checked with prison authorities in Michigan, to discover that Williams had repeatedly bragged about murdering Mineo. Guard Albert Lemkuhl reported that Williams had laughingly told him how he killed the actor but that Lemkuhl had ignored the remarks, thinking them nothing more than "jail talk." On another occasion Williams was overheard talking to a fellow prisoner, by a cook who later quoted him as saying: "Have you ever killed anybody? It's very easy." With that, Williams demonstrated his knife-wielding style.

Los Angeles officers grilled the prisoner, but Williams adamantly denied having anything to do with Sal Mineo's murder. However, one of the officers noticed a large tattoo on Williams's arm depicting a knife exactly like the one he had used to kill the actor. "It was almost like he put the mark of Cain on himself," commented Michael Genelin, prosecutor for Los Angeles County.

Because of legal maneuvering, Williams's trial did not open until January 1979, almost three years after the Mineo killing. His defense attorney repeatedly pointed to the fact that Mineo's killer had been described as a white man. Genelin produced photos of Williams taken after the killing when he was booked for robbery, and these showed the defendant with auburn-colored "processed" hair. The fact that Williams was a light-skinned black further convinced jurors that the Negro had been mistaken for a white man. Moreover, Genelin provided statements from witnesses near the murder that the suspect had fled in a yellow subcompact auto. The prosecutor then produced a loan agreement Williams had signed that allowed the suspect to drive a yellow Dodge Colt, the car the defendant was driving on the night of the murder. Genelin summed up his case: "This man is a predator. This was a progressive process with him. . . . He

*Sal Mineo's killer—Lionel Ray Williams. (Wide World)*

enjoyed brutalizing people. These were not just street robberies but one incident after another where he inflicted pain . . . and enjoyed it."

Williams's trial was unusual in that along with the Mineo killing, he was tried for a series of robberies in West Hollywood, Beverly Hills, and the Wilshire district. The jury found him guilty, and as the guilty verdicts were slowly read aloud, the defendant turned to his lawyer, Morton Herbert, and moaned: "My God, they're going to convict me of every one of these things." The jury almost did, convicting the killer of ten robberies out of eleven *and* the Mineo slaying.

Defense Counsel Herbert admitted after the trial that evidence against Williams "was extremely strong—and they were bad robberies. . . . Basically, this was a case of ten brutal robberies with Mineo tacked on. It was ironic that Mineo became a very minor part of the trial."

Found guilty of second-degree murder, Williams was sentenced by Judge Bonnie Lee Martin to a term of fifty-one years to life for the killing and the robberies. In sentencing Williams, Judge Martin recounted the guilty man's long record, beginning with four arrests when he was fourteen years old. She told his lawyer that Williams "should be locked up as long as the law allows. . . . I don't think he's susceptible to rehabilitation, considering his escalating conduct of committing more and more serious crimes and more and more violence."

The stocky, muscular Williams was defiant to the end, sneering at the judge and telling her: "I fault you for my going to the penitentiary."

Prosecutor Genelin felt extraordinarily triumphant in the conviction of Lionel Ray Williams, but he knew that the conviction was a rare and fortuitous event, especially when it came to the murder of Sal Mineo. "If a murder is not solved within twenty-four to forty-eight hours," he told newsmen, "you generally do not get a solution. Anyone who says people don't get away with murder is crazy. They do it all the time."

# 1976

## CLAUDINE LONGET
### A CASE OF "CRIMINALLY NEGLIGENT HOMICIDE"

A spen, Colorado, is Mount Olympus to the American mighty in the frenetic worlds of entertainment and sports, particularly skiing. Its inhabitants and visitors represent and live up to the laid-back kind of life that offers little or no intellectual stimulants but plenty of snow (when it does snow), skiing, and mostly expensive bars, one for each block in the downtown area. Moreover, it is a town where excessive drinking is commonplace and drug-taking is nothing unusual, from pot to coke. (A spokesman for the Federal Drug Enforcement Agency once labeled Aspen "the cocaine capital" of the country.) In keeping with its idle pursuits, Aspen's community festivities are often adolescent, even imbecilic.

One of the more quaint customs of this superjock town is Aspen's rite of spring, an end-of-the-season blowout where women of all ages appear in T-shirts, following a long evening of drinks and drugs, to compete in the Best Breast contest. To induce the modest or shy to disrobe and bare their breasts, new skis or money are offered. Ashley Anderson, the twenty-nine-year-old deputy district attorney who was to prosecute Claudine Longet for murder, once stated that these rites were "terrific. All the girls get drunk and take their clothes off."

Another tribal rite of Aspen's citizens is Winterskol, a winter carnival taking place in January, at which time naked skiing from a ski jump into a swimming pool is the highlight, one exercised chiefly by females with decidedly exhibitionist tendencies. In Aspen it's "drink and be merry for tomorrow you may break your neck on a slope," and if you don't ski, then you really need no excuse other than the altitude to drink yourself into a stupor or conk out on cocaine.

198

*Singer-actress Claudine Longet with her lover Vladimir "Spider" Sabich.*

Into this rarefied atmosphere moved Claudine Longet in 1975, when she took up residence with Olympic skier Vladimir "Spider" Sabich, who was to remain her lover for two years. The onetime Las Vegas dancer—a petite, curvy dark-haired woman—was not generally liked in the community, which thought her aloof and haughty. Sabich, on the other hand, was a freewheeling athlete who was much respected and liked in the town.

Sabich, the son of a Placerville, California, cop, was considered one of the top skiers in 1968 when he finished fifth in the slalom at the Grenoble Olympics. He turned professional in 1971 and began to earn large amounts of money in competition, gleaning $50,000 in prize money in 1972, matching that amount with fees from endorsements of ski products and coffee. Sabich's star went into eclipse in 1973 when he was beaten out in a race by French skier Jean-Claude Killy. He later had a terrible spill in which he split several vertebrae. In 1974 he suffered a knee injury that never properly healed, and by 1976 his fortunes had dwindled to the point where he earned a meager $800.

By then he was deeply involved with—and, many said, on the verge of breaking up with—the divorced thirty-four-year-old Claudine Longet, whose three children also lived with her and Sabich at the skier's $250,000 chalet, a luxury home he reportedly built for her shortly after meeting Claudine at a celebrity ski race in Bear Valley, California, in 1972.

French-born Claudine had been a scantily clad dancer in the Folies-Bergère Revue in Las Vegas in 1961 when she met and married singer Andy Williams, then the favorite singer of President John F. Kennedy. They produced three children and remained married for fourteen years, but separated long before their divorce to become "items" in the gossip columns when they appeared at Hollywood social functions with different attractive companions.

Claudine thought she had found the perfect man in Sabich, and in 1974 she moved herself and her three children into the skier's chalet. By early 1976, the year of her divorce from Andy Williams, it was stated by some Aspenites that Claudine not only had alienated many in the community with her "tart tongue" but had become estranged from Sabich. The skier was quoted as telling a close friend that "it's either going to end or we'll be married within a year." Within a month he was dead at the hands of Claudine Longet.

Claudine apparently had been making plans to move out of Sabich's chalet. She had rented a Victorian house and busied herself by twice a week attending her son's second-grade class, where she was a volunteer French teacher.

On a bright Sunday afternoon, March 21, 1976, Claudine, according to one account, spent "a couple of hours on the slopes and several more reportedly drinking with some male companions at a popular watering hole." She returned to Sabich's home before 5 P.M. About an hour and a half later Aspen police received an urgent phone call from Claudine to come to the skier's home in the exclusive Starwood subdivision. Chief of security for the area, Roy Griffith, led officers to the home, telling Lieutenant William H. Baldridge: "Watch it, this gal is *ringy* today." The word "ringy" was later construed by some during Claudine's whirlwind trial to mean that she was "crazy." Upon entering the Sabich home, police found Claudine, in the words of Griffith, "confused and upset." Her fists were clutched to her chest, and Griffith first thought that she might be wounded.

"Who shot who?" Griffith asked.

"I shot Spider," replied Claudine.

Spider Sabich was lying on the floor of the master bedroom in blue thermal underwear. He had been washing his face, Claudine told police, when she approached him with a black, German-made .22-caliber Irma pistol, asking how to use it in case of intruders, and the weapon had gone off accidentally, one bullet ploughing into Sabich's abdomen, striking an artery in his left side. Detective David Garms was later to testify that the singer told him following the shooting that "I raised the gun and playfully went 'Boom, boom,' and it went off."

By the time the ambulance attendants arrived to rush the skier to the hospital, he was dead. Claudine rode in the ambulance as it raced toward Aspen Valley Hospital and tried with the attendants to revive Sabich, but it was no use.

Police on the scene found Claudine's diary and took it along as evidence. They also later took blood and urine samples from the singer. In the first instance, it was reported, the diary would prove that Claudine's passion for the skier had turned into in-

*Claudine Longet on her way from the courthouse in Aspen, Colorado, where she was being tried for murder.*

tense dislike, and she therefore had a motive for murder. Officers gathered reports stating that Claudine "quarreled frequently with [Sabich], publicly and privately, and that their relationship was on the skids." It was also stated that Sabich had decided to order Claudine and her children from his house because he could no longer tolerate her wild jealousy.

Though many were willing to state anonymously that they believed the singer purposely responsible for the skier's death, one sterling Aspen citizen later stepped forward to say in court: "I believe [Longet] is guilty." This was none other than thirty-one-year-old Stacy Standley, the mayor of the town, who once posed nude for an Aspen calendar.

Released on a small bond, Claudine was joined by her former husband, Andy Williams, who arrived in Aspen the day after the shooting to see his children and comfort Claudine. He reportedly told an Aspen neighbor that Longet was a "crazy gal who likes to drive fast, ski fast and take chances." When confronted with this statement, Williams promptly denied it. He, Claudine, and their children moved into the Starwood home of John Denver as the folk singer's guests, to await trial.

Claudine's 1977 trial received enormous publicity, along with the town of Aspen, which *The New York Times* likened to "a hedonistic place where the rich, the young, the haunted and the newly divorced come to find a new sense of self." The paper went on to point out that Chrysler had named a new-model Dodge after the town, and that a paperback novel described Aspen as " 'a wild place . . . a savage world of sensuous indulgence . . . where the driving forces of power, money and sex culminate in violence and murder.' "

The prosecution sought a murder conviction in the Longet-Sabich killing, second degree, at least. Yet the presiding judge would not admit Claudine's diary, which police had taken from Sabich's chalet. He stated that it, and the urine and blood analysis taken from Claudine, ostensibly to prove she was drunk at the time of the shooting, were inadmissible, having been taken without proper permission from the defendant.

Throughout the short trial Claudine insisted that she was innocent of any crime in the killing of Sabich. She had pled not guilty, and took the stand on her own behalf. She refuted the charge that she was not playing around with the weapon, which went off accidentally while her lover was showing her how to use it and fatally wounded him. Upon returning home on the evening of the shooting, Claudine said that she saw the gun in a closet. "I reminded myself to ask Spider one more time what this gun was about." Earlier, she claimed, Sabich had showed her how to load the weapon. She took the pistol from the closet. As she testified Longet became nervous; her composure started to erode.

Claudine described how she walked down a hallway carrying the gun, which she held flat in one hand, the other hand folded over it. "Somehow," Claudine went on, "I don't really quite know how—I pushed a button and somehow the container [the clip holding the bullets] fell. I picked it up and put it back in." She added that she hadn't known whether or not she had reloaded the weapon properly. She walked to Sabich, who was undressing next to a sunken stone tub. "It happened very fast. I said, 'Spider, I want to know more about this gun.'"

Her attorney, Charles V. Weedman, put a weapon in Claudine's hand so she could demonstrate from the witness stand. Claudine stated that she had asked Sabich at that moment: "When the lever is on the red spot, is it safe? It won't fire?" "'You've got it,'" Claudine quoted Sabich's response.

It was at this moment, the defendant insisted, that the gun went off, a bullet striking the skier in the side. "Spider called my name many many times," Claudine said in a quavering voice. "He sort of slid down and I told him I would call the hospital and not to move." She described how Sabich began to lose consciousness. "I told him to try to make it, to talk to me, and I saw he was sort of fainting, so I tried to give him mouth-to-mouth resuscitation."

Claudine then denied that she had playfully held up the weapon to Sabich, as the police had reported, and said, "bang, bang!" or "boom, boom," before it went off. "I wouldn't joke with a gun . . . I might have said it went bang."

Prosecutor Ashley Anderson studied the petite Claudine for a moment; she was dressed in a black sweater over a white blouse and a blue miniskirt. "Isn't it a fact that you were asked to move out [of Sabich's home]?" asked Anderson.

"No," responded Claudine.

Defense Counsel Weedman objected to this line of questioning, and, with the jury removed, District Judge George E. Lohr

*Singer Andy Williams escorting his former wife, Claudine Longet, to court. (UPI)*

ruled that the line of questioning was prejudicial, and dismissed it.

The case against Claudine Longet came to an end on January 14, 1977, two days after she had testified. She had wept openly in court. So had her ex-husband, Andy Williams. Actor Jack Nicholson, seated in the reporters' gallery, was not seen to weep at all.

The jury returned within forty minutes, its members smiling broadly. They found Claudine Longet guilty of "criminally negligent homicide" instead of the "reckless manslaughter" charge the prosecution had sought.

Claudine left the court to await sentencing, choking back tears to tell reporters: "I have too much respect for human life to have been guilty . . . I am not guilty." The charge called for a maximum sentence of two years in jail and a $5,000 fine. Claudine Longet received neither. On January 31, Claudine went before Judge Lohr, pleading with him not to send her to jail so as to avoid the stigma of prison that might attach itself to her children. She added that her children, if she were jailed, would become resentful "against a system that would send to jail [the] mother they trust and believe in."

Judge Lohr, apparently moved by Claudine's tearful plea, ordered her to spend thirty days in jail "at a time of her own choosing," and put her on two years' probation, fining her $25 to pay the costs of the probation reports. The judge stated that if he had given Claudine probation without a jail sentence, the decision "might have undermined the law."

Despite a plea that she be let out of jail to spend Mother's Day with her children, Claudine was ordered to serve out her sentence, which she did, spending April 18–May 18, 1977, in a cell.

The citizens of Aspen, enduring the worst snow season in forty years and feeling some bitterness over Sabich's death, summed up the affair in a flurry of bumper stickers that suddenly appeared and that read: IT'S ALL CLAUDINE'S FAULT.

# 1978

⌘

# DAN WHITE

## DEATH AT
## THE SEAT OF POWER

San Francisco Supervisor Dan White had been brooding for a long time, perhaps weeks. On November 10, 1978, White had resigned his post as one of the city's eleven supervisors, having served as the representative from the Eighth District beginning in 1977. The thirty-two-year-old politician had quit an $18,000-a-year post with the fire department to run for the office, but his supervisor's salary of $9,600 a year (as a part-time city employee) was not enough to support his wife and infant son, he said. He quit the job but four days later asked Mayor George Moscone to reinstate him.

Moscone hedged; he intended to name Don Horanzy, bank analyst, real estate broker, and liberal politician, to the post. Horanzy was also White's political enemy, or at least White considered him as such. White persisted in asking Moscone for reinstatement but the mayor knew that legally he was not obligated to do so, and he did not intend to. Outwardly, Moscone appeared to support White, saying when White resigned: "I'm sorry to see him go. I think he's a good guy." He went ahead with his plans to install Horanzy who, with his family, was invited to the mayor's office in City Hall on the morning of November 27, 1978. The Horanzys were met by the mayor's press aid, Mel Wax, who had them wait in an outer office. He was afraid that there would be a scene with Dan White, whom Wax had just spotted entering the mayor's offices at 10:15 A.M.

White had been picked up at his small bungalow on Shawnee Avenue about an hour earlier by an unknown woman driving a red sports car who took him to City Hall. The former supervisor went to the north side of the aging granite building, to tap on a window next to the north ramp. A janitor he knew pushed open the window, and White told him that he had forgotten his keys to the side door that supervisors were permitted to use.

The janitor did not have the key either but let White in through the window. The former supervisor then walked to the second floor, where the mayor's offices were located. (It was later stated that he purposely avoided going through the main entrance of the ornate building so that the metal detector would not pick up the .38 snub-nosed Smith & Wesson Chiefs Special revolver and a pocketful of shells he was carrying.) White approached the mayor's secretary, Cyr Copertini, asking to see Moscone.

Miss Copertini entered Moscone's office, closing the huge oak door behind her. "Dan White is outside," she told the mayor. "He'd like to see you." Moscone, who was working in his shirt-sleeves at his desk, grimaced at the mention of White's name. Copertini offered to make excuses, but Moscone told her that he would see the former supervisor.

Moments later the mayor emerged from his office, smiling and still in his shirt-sleeves, to shake White's hand. Moscone's secretary asked him if he wanted anyone to sit in on the meeting. "No, I'll see him alone," laughed the mayor. He then led White down a hallway of offices to his inner sanctum where they could have a drink. This was customary for Moscone, who had been elected San Francisco's liberal Democratic mayor in 1977, the same year White had won his own office. Mel Wax later told newsmen: "When he [Moscone] wants heart-to-heart with somebody, the back office is a more informal setting. He liked to sit on the couch."

Cyr Copertini heard several popping noises just after 11 A.M. "I had an awful feeling," she later said. "I went over to the window and looked out, thinking they were shots, but hoping they weren't."

Rudy Nothenberg, the Deputy Mayor, then arrived in Moscone's office for an 11 A.M. meeting. When he saw that the mayor was not in his main office, he walked back to the "den." Nothenberg saw White running down a hallway, and entering the den, found Moscone lying on the floor, face downward, his body wedged between the couch and the coffee table. He had been shot four times and was bleeding heavily. The mayor had taken two bullets in the chest and two more shots, the coup de grace, had been sent into his head behind the right ear. He was dead. No-

*Former San Francisco Supervisor Dan White, the all-American boy turned killer. (Wide World)*

thenberg ran into the corridor and shouted: "Police! Get the police!"

At that moment Dan White was jogging steadily through a maze of hallways and offices, making his way to the other side of City Hall to his old office, a hundred-yard run to Room 250, which contained several cubicle offices. There he shouted to one of his own staff members who had not yet moved out: "Give me my keys! Give me my keys!" The staffer gave him the keys to his old office. White dashed from that main reception area to Room 237, which contained the supervisors' offices. He passed the office of Supervisor Dianne Feinstein, who looked up briefly as he ran by. White stopped at the small office occupied by Supervisor Harvey Milk, the leader of San Francisco's homosexual community who had opposed his reinstatement and had repeatedly opposed him on almost every issue in city council meetings.

"Harvey, may I see you for a moment?" he asked Milk. The supervisor accompanied White into the former supervisor's old office; White's name had already been removed from the door.

Minutes later Supervisor Feinstein, sitting at her desk, heard the distinct sounds of five shots, slowly repeated. She immediately picked up a phone and called the police. White emerged, red-faced and huffing, moving quickly down a corridor to return to the reception area in Room 250, where he demanded an aide give him her car keys. She did, and the ex-supervisor raced off, leaving City Hall at the McAllister Street side and driving away in the aide's car.

As he was descending the stairs to the exit, White passed scores of running policemen, their weapons drawn. They rushed by him on the stairs, ignoring him. Moments later Supervisor Harvey Milk was found shot to death, a bullet in his back, two more bullets in his body, and two additional bullets in the head. Later reconstruction of the murders described how White had killed both Moscone and Milk by first shooting them to knock them down, then standing over them and firing the coup de grace shots that brought death. He had prepared well, it seemed, reloading the five-shot revolver after killing the mayor, so that he would face Milk with a fully loaded weapon.

After leaving City Hall, Dan White phoned his wife, Mary Ann, at the Hot Potato, a fast-food stand the couple ran on Fisherman's Wharf that White had started to supplement his meager supervisor's income. White told his wife, a onetime schoolteacher, to meet him at St. Mary's Cathedral. When she arrived, he walked toward her crying. "I've just shot the mayor and Harvey," he told her. They walked down Van Ness Avenue and White waved to one of the many auto dealers along this strip before entering the Northern Police Station, only five blocks from City Hall, where he turned over his weapon and extra cartridges and admitted the killings. Oddly enough, White had served as a policeman out of this very station. He was locked in a cell pending a hearing.

The news of the double slaying burst through the nation's press, and citizens everywhere, particularly in San Francisco, went into shock. The city's gay community, which felt as one person that the killings were motivated by hatred for homosexuals, reacted angrily, thousands gathering to protest the killings. As evidence later showed, their anger and subsequent rage was misdirected. White had killed Moscone and Milk simply because they both opposed his reinstatement as a supervisor, not out of sexual prejudice. This was the motive White consistently gave at his later hearing and trial.

White stated that minutes after he had his meeting with Moscone, the mayor began to treat him cavalierly, indicating that he had no intention of ever allowing the ex-supervisor to regain his post. Moscone, as a way of excusing his decision, said White, had blurted: "It's only politics." With that, White shot him. White went after Milk and killed him because Harvey Milk was his chief opponent in preventing him from rejoining the city council and because he had seen Milk "smirk" one time when White was asking the mayor to reinstate him.

To White, Moscone and Milk were holding him up to ridicule and making a public "scapegoat" out of him. In a strange twist of fate, it was Moscone and Milk who had bitterly opposed a recent statewide referendum expanding the death penalty to cover, among other issues, the murder of a public official in pursuit of his duties. That November the referendum was overwhelmingly put through by California citizens (excepting large segments of traditionally ultraliberal San Franciscans), and was strongly supported by Dan White himself. He now stood, if convicted of first-degree murder, to go to San Quentin's gas chamber under the new measure.

As White awaited trial his background and those of Moscone's and Milk's were examined in the press, the minutiae of their lives chronicled to the point of their intertwining destinies. White, up to the time of the killings, had had a sterling reputation as a rugged, fearless, and upstanding citizen. He was born in San Francisco, one of seventeen boys. His mother had married twice, both times to firemen. White had been an all-American boy,

*San Francisco Supervisor Harvey Milk (left) and Mayor George Moscone. (Wide World)*

prompting one politician to remark later that if "he had been a breakfast food he would have been Wheaties." He boxed and played football in his teens and served heroically in Vietnam, earning three medals as a paratrooper.

White returned from service in 1967 and joined the police force, where he served with distinction, although he enjoyed a full bachelor life, spending his money on gambling junkets to Reno and purchasing sports cars, first an $8,000 Jaguar, then a $15,000 Porsche. He moved to Marin County to live on a houseboat before taking a leave of absence from the police force in 1972, when he decided to see the country on a hitchhiking tour. He wound up in Alaska, where he worked as a high school guidance counselor and truant officer.

In 1977, when he was running for the post of supervisor, White told a reporter: "I guess I'm something of a romantic. I am a great Jack London fan, and I do some writing, mostly short stories. So I hitchhiked around the country." After his travels White returned to San Francisco, where he joined the fire department and married, buying a $70,000 house in the Vistacion Valley section.

He and his wife had a son shortly before he ran for office, and neighbors were delighted when the Whites held an open house for the boy's christening. Even after White won his supervisor's post, he continued his job with the fire department and was responsible for helping to save a woman and a child trapped on the seventeenth floor of a burning building. He received a medal for heroism for this act from the fire department, bestowed upon him after he had killed Moscone and Milk.

White's victims were both liberal Democrats and shrewd politicians who played to the many ethnic and social minorities that made up San Francisco's 650,000 population (approximately 50,000 to as many as 150,000 were self-proclaimed homosexuals; an exact gay census has never been taken). Mayor George Moscone had been a foe of capital punishment ever since his father, who had been a guard at San Quentin, showed him the gas chamber as a little boy. He and Harvey Milk had also been staunch supporters of Jim Jones and continued to be so even after the religious fanatic moved his entire People's Temple following to remote Guyana. The mass murder and suicide in Guyana, which occurred only a week before White went on his killing spree, caused both Moscone and Milk to weep. "I cried and then vomited," said Mayor Moscone. Milk later flippantly remarked about the 911 deaths in Guyana: "It would have made a great opera. I'd like to have the rights to it."

Moscone had worked his way through the College of the Pacific and Hastings Law School. He had served in the Navy and had four children with his wife, Gina (Bondanza), whom he married in 1954. After practicing law for fifteen years, Moscone entered politics, working his way through San Francisco's tricky Italian-American political system until he emerged as a candidate for mayor, winning the post in 1977.

Though he campaigned on an anticrime theme, Moscone's critics accused him of being soft on crime once he took office. Robbings, shootings, bombings, and murder threats increased drastically during Moscone's reign until he was forced to institute a crash anticrime program that did little to alleviate the crime wave. The freewheeling, affable mayor further incensed critics by espousing all manner of liberal causes. He marched with the United Union of Farmworkers led by Cesar Chavez. He backed wide-

spread welfare programs, and he appointed a phalanx of homosexuals to various city commissions and even ordered the City
Hall flag flown at half-mast after a San Francisco homosexual was
murdered. The forty-nine-year-old mayor was not, as was later
reported, out to fill his own coffers through his powerful position.
He was $200,000 in debt when he was killed, and had less than
$2,000 in the bank.

Harvey Milk shared Moscone's liberal philosophy and, as a
supervisor, proudly stated that he was San Francisco's first acknowledged homosexual official. A native New Yorker, the
forty-eight-year-old Milk had moved to San Francisco in 1969 to
work in the financial district. He tried several times to run for the
post of supervisor, stressing his homosexuality, but received only
token votes. In 1977 he was narrowly elected to the post, as was
Moscone to his. After the election, at the reception where officials
were to introduce their wives, Milk presented Jack Lira, age
twenty-four, whom he introduced as "my lover, my partner in
life." Lira committed suicide three months before Milk was killed
by Dan White. Milk's running joke was to refer to City Hall as
"silly hall."

The homosexual question repeatedly pitted Harvey Milk and
Dan White against each other in council debates. On one occasion Milk was instrumental in passing an ordinance guaranteeing
the rights of homosexuals, one of the most stringent in the country. The only supervisor voting vehemently against it was Dan
White.

By then White was an open foe of deviants and "perverts" in
San Francisco, which had become a haven for social dropouts and
misfits. Bernard Diamond, a psychiatrist and professor of law at
the Berkeley campus of the University of California, was quoted
at the time as saying that "many people who can't adjust elsewhere find Northern California an extremely attractive place. In
the Bay Area, disturbed people can do their own thing. There is
a tolerance for deviants of all kinds."

Dan White concurred. In fact, the main thrust of his campaign
was his antideviant attitudes. One of his brochures read:

You must realize there are thousands upon thousands of
frustrated angry people such as yourself waiting to unleash
fury that can and will eradicate the malignancies which

blight our city. Should we continue to be maligned and shamed throughout the nation? I say no.

I am not going to be forced out of San Francisco by splinter groups of radicals, social deviates, incorrigibles. . . . By choosing to run for supervisor of District Eight I have committed myself to the confrontation which can no longer be avoided by those who care.

After Moscone and Milk were killed, reporters were stunned to learn that both men had voiced their apprehension of being assassinated. Milk had made a tape recording predicting that he might meet such a violent end. George Moscone had openly said: "As a practical matter, anybody who wants to knock me off can do it regardless of whether I have Dick Tracy or anybody else with me."

As White awaited trial on the fifth floor of the Hall of Justice, thirty thousand mourners gathered in a torchlight parade. Many of those in attendance vowed vengeance if Dan White escaped the gas chamber. At the time, Douglas Schmidt, White's attorney, was preparing a defense that would achieve exactly that end.

Schmidt knew that he could not plead his client not guilty by reason of temporary insanity; the experts would easily disprove such a claim. He did plead his client not guilty but attempted to prove that White had lost his reason through eating junk foods. White, claimed Schmidt, was a manic-depressive who had acted compulsively all his life and who was laboring under unbearable financial pressure because of a heavily mortgaged house, a failing fast-food stand, and the nagging thought that he could not support his wife and child, further aggravated by the fact that Moscone and Milk had blocked his path to resuming his supervisor's seat.

Dan White had nervously wolfed down junk food, Schmidt told a jury, during the period immediately before the killings, gobbling Twinkies, Cokes, candy bars, doughnuts, all of which allowed too much sugar to enter his bloodstream and caused him to be temporarily deranged. Psychiatrist Jerry Jones echoed Schmidt's statements, adding that White was suffering at the time of the killings, "not the blues, what you and I call being depressed." The junk food had produced a genetic melancholia "as if the world were viewed through black glasses."

Thomas Norman, the prosecutor, tried to sweep away this theory by arguing that White was guilty of cold-blooded, premeditated murder, emphasizing to the jury of seven women and five men that White had "leaned over the prostrate bodies of his victims and finished them off with point-blank shots into their skulls."

White sat frozen throughout the trial without showing emotion other than to cry periodically when the killings were discussed. He showed no response when prosecutor Norman repeatedly demanded that the jury find him guilty of first-degree murder and send him to the gas chamber.

The trial grew to a close on May 21, 1979; the jury shocked the press and public alike with a verdict of voluntary manslaughter, which carried with it a maximum sentence of seven years and eight months.

When word of the verdict reached the gay community, angry crowds began to gather, shouting threats. Leading homosexuals began to yell that the Establishment had betrayed them. That evening, runners suddenly appeared as if part of an orchestrated program, dashing into bars and yelling: "Out of the bars and into the streets!" By 8 P.M. more than three thousand persons had assembled outside City Hall, a lynch mob screaming "Junk Food Murderer!" and "Kill Dan White!" The few persons in the crowd who attempted to quell the rioters were smashed down.

Inside City Hall, officials were held captive for hours. Acting Mayor Dianne Feinstein, who was president of the board of supervisors and had succeeded to Moscone's post, briefly appeared in an attempt to quiet the demonstrators. As soon as the rioters saw her, they began to chant: "Dump Dianne! Kill Dianne!" She was hastily pulled back into the building by her fiancé, banker Richard Blum. With a look of bewilderment on her face, the acting mayor said: "I wanted to speak to the crowd. I would have been a lightning rod."

Then Supervisor Carol Ruth Silver, who had long been a favorite of the gay community, stepped out on a balcony to try to calm the protestors. Before she could address the crowd, she was struck by a rock and later required twenty stitches.

Police arrived, muscling the crowd from City Hall. Rioters at this time went berserk, attacking the public library and looting the nearby stores, setting fire to the gas tanks of police cars,

*More than 25,000 San Franciscans, most of them gays, gather outside City Hall to mourn the slaying of Supervisor Milk and Mayor Moscone. (Wide World)*

showering officers with rocks and bricks. Police drove them back with nightsticks, some officers reportedly shouting: "Get out of here, you goddamned queers!" For six hours the bloody riots raged, subsiding only after 119 persons were injured, including 60 policemen. Twelve police cars had been torched and more than $1 million damage had been done to public buildings.

The senseless riot had left City Hall a shambles, its windows smashed, its front entranceway splintered where a mob had tried to knock down the front doors with a battering ram. Acting Mayor Feinstein (who would soon be elected mayor) later empathized with the rioters, stating that the verdict in the White case was "shameful." The verdict, however, stood, and White was sentenced to serve seven years and eight months.

# 1980

## JEAN STRUVEN HARRIS
### A "WRONGED" WOMAN'S FURY

Juanita Edwards, a woman in her sixties, sat in the examining room while Dr. Herman Tarnower took her pulse. At the time, Tarnower was not only a leading cardiologist but one of the most celebrated authors in America, his book *The Complete Scarsdale Medical Diet,* written with Samm Sinclair Baker, having sold more than three million copies and grossed more than $11 million since its publication in January 1979. Before Tarnower completed his examination of Mrs. Edwards, the doctor was called to the phone by his assistant, Mrs. Lynne Tryforos, a slim, attractive thirty-eight-year-old blonde.

Tarnower picked up the phone in the examining room, then told his assistant: "I'll take this call in my office." He excused himself, leaving the phone off the hook so that Mrs. Edwards accidentally heard part of his conversation whenever he raised his voice. "Goddamnit, Jean," Mrs. Edwards heard Tarnower yell over the phone, "I want you to stop bothering me!" There was some muffled conversation, then the doctor again yelled: "You've lied and you've cheated!" Later he was heard to say: "Well, you're going to inherit $240,000." The sixty-nine-year-old doctor hung up and returned, visibly agitated, to finish his examination of Juanita Edwards.

The "Jean" he had just brushed off was his fifty-six-year-old mistress, Jean Struven Harris, whom he had been seeing for fourteen years. Dr. Tarnower would see her once again on this last day of his life.

Actually, there had been many mistresses in the long and lucrative life of Herman Tarnower, dozens of them whose names and addresses he kept in a little black book. Jean Harris had lasted the longest, but only because she had willingly become his slavish pawn, a role that she came to loathe, one that caused a self-hatred and a seething passion for either vindication or vengeance. On March 10, 1980, Mrs. Harris chose the latter course.

That Monday afternoon Jean Harris left her duties at the Madeira School and slipped behind the wheel of her blue 1973 Chrysler. She drove through a rainstorm for five hours from McLean, Virginia, an exclusive Washington, D.C., suburb, to the $500,000 six-and-a-half acre estate of Herman Tarnower outside of Purchase, New York, near Scarsdale in Westchester County and nineteen miles out of New York City. She had swallowed several amphetamines, and inside her purse rested a .32-caliber revolver with extra cartridges.

While Jean Harris was still on the road battling rain-coated roads, Dr. Tarnower was dining with intimate friends, including his attractive blond assistant, Mrs. Lynne Tryforos. His guests left the sprawling Tarnower home—with its Japanese motifs, its huge swimming pool, tennis courts, and private duck pond—by 9 P.M. A little less than two hours later Jean Harris arrived at the estate and made her way through the darkened mansion to a second-floor bedroom to face a pajama-clad Herman Tarnower.

Some minutes later shots rang out that awakened Suzanne van der Vreken and her husband, Henri. The housekeeper-cook told her husband, who was the grounds keeper for the estate, to go upstairs and check on the noise. He cautiously entered the doctor's room, to find his employer lying between twin beds and dying of four bullet wounds in the hand, chest, shoulder, and arm. His wife, meanwhile, had called police in nearby Harrison, New York. Putting down the phone, the housekeeper went to the window to see a blue Chrysler sedan parked in the circular driveway. Someone was sitting behind the wheel.

As she stared straight ahead into the dark drizzle that awful night, Mrs. Jean Struven Harris, a worldly, educated, and highly refined woman, must have thought deeply and desperately back to the time when fate had brought her into contact with Herman Tarnower. It was a time when she had been made to feel like Cinderella by a charming, urbane, but domineering man who had over the years utterly captivated her heart and mind (or so she later insisted) and, through his betrayals and her insane jealousy, brought about her ruination as well as his own violent death.

*Millionaire diet doctor Herman Tarnower, the object of Jean Harris's love and hate.*

Jean Harris's background was one that would brighten the hustling heart of any personnel agent inspecting her resumé. Born in Cleveland, Ohio, to a career military officer, she lived as a child in the exclusive suburb of Shaker Heights and attended the Laurel School, a private academy for girls from upper-class families. She graduated with honors and then during the war years moved on to Smith College, where she graduated magna cum laude and Phi Beta Kappa in 1945.

Marrying James Harris, the son of a Detroit industrialist, who worked as an executive for the Holly Carburetor Company, Jean settled down in exclusive Grosse Pointe, where she taught history at the Country Day School. From 1950 to 1954 she stayed at home to raise her two sons, David and James. They were to grow up calling her "Big Woman" in reference to her proper manner and insistence on etiquette; she was a gentle but persistent disciplinarian.

Mrs. Harris returned to teaching at the University Liggett School in Grosse Pointe. In 1964, Jean made two major decisions. She divorced her husband on grounds of cruelty and, after she was passed over as assistant to the president of her school, moved on to become the director of an exclusive Philadelphia girls' school, Springside, living with her two sons in the well-to-do suburb of Chestnut Hill. In 1972 she became the director of the now defunct Thomas School in Rowayton, Connecticut, another exclusive girls' school. It was here that Mrs. Harris first began to show signs of instability; she was subject to "unexplainable emotional outbursts," according to one faculty member. Her unruly temper may have caused her to look elsewhere for employment in 1977 after board members criticized her behavior.

It was in that year that Jean Harris became the headmistress for the Madeira School for girls in McLean, Virginia, which had graduated the likes of Katharine Graham, chairman of *The Washington Post*. Mrs. Harris had arrived at the top of her profession when she assumed the position at one of the most exclusive schools in America. It was here that Mrs. Harris earned the sobriquet of "Integrity Jean" for her obsession with honesty and her near-rabid emphasis on discipline. Two weeks before driving to the Tarnower estate with a gun in her purse, Jean Harris had arbitrarily expelled four girls—from some of the wealthiest families supporting Madeira—for drinking and smoking marijuana.

Mrs. Harris's attitude during this period was undoubtedly in-
fluenced by the vexing thought that her lover of fourteen years,
the indefatigable Dr. Tarnower, was about to throw her over for
another woman, a younger woman, a sleek, calculating blonde
who, in Mrs. Harris's troubled mind, was out to destroy her. Her
constant obsession with honesty, was, no doubt, a reaction to the
incessant betrayals she experienced with Tarnower. In her public
life as the prim and proper headmistress of Madeira, Mrs. Harris
exhorted her female charges to concentrate on emotional integrity, not outward gloss and polish.

In one address to seniors at Madeira she stated:

I have often talked with you about those useful study skills
and good manners that we hope you have woven into the
fabric of your lives during your years at Madeira. But it
occurs to me I have seldom mentioned that most important
ingredient of all, a stout and loving heart. It is not easily won
and yet is one of those things we each assume we have and
so neglect to give it the attention it deserves. Hard work,
good intentions, politeness, even genius are not substitutes
for it.

Mrs. Harris's own heart was lost long before to Dr. Herman
Tarnower, to her beloved "Hi," as intimates called him. The two
first met on December 9, 1966, at a Manhattan dinner party given
in the home of Leslie and Marjorie Jacobson. "It was an instant
take," Marjorie Jacobson later testified when referring to that first
meeting between Tarnower, whom she had known for twenty-
five years, and Mrs. Harris, who had been a childhood friend.

Herman Tarnower must have seemed to Jean Harris an exceptional man, if not a trifle odd in that he was eminently successful
and had been for most of his life, yet he had never married.
Tarnower was born into wealth; his father was a prosperous hat
manufacturer in New York City. He had been expected to go into
the family business but ignored that idea and entered Syracuse
University, studying medicine and graduating in 1933. He served
his residency at Bellevue. He traveled extensively through
Europe on a 1936–37 postgraduate fellowship, specializing in the
study of cardiology in London and Amsterdam.

He returned to White Plains Hospital in 1939 as an attending cardiologist. During World War II, Tarnower served as a medical officer in the U.S. Army Air Corps. After Japan surrendered, the doctor was a lieutenant colonel and a member of the Casualty Survey Commission, examining Japanese civilians injured in the A-bomb blasts of Hiroshima and Nagasaki, an unforgettable if not traumatic experience for Tarnower that he spoke of frequently during the remainder of his long and lucrative life.

After being mustered out of the Army, Tarnower moved to Scarsdale to open a medical practice. As his practice expanded he grew rich, establishing his own Scarsdale Medical Center in 1959. The doctor spent his leisure time traveling about the world and shooting big game, delighting in annual African safaris where he shot kudu, lion, rhino. The heads of these beasts Tarnower mounted on the walls of his new $500,000 house in Purchase, New York. The mansion itself, sitting on more than six acres, with its Japanese-style brick-and-glass architecture, was another trophy. Into it he brought art treasures and antiques and, at night, women of all kinds. Some were his patients, others were members of New York society. All of them were, like Jean Harris, sophisticated and intelligent. By the time Herman Tarnower met Mrs. Harris, he had the reputation of a ladies' man if not an out-and-out playboy. Yet she didn't seem to mind. His wealth and social position made him a prize catch for any woman, yet in affairs of the heart the doctor was like a wily trout, experienced at nibbling the worm away without ensnaring himself on the hook.

Three weeks after her first meeting with Tarnower, Jean received a "nice note" from the cardiologist, who later told her over the phone that he was leaving on an African safari but would like to see her in New York upon his return. The couple did meet, dining in New York; and then, related Jean, "we went to the bar at the Pierre [Hotel] which I have loved ever since. We danced. Hi was a wonderful dancer and I got better."

Within a month Mrs. Harris was celebrating Tarnower's fifty-eighth birthday with him at his estate, with her two sons in attendance. Then Tarnower, after a few visits to see Jean in Philadelphia, began sending her roses regularly and calling her every night at 6:30 P.M. The doctor gave Mrs. Harris an enormous emerald-cut diamond in May 1967 and at that time asked her to marry him. Mrs. Harris accepted, and Tarnower made hasty plans to add a wing to his house to accommodate Jean's two growing boys.

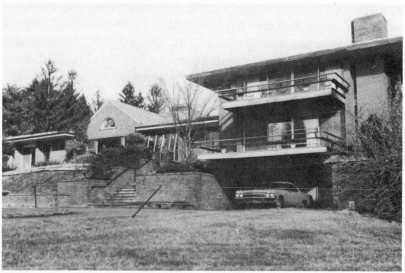

*The Tarnower estate in Purchase, New York. (Wide World)*

The wedding plans never went beyond the talking stage, however. In August, Tarnower informed Mrs. Harris, according to her own later statements, that the wedding was off. Jean returned the ring, which she said was worth approximately $50,000, telling the doctor: "You really ought to give it to Suzanne. She's the only woman you'll ever need in your life." This remark, of course, was a reference to Tarnower's devoted housekeeper of sixteen years who not only maintained the doctor's palatial home but dutifully picked up after the many women who made regular nocturnal visits to see Tarnower. (The housekeeper had strict instructions to make sure that no female undergarments were ever left in his bathroom, an apparently overlooked chore on the night of Tarnower's murder.)

Tarnower's exceptionally active sex life, which appeared to be extraordinary for a man in his late sixties, might have been in keeping with his philosophy of good health and an energetic body and heart; his bedroom prowess certainly provided ample exercise. He also made light of his sexual dexterity. Above one of the twin beds in which Jean Harris slept on weekends at the Tarnower estate was a picture of the lizard-like-looking doctor with a caption beneath it reading: "No strings on me."

Another woman, one of many who also reportedly slept in that bed, was the tall and aesthetic-looking Lynne Tryforos, the doctor's assistant. According to Mrs. Harris the assistant slept with Tarnower whenever she was not present; before Mrs. Harris arrived on a weekend in Scarsdale, Mrs. Tryforos would sleep with the doctor, departing just before Jean arrived and returning just after she left for Virginia.

The nurse had dropped out of Endicott Junior College to marry Nicholas Tryforos, part owner of a florist shop. They divorced in 1976, and Mrs. Tryforos and her daughters, age ten and fourteen, moved to a small house in Scarsdale. Lynne was hired as Tarnower's assistant after the doctor took one look at her. From 1977 on she was the doctor's constant social companion whenever Jean Harris was not present, attending parties and dances with Tarnower. The doctor subtly acknowledged her presence in his diet book by wedging into the many recipes therein something called "Spinach Delight à la Lynne" (creamed spinach made with yogurt).

Mrs. Harris discovered the presence of Lynne in Tarnower's personal life as early as 1977, when she found Mrs. Tryforos's coat in a hall closet at the doctor's estate. Jean confronted Tarnower, but he ignored her mild accusations. Over the next three years, Mrs. Harris insisted, Lynne tried to unnerve and agitate her by making anonymous phone calls to her, calling her when she was alone in Virginia or even phoning her when she was on trips to Paris or Miami with Dr. Tarnower. On New Year's Day, 1980, while Jean was vacationing with Tarnower in Palm Beach, she said she picked up a copy of *The New York Times* to find the following ad: "Happy New Year, Hi. Love always. Lynne." She showed this to the doctor and said: "Herman, why don't you use the Goodyear blimp next year. I think it's available."

"I hope none of my friends see it," Jean quoted Tarnower as responding. She was later to quip: "I was one of his friends, and I saw it."

Lynne Tryforos's presence at the doctor's estate was another matter. The nurse first appeared in front of Jean with her two daughters, carrying buckets of paint. Mrs. Harris ordered her from the premises, but the nurse proceeded to paint the lawn furniture with her daughters, saying "I'm allowed."

The women, according to housekeeper van der Vreken, then took to open warfare, each cutting up the other's clothes whenever they found them on Tarnower's premises, and, when this tactic proved ineffective, spreading human feces upon designer gowns belonging to each other. According to Mrs. Harris, she persistently complained to Tarnower that Lynne was making obscene anonymous phone calls to her. The doctor, with the assistant "simpering" next to him, banished Jean for a month from his Xanadu for making such wild accusations.

It was about this time, in November 1978, that Mrs. Harris visited Irving's Sports Shop in Tyson's Corner, Virginia, a few miles from the Madeira School, and purchased a .32 Harrington and Richardson revolver from clerk James Forst. It was for her own protection, Jean had told the clerk, since she lived "back in the woods in a secluded area." This was the very weapon that Mrs. Harris carried in her handbag on the night of March 10, 1980, a gun she intended to use on herself, she later told police.

Though Tarnower appeared to need Jean Harris less and less as a sexual prop, he did use her extensively in the preparation of his book. One report stated that Suzanne van der Vreken provided the recipes and Jean polished the manuscript, although she disliked the idea of the book and, like Lynne Tryforos, felt that it "denigrated him" to where he was known as the "Diet Doc." The book, which became a stupendous success, promised readers that they could lose a pound a day if they followed the high-protein, low-carbohydrate regime dictated by Tarnower.

In the acknowledgments Tarnower thanked Jean Harris "for her splendid assistance in the research and writing of this book," but co-author Samm Baker later thought this nod of gratitude specious, stating: "Whatever she did for him, I don't know." Baker later stated that Tarnower was a dedicated physician: "Medicine is his life." Another friend labeled Tarnower at the time of his book's great success as unconcerned about his sudden fame. He was already wealthy and did not really need the fortune the diet book brought him. One person thought the doctor "austere, humorless and egotistical." Another, Sidney Salwen, said that the book's success never changed Tarnower, that "the last thing he would have wanted was to be known as the diet man. The diet was incidental. He was first and foremost a cardiologist."

In the eyes of Jean Struven Harris, however, Herman Tarnower had become, in March 1980, a man who was destroying her confidence, self-esteem, and sanity piece by piece through his mistreatment of her and his flagrant affair with Lynne Tryforos. She began to lose control at the Madeira School, with peers and board members criticizing her severe policies. She felt "traumatized. I functioned until I couldn't function anymore." She was, she claimed further, in a drugged state half the time, swallowing by the handfuls such addictive drugs as Desoxyn, which the doctor had prescribed for her ten years before when she began to complain of exhaustion. Other drugs urged upon her by the doctor included Valium, Nembutal, Percodan, Plexonal. She took pain-killers, sedatives, stimulants, uppers and downers; Dr. Tarnower had Jean Harris popping pills almost on an around-the-clock basis.

As a final gesture toward reconciliation with her wayward lover, Jean wrote Tarnower a voluminous letter in which she poured out her heart, her insecurity, her bottomless sense of self-degradation, and her venomous hatred for Lynne Tryforos and for the way he had treated her. It was this letter that Mrs. Harris later fought desperately to suppress during her murder trial. That she had shot and killed Dr. Tarnower on the night of March 10, 1980, Mrs. Harris never denied; that it was murder, she would never admit.

When police cars arrived that night with sirens screaming and deck lights flashing in the Tarnower driveway, they passed Mrs. Harris, who was about to drive away. Patrolman Brian McKenna approached her.

"There's been a shooting in the house," she told the officer.

He rushed inside, going upstairs to find the doctor on the floor of his master bedroom, mortally wounded. By then Mrs. Harris had reentered the house and was standing in the foyer. Patrolman Daniel O'Sullivan came near to her, and she looked at him squarely, saying: "I shot him. I did it."

O'Sullivan and Detective Arthur Siciliano took Mrs. Harris into the dining room. She quickly explained that she had just driven up from Virginia, where she was the headmistress of the Madeira School, "with the hope of being killed by Dr. Tarnower."

The policemen squinted at her in wonder. "He wanted to live, I wanted to die," she went on. "I'd been through so much hell. I loved him very much. He slept with every woman he could. I had no intention of going back to Virginia alive." She described how she had gone to the doctor's room and begged Tarnower to kill her, and how he had shouted at her: "You're crazy! Get out of here." She had produced her revolver and they struggled with it. Then the gun went off several times.

Siciliano asked her: "Who had control of the gun?"

"I don't know," Mrs. Harris responded.

"Who owns it?"

"It's mine."

"Who did the shooting?"

"I remember holding the gun and shooting him in the hand."

Mrs. Harris led police to her car and opened her purse, retrieving the revolver and turning it over to the officers. They walked back into the house, where Jean began to recite a litany of complaints against Tarnower, indicting him again and again for sleeping with numberless women. "I had it!" she shouted, and made a wild gesture with her hands.

An officer came downstairs to report that there were fresh knicks on the bathroom tile, and Jean stated that that was where she had thrown the gun several times during her struggle with Tarnower.

She handed Detective Siciliano a list of names, telling him that they were the names of friends and relatives who were to be contacted after she had taken her own life or if Tarnower had been good enough to kill her. She mumbled something about shooting herself at the edge of the estate's duck pond "where the daffodils bloom in the spring." Mrs. Harris remembered staring down at the wounded Tarnower after the struggle for the gun, asking him: "Why didn't you kill me, Hi?" She jerked her head from one officer to another. "Why should he die? Can I see him? Who did he have over for dinner?"

The place was soon filling up with police. Ambulance attendants rushed upstairs with a stretcher to pick up the fatally wounded Tarnower. Police Lieutenant Brian Flick stood staring down at Mrs. Harris, who was seated in a chair. She looked up at him, saying: "Isn't it ironic? He's dying and I'm alive. I wanted to die and he wanted to live."

She began to get out of the chair but appeared faint and sank back, breathing heavily. She said she wanted to make a phone call, and Patrolman Robert Tamilio accompanied her to a phone in an adjoining room. Mrs. Harris called a friend who was a lawyer, blurting: "Oh, my God, I think I've killed Hi!"

As she was led back into the living room, Jean Harris passed a mirror, stopped, and stood close looking at herself, noticing bruises on her face and arms. She touched a bruised lip and said in a soft voice: "He hit me, he hit me a lot."

Once more seated in the dining room, Mrs. Harris heard the hospital attendants upstairs. Tears welled up in her large eyes and she stood up, walking to Detective Siciliano. "Can I see Hi?" she asked him.

"I don't think it's a good idea at this time," he told her.

Just then the ambulance attendants appeared on the stairs, carrying the stricken Tarnower. They passed Mrs. Harris, whose eyes were riveted to the doctor's exposed face. Jean suddenly grabbed Detective Siciliano, as if to steady herself, seeming to slip downward in a dead faint.

"Get a doctor!" shouted Siciliano as he lowered her to the floor.

"The police doctor just got here!" a voice shouted back from the open front door. "He'll be right in!"

Siciliano was shocked to see Mrs. Harris make an immediate recovery, almost jumping up from the floor, brushing herself off, and saying in a calm voice: "I don't need a doctor." This abrupt turnabout in posture—from a fainting, confused person to a self-reliant and purposeful woman in a matter of seconds—had been repeated several times by Mrs. Harris in recent weeks. Only days before, Jean had written in the Madeira alumnae magazine: "If my educational philosophy has a schizophrenic ring to it, perhaps the same could be said of myself as a woman."

An hour after he was removed from his elegant estate, Dr. Herman Tarnower was dead of four gunshot wounds. A fifth shot had been fired, police learned a short time later, but had failed to strike the "Diet Doc."

Police booked Mrs. Harris on charges of second-degree murder. Two days later she was released on a $40,000 bond and immediately checked into a Westchester hospital for treatment. Her lawyer, Joel Aurnou, first stated that he would plead his client not guilty by virtue of self-defense. He described Mrs. Harris's many bruises, one on the lip, one near an eye, and a seven-inch bruise from her left elbow to her armpit. "She is a poor, sick woman," Aurnou told reporters.

Newspaper and TV reporters went wild with the case, gathering every morsel of gossip and rumor available, and there was much of that before Jean's trial commenced. It was high-society murder and millions were at stake, Tarnower's millions. His will was quickly unearthed. In it he had left Mrs. Harris $220,000 (not the $240,000 he was overheard to tell Jean by Mrs. Edwards) which would be forfeited if she was convicted of murdering him. He also bequeathed $200,000 to nurse Lynne Tryforos. Another $20,000 each was willed to Lynne's two daughters, along with a large sum for their college educations. The rest was divided among a phalanx of relatives, with Pearl Schwartz of Larchmont, New York, Tarnower's sister, to receive his fabulous estate.

In Virginia shocked board members of the Madeira School quickly drafted a letter informing alarmed parents that the school would survive in spite of "the tragic events involving Mrs. Harris." Students came forward with reports of how Mrs. Harris had driven off on the day of the murder, leaving the front door to her home wide open. Some of them looked inside to see the place "a perfect mess." She was strict, some students carped to reporters, too strict. She had recently found orange peels littering the grounds of the school and had banned oranges on campus. "Outlawing oranges," sneered one girl. "Can you *imagine*?" Another girl said: "She was very intense. Even the littlest things seemed to get her off."

"Mrs. Harris is most genteel," *New York* magazine quoted one Madeira alumna. "She's so very proper. The whole thing sounds so *incongruous.*"

Mrs. Harris's soap opera trial commenced the following November in a White Plains courtroom where she was tried before Judge Russell R. Leggett and a jury of eight women and four men. The public clamored for every word of testimony from the ninety-seven witnesses oozing scandal and sin in wealthy Scarsdale society. Hundreds, mostly women, packed the courtroom during the trial, spilling out into a hallway, fighting each day for a place in the visitors' gallery.

Jean Harris appeared composed throughout the many weeks of her trial. She busied herself with studying photographs and making notes, which she passed to her three lawyers—Joel Aurnou, Bonnie Steingart, and Victor Grossman. She reacted to witnesses in an animated fashion, frowning at those who made derogatory

*Jean Harris (center) conferring with her defense team (left to right)—Barbara York, Joel Aurnou, Bonnie Steingart, and Victor Grossman. (Wide World)*

remarks about her, laughing—perhaps a bit too long and loud—with the court when any tidbit of humor presented itself.

The policemen who arrived at the scene of the killing gave their testimony, describing Mrs. Harris's actions and quoting her strange and damning words verbatim. Suzanne van der Vreken also testified. (She and her husband, Henri, received $32,000 each in Tarnower's will, $2,000 each for every year of loyal service to him.) Mrs. van der Vreken was neither sympathetic nor antagonistic to Mrs. Harris's cause, but she did say that Jean in one conversation "used some words not very nice about" Lynne Tryforos. She quoted Mrs. Harris at the time as saying: "I will make their life miserable."

Jean herself took the witness stand in her own defense, and for six days she fenced with a determined prosecutor, Assistant District Attorney George Bolen. She displayed at first a cautious, even shrewd, demeanor, answering questions directly but always adding a bit more with each response as she became indignant and often angry at Bolen's queries. She was a lady of quality, her refinement and upbringing were apparently paramount to her as she sat stiffly in the witness chair, dressed all in black.

Jean told Bolen that three weeks before the doctor's death she and Tarnower had made love and that she had given him a gold tie clasp. She added that she was not seeking "The Good Housekeeping Seal of Approval," and that she understood from the start that Tarnower was "not the marrying kind." She smiled broadly, almost triumphantly, at prosecutor Bolen when she said: "He made love to me that morning. We had a lovely conversation and that's when I gave him the gold caduceus." (A tie clip with the medical symbol on it.)

When Lynne Tryforos's name was mentioned, Jean bristled, then blurted how her hated rival had slashed her thousand-dollar wardrobe and had even attempted to seduce the caretaker, Henri van der Vreken. "This gets dirtier and dirtier," moaned Mrs. Harris, but she plunged on, at Bolen's instigation, to say that "I dried Suzanne's eyes when she came to me saying Lynne was trying to seduce Henri." Then she added: "I thought of possibly suing Tryforos when $1,000 of my clothes were destroyed."

Bolen asked if Jean's salary in 1966, the year in which she met the doctor, had been relatively low.

"Yes," she replied.

"And Doctor Tarnower took you on trips around the world?" inquired Bolen.

"I don't really like your saying he 'took me.' I sound like a piece of baggage! We went together."

Always Bolen returned to Lynne Tryforos, attempting to show that out of hatred for this woman and her affair with Tarnower, Mrs. Harris had ruthlessly planned premeditated murder.

In an adroit move the defense produced a huge Christmas card that Jean had once sent to Tarnower, one in which she poked what lawyer Aurnou hoped the court would think good-natured fun at the doctor's many female lovers and which would prove that Jean Harris was never jealous of Tarnower's female companions, certainly never to the point of killing him in a jealous rage. Jean's parody of "A Visit from St. Nicholas" was read aloud by her attorney to the delight of a courtroom packed with sensation-seeking reporters and spectators:

'Twas the night before Christmas, . . . In the guest room lay Herman, who, trying to sleep, was counting the broads in his life—'stead of sheep! On Hilda, on Sigrid, on Jinx and Raquel, Brunhilda, Veronica, Gretel, Michelle. Now Tania, Rapunzel, Electra, Adele; Now Susie, Anita—keep trucking Giselle. . . . ingenues, Dashers and Dancers and Vixens. I believe there was even one Cupid—one Blitzen! He lay there remembering with a smile broad and deep, till he ran out of names, and he fell asleep.

(Let me mention, my darling, if this muse were inclined toward unseemly thoughts or an off-color mind, it wouldn't be easy to keep this thing refined!) But 'tis the time to be jolly—and very upbeat—and for now that's not hard because Herman's asleep! Beside him lay Jeannie, headmistress by jiminy—who was waiting for Santa to come down the chimney. . . . Then all of a sudden there arose such a clatter, Herm awoke from his sleep to see what was the matter.

And with Jeannie obediently three paces back, They tiptoed to the living room to watch [St.] Nick unpack. . . . Now let's see—there's Herman—with Tarnower for a monicka [sic]. It seems to me he got his best stuff for Chanukah. . . . But here's one little thing that I *know* he will use, If his evenings are lonely he'll have no excuse . . .

Here's some brand new phone numbers in a brand new black book (I'm not quite the innocent gent that I look!). This book holds the key, and the hope, and the promise, of a whole bunch of fun with some new red-hot mamas.

The result of exposing Mrs. Harris's kitsch to the world only emphasized her knowledge of Tarnower's prolific lovemaking while betraying the real thoughts that lay just below the surface of her nail-scratching lines. The revelation of the poem also held her up to ridicule, and there was plenty of that the following day. One newspaper ran the headline: SLAIN "DIET" DOCTOR WENT FROM BED TO VERSE.

On the following day prosecutor Bolen returned to the subject of Lynne Tryforos, asking Jean what she thought about her.

"I think she denigrated Hi and gave me a great deal of trouble with my own identity," replied Mrs. Harris in a calm voice.

"Was it a question of her education?" probed Bolen.

"She lacked common sense and taste."

"No taste?"

"You have to judge taste by the things people do," replied Jean, as if instructing the prosecutor. "Writing to a man for eight years while he was traveling with another woman is tasteless."

"How many times did you tell the doctor that you were upset about Lynne Tryforos?"

"Not all the time I felt it. I didn't count."

Bolen had repeatedly attempted to introduce into evidence the much-debated letter Jean Harris had sent to Tarnower on March 10, 1980, the day of his murder, but Judge Leggett stated that he would read the letter and decide later on its possible admission to the trial. Still Bolen persisted, trying to slip points made by Jean in the letter into her testimony. In one reference to the letter he asked: "Did he accuse you of stealing two books and some money?"

"We read each other's books all the time," replied Jean coolly.

"Why did you use the word 'steal' in the letter?"

"Hi couldn't find them and I didn't have them." She added, as she was doing increasingly in her long testimony: "By Saturday and Sunday I was very deeply depressed, and I covered it up. Anything unkind from Hi was disturbing."

"How did you refer to Lynne in that letter?"

"In many unattractive ways, as I had experienced her—dishonest, adulterous, a whore—that pretty well does it."

Bolen raised his voice when he then asked: "Did you say, 'your whore'?"

"The letter was to Hi," replied Jean stonily.

"And did you refer to 'your psychotic whore?' "

"That's what Suzanne [van der Vreken] called her. Suzanne thought she was crazy."

"What did Suzanne think of you?"

"I hate to think," retorted Jean Harris wryly as the court let loose a ripple of laughter.

Bolen doggedly continued quoting Jean's letter, asking her if she used the word "slut" in referring to Lynne Tryforos.

Jean turned in the witness chair, annoyed, her face flushed, asking Judge Leggett: "At what point—?"

"Mr. Aurnou is your attorney," Judge Leggett pointed out. "He can object."

After a while Bolen went back to the same subject, asking Mrs. Harris to explain the word "whore."

Jean's face tightened and she replied: "A whore is a whore is a whore."

"Is that your usual language?"

"Those are not words I customarily use. I was in a struggle with my own integrity. I couldn't walk away, and I couldn't come to terms with it."

Later, Bolen asked Jean if she had realized how relaxed Dr. Tarnower had become with Mrs. Tryforos, that he actually found himself "going out to get a pizza" with her. (Such posthumous heresy about Tarnower's eating habits raised many eyebrows; the doctor had once been quoted as saying: "My cravings are not for Big Macs, but for low-calorie Italian white truffles.")

Munching on pizza, Jean responded, did not sound like Dr. Herman Tarnower. "He was the only man I know who didn't know who Charlie Brown was, the kind of person who read Herodotus for fun."

How did she feel about finding things of Lynne Tryforos's at the Tarnower estate, Jean was asked. She shrugged indifferently, then admitted that she "threw some 'Super Doctor' buttons" left by Lynne "into the pond," along with "Valentines left on the front seat of his car," items she said had been left on purpose by Mrs. Tryforos before Jean's regular arrival at the doctor's home. All of it was "inappropriate" in Jean's estimation. She was cool at this point but then appeared to become upset and related how "frustrated and hurt" she had been at finding Lynne's "negligee" in "her" bathroom. This item, a green negligee, the prosecution would later contend, which was spotted by Jean Harris on her last visit to Herman Tarnower, found in "her" bathroom, tacit proof that she was being two-timed by a "tasteless" nurse, was a negligee that caused her to go for her gun and send four bullets into a cringing, begging Dr. Herman Tarnower.

The full image of the "wronged woman," or the "scorned woman" releasing fury hotter than hell was not formed for the jury until the following day. The admission of Jean's March 10 letter was a bombshell that exploded the myth of Mrs. Harris as a woman who had jokingly accepted Tarnower's peccadillos and had remained aloof and unperturbed by his philandering. She was, as most concluded after hearing the letter, one certainly filled with pain and agony and lovesick hopelessness, capable of hating as deeply as any mass murderer in the history of crime.

February 4, 1981, was a high-water mark for the prosecution. George Bolen read Mrs. Harris's inflammatory letter to Herman Tarnower, which had been mailed by Jean at 8:30 A.M. from Virginia on the day of the doctor's murder and had arrived a day later. The lengthy missive had been in the hands of the defense team, but Bolen had managed to pry it loose so that Judge Leggett could pass on it. The judge, in a surprise move, allowed Bolen to introduce the letter as evidence. Bolen stood before the court and slowly read Mrs. Harris's self-damning words. The infamous "Scarsdale letter" read:

I will send this by registered mail only because so many of my letters seem not to reach you—or at least they are never acknowledged so I presume they didn't arrive.

I am distraught as I write this—your phone call to tell me you preferred the company of a vicious, adulterous psychotic was topped by a call from the dean of students 10 minutes later and has kept me awake for almost 36 hours. I had to expel four seniors just two months from graduation and suspend others. What I say will ramble but it will be the truth—and I have to do something besides shriek with pain.

Let me say first that I will be with you on the 19th of April because it is right that I should be. [This is a reference to an upcoming dinner sponsored by the Westchester Heart Association at which Dr. Tarnower was to be honored for his contributions to cardiology; Tarnower had apparently told Mrs. Harris on the day of his death that he would not only be taking Lynne Tryforos to this dinner but had proposed marriage to the nurse and she had accepted, the action that sparked Mrs. Harris's vitriolic missive.] To accuse me of calling Dan [a Tarnower friend who was making preparations for the dinner] to beg for an invitation is all the more invidious since it is indeed what Lynne does all the time—I am told this repeatedly, "She keeps calling and fawning over us. It drives us crazy." [An oblique quote attributed to housekeeper Suzanne van der Vreken.]I have and never would do this—you seem to be able to expiate Lynne's sins by dumping them on me. I knew of the honor being bestowed on you before I was [ever] asked to speak at Columbia on the 18th.

Frankly I thought you were waiting for Dan's invitation to surprise me—false modesty or something. I called Dan to tell him I wanted to send a contribution to be part of those honoring you and I assured him I would be there.

He said, "Lee and I want you at our table." I thanked him and assured him I would be there "even if the slut comes—indeed, I don't care if she pops naked out of a cake with her tits frosted with chocolate!"

Dan laughed and said, "And you *should* be there and we want you with us."

I haven't played slave for you. I would never have committed adultery for you—but I have added a dimension to your life and given you pleasure and dignity, as you have me.

As Jackie [a mutual friend] says, "Hi was always a marvelous snob. What happened?"

I suppose my check to Dan falls into the "signs of masochistic love" department, having just, not four weeks before, received a copy of your will, with my name vigorously scratched out, and Lynne's name in *your* handwriting written in three places, leaving her a quarter of a million dollars and her children $25,000 apiece—and the boys and me nothing.

It is the sort of thing I have grown almost accustomed to from Lynne—that you didn't respond to my note when I returned it leaves me wondering if you send [*sic*] it together. It isn't your style—but then Lynne has changed your style. Is it the admiration of 14 years of broken promises, Hi—I hope not—"I want to buy you a whole new wardrobe, darling," "I want to get your teeth fixed at my expense, darling." "My home is your home, darling." "Welcome home, darling." "The ring is yours forever, darling." "[If you leave it] with me now I will leave it to you in my will." "You have, of course, been well taken care of in my will, darling." "Let me buy an apartment with you in New York, darling."

It didn't matter all that much, really—all I ever asked for

was to be with you—and when I left you to know when we would see each other again so there was something in life to look forward to. Now you are taking that away from me too and I am unable to cope—I can hear you saying, "Look, Jean, it's your problem. I don't want to hear about it."

I have watched you grow rich in the years we have been together, and I have watched me go through moments when I was almost destitute. . . .

. . . I don't have the money to afford a sick playmate—you do. She took a brand new nightgown that I paid $40 for and covered it with bright orange stains. You paid to replace it —and since you had already made it clear you simply didn't care about the obscene phone calls she made, it was obviously pointless to tell you about the nightgown.

The second thing you paid for (I never replaced it) was a yellow silk dress. I bought it to wear at Lyford Cay [an exclusive club in Nassau in the Bahamas] several years ago.

Unfortunately I forgot to pack it because it was new and still in the box, rolled up, not folded now, and smeared and vile with feces.

I told you once it was something "brown and sticky." It was, quite simply, Herman Tarnower, human shit. [Mrs. Harris had accused Mrs. Tryforos of smearing this on her finest gown.]

I decided, and rightly so, that this was your expense, not mine. As for stealing from you, the day I put my ring on your dresser my income *before taxes* was $12,000 per year.

I had two children in private school. They had been on a fairly sizable scholarship until I told the school I wouldn't need it because we were moving to Scarsdale. It was two years before we got it back.

*That* more than anything else is the reason David [her son] went to Penn State instead of the Univ. of Pennsylvania. He loathed every minute of it—and there is no question that it changed his life.

That you should feel justified and comfortable suggesting that I steal from you is something I have no adjective to describe.

I *desperately* needed money all those years. I *couldn't* have sold that ring. It was tangible proof of your love and it meant more to me than life itself.

That you sold it the summer your adulterous slut finally got her divorce and needed money is a kind of sick, cynical act that left me old and bitter and sick. . . .

You have never once suggested that you would meet me in Virginia at *your* expense, so seeing you has been at my expense—and if you lived in California I would borrow money to come there, too, if you would let me.

All my conversations are my nickels, not yours—and obviously rightly so because it is I, not you, who needs to hear your voice.

I have indeed grown poor loving you, while a self-serving, ignorant slut has grown very rich—and yet you accuse me of stealing from you. How in the name of Christ does that make sense?

I have, and most proudly so—and with an occasional "right on" from Lee [a mutual friend] and others—ripped up or destroyed anything I saw that your slut had touched and written her cutesie name on—including several books that *I* gave you and she had the tasteless, unmitigated gall to write in.

I have refrained from throwing away the cheap little book of epigrams lying on your bed one day so I would be *absolutely sure* to see it, with a paper clip on the page about how an old man should have a young wife.

It made me feel like a piece of old discarded garbage—but at least it solved for me what had been a mystery—what had suddenly possessed you to start your tasteless diatribe at dinner parties about how everyman [*sic*] should have a wife half his age and seven years.

Since you never mentioned it to anyone under 65, it made the wives at the table feel about as attractive and wanted as I did.

Tasteless behavior is the only kind that Lynne knows— though to her credit she is clever and devious enough to hide it at times. Unfortunately, it seems to be catching.

The things I know or profess to know about Lynne— except for what I have experienced first hand—have been told by your friends and your servants, mostly the latter—

I was interested to hear from Vivian and Arthur's [mutual friends] next door neighbor in Florida—I don't remember her name though I'm sure Lynne does:

"I took her to lunch, she seemed so pathetic"—that you sat at the table while I was there and discussed Lynne and her "wonderful family—brother a Ph.D."

I can't imagine going out to dinner with you and telling my dinner partner how grand another lover is. . . .

My phone tells me this—that "mysterious" caller—I hope to God you don't know who it is! Who pays him? [Apparently an oblique reference to the obscene calls Mrs. Harris said she had recently been receiving before Tarnower's death.]

When my clothes were ripped to shreds Suzanne said, "Madam, there is *only* one person who *could* have done it. You must tell him."

In my masochistic way I tried to downplay it in my notes to you, although in all honesty I thought it was so obvious you would know who did it. Instead you ignored it and went happily off to Florida with the perpetrator. Suzanne told me —and I would think would say so in court.

1. The clothes were not torn when she went into the closet to find something of Henri's on "Wednesday or Thursday" while we were away.

2. On the Sunday morning before we came home Henri and Suzanne both saw Lynne drive hurriedly up to your house. They were outside and she did not see them. They saw her go in but not out.

3. Lynne knew you were coming home that evening and that she would see you by 8:00 the next morning. What business did she have at your home that morning?

4. When I discovered the clothes destroyed Suzanne was sitting in the dining room at the wooden table right next to the door. I said, "My God—Suzanne, come look!" and she was right there.

When I called your slut to talk to her about it and see what she was going to do about it, she said, "You cut them up yourself and blamed it on me."

That was the first time it occurred to me they had been "cut," not ripped. Only someone with a thoroughly warped mind would decide that a woman with no money would ruin about one-third of her wardrobe for kicks. Suzanne still believes Lynne did it and I most certainly do, too. I think this is enough evidence to prove it in court!

The stealing of my jewelry I can't prove at all—I just know that I left some things in the white ash tray on your dresser as I have for many years. When I thought of it later and called, Lynne answered the phone.

When I called again and asked Suzanne to take them and put them away, they were gone. I only hope if she hocked them you got something nice as a "gift." Maybe I gave you some gold cuff links after all and didn't know it. I [don't for one instant] think Henri or Suzanne took them. . . .

Going through the hell of the past few years has been bearable only because you were still there and I could be with you whenever I could get away from work, which seemed to be less and less.

To be jeered at, and called "old and pathetic" made me seriously consider borrowing $5,000 just before I left New York and telling a doctor to make me young again—to do anything but make me not feel like discarded trash—I lost my nerve because there was always the chance I'd end up uglier than before.

You have been what you very carefully set out to be, Hi —the most important thing in my life, the most important human being in my life, and that will never change.

You keep me in control by threatening me with banishment—an easy threat which you know I couldn't live with —and so I stay home alone while you make love to someone who has almost totally destroyed me. . . .

I always thought that taking me out of your will would be the final threat. On that I believed you would be completely honest. I have every intention of dying before you do, but sweet Jesus, darling, I didn't think you would ever be dishonest about that. . . .

I wish 14 years of making love to one another and sharing so much happiness had left enough of a [mark] that you couldn't have casually scratched my name out of a will and written in Lynne's instead. . . .

Give her all the money she wants, Hi—but give me time

with you and the privilege of sharing with you April 19th. There were a lot of ways to have money—I very consciously picked working hard, supporting myself, and being with you.

Please, darling, don't tell me now it was all for nothing.

She has you every single moment in March—for Christ's sake give me April. T. S. Eliot said it's the cruelest month— don't let it be, Hi.

I want to spend every minute of it with you on weekends. In all these years you never spent my birthday with me. There aren't a lot left—it goes so quickly.

I give you my word if you just aren't cruel I won't make you wretched. I never did until you were cruel—and then I just wasn't ready for it.

Jean Harris had sat like a stone Buddha through the reading of the much-heralded Scarsdale letter, and when Bolen finished reading it, she continued to show a blank expression to the court. There was, however, a sigh en masse from those packing the courtroom, as if in relief that the truth was finally known: Mrs. Jean Harris had been jilted, thrown over completely by Tarnower for his nurse, the younger, attractive woman whom he vowed to marry and make his considerable heir. It took little imagination to envision Mrs. Harris's terrible thoughts after mailing the letter and how she must have exploded in rage to where she grabbed her revolver, hopped in her car, and set out for Scarsdale, a teeth-clenching, hand-clutching drive spurred on by jealous anger and having only one intent—murder.

Prosecutor Bolen hammered home the point again and again after having read the letter, asking if Tarnower had told her just that morning that he was through with her and would wed Mrs. Lynne Tryforos.

"No," replied Jean. "Did he tell *you*, Mr. Bolen?" she added bitterly.

"Isn't it a fact that the doctor told you he preferred Lynne Tryforos over you?"

"No."

"And in that March 10 morning telephone call did he tell you that you had lied to him and that you had cheated?"

"No, indeed. That would have been a strange word from him."

"And did he tell you that you were going to inherit $220,000?"

Defense lawyer Joel Aurnou stood up and shouted: "I move for a mistrial!"

Judge Leggett denied his motion.

"No, he didn't," Mrs. Harris finally responded.

"Didn't he say, 'Goddamnit, Jean, I want you to stop bothering me'?"

Jean's face reddened and she shouted back at Bolen: "No!" Then she turned to Judge Leggett. "Is this going to go on forever?"

At this point the prosecution and defense lawyers exchanged challenges with Judge Leggett, asking if there was a witness to Tarnower's remarks. Bolen replied there was, meaning Juanita Edwards, and that he would later produce her as a witness for the prosecution.

Bolen finally turned dramatically once more to Jean, asking her his final question. "And isn't it true, Mrs. Harris, that you intended to kill Dr. Tarnower and then kill yourself because if you couldn't have him nobody else would?"

Her response was soft and determined: "No, Mr. Bolen."

The prosecution had made telling and damning points during the six-day interrogation of Jean Harris. She had admitted killing Tarnower but insisted that it was accidental, that she had wanted him to kill her. She had tried to place the blame for her unhinged state on her troubles at Madeira, not Lynne Tryforos, saying that the hassles from the school board in recent months had destroyed her life. "I couldn't function from then on," she had testified. "I wasn't sure who I was. I was a person sitting in an empty chair."

She had decided to die, period. "My only worry was what I would do if Hi said something that spoiled my resolve to die." She admitted finding Mrs. Tryforos's green negligee in Tarnower's bathroom and then claimed that Tarnower had hit her repeatedly when she made a scene about Lynne's undergarments. "The script was not working as I intended," she had told the jury, and she remembered begging Tarnower at that moment to "hit me again, and make it hard enough to kill me!"

It was then, she admitted, that she reached into her purse and pulled out the revolver, reportedly saying, "never mind, I'll do it myself." She struggled with Tarnower over the weapon. She remembered "an instant where I thought I felt the muzzle of the gun in my stomach. I pulled the trigger. I thought: 'My God, that didn't hurt at all. I should have died a long time ago.' "

But, of course, it was Herman Tarnower who had been shot and it was Herman Tarnower, celebrity cardiologist and aging ladies' man who crashed to the bedroom floor, gushing blood from four bullet wounds.

In the final arguments Aurnou and Bolen put on a battle royal. The defense attorney brought to bear every plea for Jean Harris's sorry plight and how she had been driven half mad at the thought of losing every worthwhile thing in life. To Aurnou the entire affair was a tragic accident that took place when Mrs. Harris, "masochist" to the end, tried to kill herself.

"She was obsessed with dying," pleaded Aurnou. "Everything that happened in that room that night had meaning to her only in terms of stopping the pain of dying." He portrayed Tarnower as an ungrateful lover who was "incapable of accepting the greatest gift a woman has to give," but the doctor did try to save the woman's life and in the attempt was accidentally shot to death. "There is no evidence that Jean Harris ever intended to kill Tarnower," Aurnou pointed out to the jury. "This suicidal, sick woman . . . was obsessed with dying. That's why she's not guilty of murder."

Bolen addressed the jury to make only one thunderous point: Jean Harris murdered Herman Tarnower after finding Lynne Tryforos's negligee in the doctor's bathroom. "She goes into the bathroom and sees the belongings of Lynne Tryforos for the first time. All the inward hostility to Lynne Tryforos—and how, in her mind, Lynne Tryforos had usurped her role as far as the doctor is concerned—emerges.

"She's enraged. She gets the gun. She's in control. She has the power now. If Herman Tarnower won't deny himself of Lynne Tryforos, she'll do it for him: 'If I [Mrs. Harris] can't have him no one can.'

"She intended to kill him, take him from Lynne Tryforos, then take her own life. The defendant confronts Herman Tarnower with the gun, points it, shoots it and the bullet breaks through Dr. Tarnower's outstretched hand and into his chest." Bolen described how more bullets were sent into the errant lover, while "the defendant retreats," going into the bathroom where "she's enraged, she's throwing, she's tossing" Mrs. Tryforos's belong-

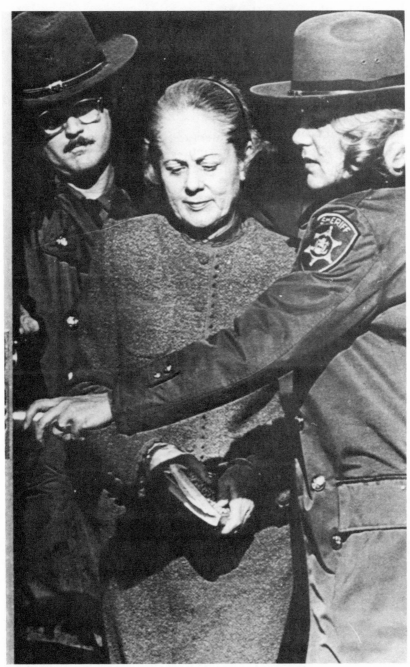

*Handcuffed, Jean Harris is led away to prison in March 1981 to begin serving a fifteen-year term for murder. (Wide World)*

ings. Bolen then reminded the jury in mocking terms how Mrs. Harris had earlier insisted that at that point she went to get help.

"She's so concerned about the doctor," Bolen sneers, "she remembers to take her fur coat and gun." The prosecutor paused, then added sarcastically: "Yeah, she went to get help."

He went on to demand that Jean Struven Harris be convicted of murder in the second degree, the highest form that she could be convicted of in New York State, first-degree murder applying only to the killing of law enforcement officers and prison guards, the maximum penalty for both being the same, twenty-five years to life.

On Tuesday, February 24, 1981, after eight days of deliberation, the jury of eight women and four men returned a verdict of guilty of second-degree murder. Foreman Russell Von Glahn pronounced the word "guilty" three times for the murder charge and two weapon counts. Defense lawyers burst into tears when hearing the verdict, but Jean Harris gave the court and newsmen her "stiff-upper-lip" expression, even leaning over sympathetically to console lawyer Bonnie Steingart by patting her knee.

On March 20, 1981, Mrs. Harris was sentenced to the minimum term for her crime, fifteen years to life. She had earlier told her lawyers: "I can't sit in jail." After being sent to prison, the one-time arbiter of social taste went on a brief hunger strike, saying that she "only wanted to die." She did not die, but gave up the strike and slowly adjusted to prison life.

Her ordeal was finally over; she no longer had to worry about sharing Herman Tarnower's affections with other women, or about the manners and morals of spoiled children from upper-class families, or count the sharp rungs on the social ladder she had tried to scale. She had time to reflect upon the social strata and life-style she valued beyond measure, one that undoubtedly gave her the notion, as it has many before her, that she could murder with alacrity and escape back into an insulated world that protects its own. She has plenty of time to think about it, at least a decade behind bars.

# 1980

## ALLARD LOWENSTEIN
## DEATH OF A DO-GOODER

Only an hour before he was shot to death by Sirhan Sirhan in 1968, Senator Robert Kennedy asked an aide to call Al Lowenstein, one of America's leading activists in the civil rights movement. The Kennedys had come to form a close association with Lowenstein, who had run for Congress from New York seven times and had been elected as a U.S. Representative in 1968 at the height of the civil rights activity in America.

Lowenstein represented the academic left and had been considered a radical early in his career during the late 1950s. By 1952 his name was associated with mighty liberal causes. That year he became the president of the National Student Association and national chairman of Students for Stevenson. By 1961 he was an assistant dean of men at Stanford University in Palo Alto, California. It was here that he met the man—Dennis Sweeney, then an eighteen-year-old student—who was to murder him nineteen years later.

Like many another idealist Sweeney responded wholeheartedly to Lowenstein's ideas of activism to bring about abrupt change in American society. He saw the then thirty-two-year-old academic leader as a shining knight out to right the country's wrongs and somehow lift up wholly the downtrodden minorities and overturn a system that had held firm for some 108 years.

A graduate of Yale University, Lowenstein venerated the likes of Eleanor Roosevelt and Norman Thomas, both of whom later became his friends. He considered himself the single most important champion of what has been termed the "post–New Deal social democracy," and in many respects he was correct to think so. He was a political mover and shaker who actually brought about change, who affected the system.

Lowenstein appeared the academic even in his later years, addicted to jeans or khaki pants, a sport coat, and a tie set askew, which came to be sort of an inside physical symbol of the leftist-liberal-academic in pursuit of truth. But then, in the 1960s, political life and academic life were hopelessly intertwined, a black and white matter compared with today's legal grays, one where stereotyped images appeared blatant and went unchallenged. (The conservative of those days, the William Buckley type, invariably wore a straight-as-an-arrow tie tucked properly beneath a collar spread stiffly with hand-inserted stays.)

The six-foot Dennis Sweeney was a scholarship student from Portland, Oregon, where his stepfather worked as a printer. His real father, a military man, had been killed in an accident when he was a child. He was shy and self-conscious of his workingclass background but was just the kind of candidate Lowenstein traditionally recruited to his colors. Because of his naiveté, his staggering sincerity, friends called Sweeney "Sweet." As one of Lowenstein's first handpicked protégés, Sweeney became slavishly devoted to the political pundit.

In 1962, Lowenstein traveled through the state of Mississippi conferring with the newly organized Student Nonviolent Coordinating Committee, the precursors to the so-called freedom riders who would later invade the South on behalf of civil rights activism. Though SNCC distrusted white liberals, Lowenstein represented the kind of northern academic who could muster widespread support for its cause in the press and in high political circles. He was asked to provide clean-cut students for SNCC activities in southern states, and he did.

One of the first volunteers was Dennis Sweeney, who immediately answered the call to work in the SNCC offices in Jackson, Mississippi. He later volunteered to work in McComb, the most dangerous area of the state, a hotbed of Ku Klux Klan activity. It was here that the youthful idealist almost lost his life when a Klan bomb was thrown through the window of a Freedom School where Sweeney and other activists were asleep. The resulting explosion, fortunately, was absorbed by a thick plywood bed board, although Sweeney and the others were badly shaken and received minor injuries.

Lowenstein's reaction to SNCC's increasingly militant attitudes was to withdraw slowly to mainstream activism, whereas Sweeney became more and more committed to the maverick group's violence-prone tactics. SNCC became the loudest dissident force in the civil rights movement, attacking the Reverend Dr. Martin Luther King, Jr.'s Southern Christian Leadership Conference, of which Allard Lowenstein had become a board member. Members of SNCC, particularly Sweeney, his once-devoted follower, labeled the liberal politician a "traitor" and a "sell-out."

The final confrontation between SNCC and moderate civil rights forces came in 1964 at Atlantic City when an attempt to seat a black delegation representing Mississippi's Negro voters was turned back by the state's old white-power structure. Lowenstein had sided with the forces that counseled moderation in this affair, and when the blacks were ousted, he was accused of undermining true civil rights aims.

Sweeney, thoroughly disillusioned by these events, and along with other white liberals resenting being kicked out of SNCC activities—the organization was concentrating then on total black-power strategy—drifted back to Stanford where he drove a pickup truck and made a lame effort to study. He dropped his academic pursuits altogether and, fielding about for some sort of cause to justify his existence, threw himself into the antidraft movement, helping to organize wild protests against the Vietnam War.

He was seen by a Stanford professor in 1967 leading a rally against the Central Intelligence Agency, openly denouncing none other than his former mentor, Allard Lowenstein. At that time, the CIA was exposed as having financed for years the National Student Association to which Lowenstein had been umbilically linked, albeit the intelligence agency, it was proved, had not affiliated itself with the association until a year after Lowenstein had served as president.

This was the ultimate betrayal to the naive Sweeney. The man he had almost venerated as a political messiah had, in his opinion, been a sham from the beginning, a treacherous Benedict Arnold who was out to destroy the very people he had led so pompously into the civil rights movement. It was all reminiscent of the scene in *Mr. Smith Goes to Washington* where novice senator Jimmy Stewart discovers he has been used as a gullible idealist by his gray-haired sponsor, Claude Rains, the senatorial "white knight," for his own political ends.

Lowenstein, however, was no white knight conniving with power brokers in the Senate cloakroom but was a political work-

Left: *Former Congressman Allard Lowenstein.* Right: *Dennis Sweeney in custody shortly after he killed Lowenstein*

aholic who by the late 1960s had earned the respect of almost every political liberal powerhouse in the nation. He had led the "Dump Johnson" campaign that resulted in President Lyndon Johnson's withdrawal from the 1968 presidential race. He had convinced Eugene McCarthy to run for the presidency, although he undoubtedly knew the relatively unknown McCarthy had no real chance of winning against Richard Nixon; Lowenstein had wanted Bobby Kennedy all along, but Kennedy had been assassinated.

When Kennedy had won the California primary, he had asked an aide to call Lowenstein to give him the good word only an hour before he went to a victory celebration at the Ambassador Hotel in Los Angeles. Kennedy had sought Lowenstein's advice in his campaign and relied heavily upon him as a weather vane for the attitudes and feelings of the academic community and youthful voters in general. An hour later Kennedy was shot down by an assassin's bullet. Lowenstein, who had been campaigning for his own congressional seat from Long Island, immediately flew to Los Angeles after hearing that his favorite politician had been attacked. He arrived in time to hear a doctor pronounce the presidential candidate dead.

Along with several others, Lowenstein accompanied the body to the ground floor in an elevator that also contained Edward Kennedy. The academic pundit turned to the Kennedy brother and said for all to hear: "You're the only hope we've got left, and you're not good enough."

Despite this brash criticism of Kennedy, the lone survivor of the political brothers never failed to heap praise upon Allard Lowenstein. When Lowenstein was murdered in 1980, Senator Kennedy was quoted in *The New Yorker* as saying that the activist was "a one-man demonstration for civil rights. With his endless energy, with his papers, his clothes, his books, and seemingly his whole life jammed into briefcases, envelopes, and satchels—all of it carried with him everywhere—he was a portable and powerful lobby for progressive principles."

Lowenstein went on working for political liberal causes, but he failed to be reelected to Congress after his 1968 term. His influence waned during the 1970s until he became sort of a backwater political adviser in New York. In memory of his political heroes, Lowenstein named his three children Frank Graham, Thomas Kennedy, and Katherine Eleanor. His wife, the former Jennie Lyman, divorced him.

Sweeney's life was a nightmare compared to that of his one-time guru. By the 1970s, when pot replaced politics, Sweeney began to have regular hallucinations. He insisted that he could hear strange voices at all hours of the day and night, voices that were trying to direct his will. His mother and stepfather tried to have him committed to a state mental hospital in Oregon in 1973, but he was released after a week of examinations. Doctors said that his condition did not require confinement.

The activist became utterly convinced that he was being controlled by alien forces. He told his friends in Portland that creatures from outer space were sending messages to his brain, trying to influence his thoughts through receivers they had somehow managed to implant in his bridgework. He tore out his caps and bridgework to prevent such mind control, but he still felt that he was wired and bugged. Then he was positive that the CIA was behind his problems, that the agency had implanted a transmitter in his body somewhere so that agents could monitor his every thought. Before leaving Portland, he wrote a number of friends complaining about this strange circumstance. One letter read:

I am at the lowest ebb of my life now because of the psychological warfare that is being made on me. . . . I am simultane-
ously attuned to and programmed electronically . . . [incapa-
ble] to sort my own thoughts from the impulses running
through my skull. I am fairly certain that I have software I
wasn't born with.

In 1975, Lowenstein received an unexpected call from
Sweeney, who was in Philadelphia. "He called me out of the blue
to tell me people were trying to kill him," Lowenstein later told
Professor Clayborne Carson of Stanford University. "It was a
very sad sort of an end to a very talented person that hacked out
the fillings of his teeth because he said the CIA would use the
fillings to damage his brain. He just simply had gotten to the
point where I don't know if there was any way he could be
reclaimed from this tragedy."

The "tragedy" Lowenstein referred to was the collapse of the
civil rights movement and other activists causes, which had come
to be either ignored or rejected by an American public that would
no longer tolerate violence and chaos emanating from the radical
chic. Lowenstein labeled Sweeney at the time a "victim" of the
1960s, a period that betrayed the youth's lofty ideals, a traumatic
experience that, in the words of Allard Lowenstein, "very, very
badly damaged him."

This was the same approach many took, even after Dennis
Sweeney fatally shot Allard Lowenstein on March 14, 1980. William Buckley, as might be expected, did not. To him the "victim"
theme was nonsense; tens of thousands of youths had undergone
the sharp political transitions of the 1960s to the 1970s without
going berserk. "In the past it has been customary to withhold pity
from the murderer at least until the body was cold," Buckley
wrote in the *National Review* in April 1980. He portrayed Sweeney
as a typical crackpot among a host of crazies spawned by mentors
like Lowenstein, striking the theme of "I am my own executioner."

Sweeney was no "victim" at all, Buckley said. "They [radical
activists] dramatize themselves in terms of a mythology according to which violence is an inevitable response to oppression.
Even the looniest loners have sensed that their best chance for
social impact lies in claiming the sanction of leftist ideals; the

hijacked planes always headed for Havana or Algeria, not Pretoria or Santiago."

In Lowenstein's talk with Professor Carson, recorded in 1977, the activist appeared to show genuine signs of pity for Sweeney, but he made little or no mention of the fact that Sweeney's 1975 phone conversation with him ended with Sweeney accusing him, Lowenstein, of putting people on his trail. "Call off your dogs," Sweeney ordered him.

Lowenstein then said: "Dennis. Let me help you. I know people who can help you. I want to put you in their hands."

"So—you too," Sweeney snorted and hung up.

Sweeney became an utter loner; his wife had divorced him years earlier. (She was later to marry Dr. Peter Bourne, whose penchant for en masse drug prescriptions later cost him his job in the White House.) He visited a filmmaker in Cambridge, Massachusetts, and terrorized the man and his wife and child for six hours, telling the frightened family that all of them, including the five-year-old boy, had been broadcasting messages to his brain and they must stop it. They were all part of a "killer elite on the run since Watergate," part of "an international Jewish conspiracy" that was trying to compel him to "marry a Jewess." Before leaving, Sweeney told the filmmaker that he was not only "radioactive" but at times became "transparent."

The filmmaker thereafter armed himself and, a short time later, hired bodyguards to chase off Sweeney, who had insisted on seeing him in a park. Backing away, Sweeney warned the filmmaker never to again send messages to his brain. "The next time you've got a message for me," screamed Sweeney, "deliver it to my face!"

Sweeney moved to Mystic, Connecticut, where he took a small room and worked at odd jobs. He kept track of Lowenstein's movements, noting that his former mentor had held several positions with the United Nations. He spoke to no one in the small community but once turned to a customer in a bar and said: "You know I'm picking up signals from Mars."

By 1979 Sweeney had moved to another Spartan-like room in New London, Connecticut. He seemed content to live a quiet life, working as a carpenter. He still kept to himself and had only a few acquaintances in New London. Fellow boarder Richard Mender later remembered Sweeney as a hermitlike person who occasionally visited Mender in his room. "When he talked he never looked at you," Mender recalled later. Then Sweeney received word that his stepfather had died, and he returned to Portland for the funeral. By early March 1980 he was once more in New London, but he was a changed man, mumbling to himself on the streets, cursing violently at phantoms. Lowenstein, he told complete strangers, had caused his poor stepfather's death. It was Allard Lowenstein all right.

On March 11, 1980, Dennis Sweeney went to Raub's Hardware and Sporting Goods store in New London. He selected a seven-shot Llama .380 semiautomatic pistol for $120 but left the weapon until his application forms had been cleared. The forms demanded to know if he had ever been committed to a mental institution or had ever been convicted of a felony. He had replied no to both questions.

Within the week the purchase approval came through, and Sweeney informed his landlord that he would be leaving town shortly. Next, Sweeney called Allard Lowenstein in New York, where he was working for the firm of Layton & Sherman, and made an appointment to see him.

A little before 4 P.M. on March 14, 1980, the thirty-seven-year-old Sweeney took the elevator to the ninth floor of 50 Rockefeller Plaza, at 51st Street. He entered Lowenstein's office wearing jeans and boots, a plaid shirt and zippered blue jacket. He said nothing to the telephone repairmen who were working in the waiting room. His face was expressionless as he stared vacantly ahead, one hand in the pocket of his jacket, undoubtedly clutching the pistol he had recently bought.

Lowenstein, age fifty-one, came into the waiting room, and the men shook hands. They entered Lowenstein's office and talked for about ten minutes; the repairmen heard nothing until Sweeney's voice rose with the words: "Al, we've got to put an end to this obsession."

It was apparently at this point that he yanked forth his pistol and pointed it at Lowenstein. Repairmen heard Lowenstein yell: "No—don't do it!"

"I heard screams, then pops, three or four," one of the repairmen later told police. The door to Lowenstein's office then opened and Dennis Sweeney casually sauntered into the outer office. He put the pistol in an ashtray on the secretary's desk, calmly lit a cigarette, and sat down.

One of the telephone repairmen moved toward the weapon. A fellow worker watched as the repairman "picked up the gun and put it in the office in case the guy went berserk. It was weird. That guy [Sweeney] did not say one word."

Sweeney had many words for the police when they arrested him some minutes later. He told officers that Lowenstein had caused so many problems for his family in Oregon that the pressure prompted his stepfather to have a heart attack. Then he said that Lowenstein was behind a lawsuit brought by a client against his stepfather and this had caused his parent's end. There was no such lawsuit. As he was driven away to be booked, Dennis Sweeney snarled: "He's been controlling my life for years. Now I've put an end to it."

Lowenstein had been shot five times, two of the bullets entering his heart, another his lung. Doctors at St. Clare's Hospital worked for five hours to save him, but it was hopeless. Friends and relatives, about fifty in all, who had gathered in a hospital conference room were informed of Lowenstein's death. They broke into tears, then joined hands and began to sing a Peter, Paul and Mary song: "Weave, weave, weave into the sunshine. . . ."

Dennis Sweeney pled guilty to murdering Allard Lowenstein on February 23, 1981, by reason of mental defect and was sent to an institution for life. He is there at this moment, pacing a barred room, raging about mythical transistors implanted in his brain, sending signals, always signals.

# 1980

## DOROTHY STRATTEN
### THE RISE AND FALL
### OF A PLAYMATE

P aul Snider had always been a desperate man. Tall, lean, and relatively good-looking, he had been on his own since he quit the seventh grade in Vancouver, British Columbia, the product of a broken home and street gangs. A voluptuary and money lover, Snider possessed, if not formal schooling, the inherent gift of turning a dollar, working the seamy side of the street through his youth. By the time he was in his early twenties, Snider was pimping.

He grew moderately rich as he concentrated on peddling the flesh of only a few girls, "class ladies," as he put it. Snider took to wearing expensive furs, the traditional diamond pinky ring, and ostentatious clothes, always with his shirt front open to expose a jewel-encrusted Star of David that earned him the distasteful sobriquet of "The Jewish Pimp."

Snider scooted about Vancouver in a variety of sports cars that were either financed or on loan to him. He was a car freak who had tried to earn a living as a promoter of auto shows and motorcycle races before turning to the more lucrative practice of pimping. Snider was clever enough to steer clear of drug traffic in his business, even though drugs went hand in hand with prostitution. He successfully evaded underworld pressures to push hard drugs, which was no easy chore in that he was paying certain crime figures for protection against arrest. He was terrified of having to do a long prison sentence and had once told a friend: "I will kill myself before I go to jail."

The hustler's expensive tastes eventually got him into serious trouble with Vancouver loan sharks; when he failed to pay one premium on time, he was taken to the top of a hotel and held by his ankles out of an open window. The experience so frightened

Snider that he immediately fled to Los Angeles, where he recruited several women to work the neighborhoods surrounding Beverly Hills. Initially, the kickbacks from the girls brought Snider enough cash so that he could live in fashion, in the style of gone-to-pot Hollywood, not Beverly Hills. His high-water mark during this period, 1976–77, was being able to buy a gold limousine.

Competition in the sale of flesh, however, increased to the point where Snider's girls, about six in number, had little chance against the hordes of prostitutes lining the notorious Sunset Strip. Running low on money, Snider returned to Vancouver where he told friends that he had had a change of attitude and heart: he was going straight and would never again dabble with the illicit.

Busying himself with minor promotion jobs, Snider walked into a Vancouver Dairy Queen one afternoon and was immediately struck by the vision of a tall, buxom girl with a milk-white complexion and the attitude and motions of a mature woman, although Dorothy Ruth Hoogstraten was then only eighteen years old. She had been working part time at the Dairy Queen for four years. Her parents had separated, and she lived with her mother.

Dorothy had few ambitions. She wrote poetry gushing of lofty love but kept her verses to herself. She was planning to take secretarial courses and enter the business world as an executive secretary. Nothing about her was assuming. In fact she was shy, exceptionally well mannered, a beautiful girl who was embarrassed by her large breasts and long hands.

"She was the kind of girl you'd be proud to have for a sister or a daughter," her employer, David Redlick, was later to say. "She even used to take my kids to the beach sometimes, and she's the only girl I ever bought roses for when she left [the Dairy Queen]. I don't even do that for my wife."

Snider did not approach Dorothy directly. As was his style, he got her phone number from another girl and called her to ask her out on a date. From the beginning he showered her with flowers, inexpensive rings, and clothes, acting the proper but sophisticated older man and endlessly flattering her for her exceptional good looks.

Dorothy was, quite simply, overwhelmed by Snider. She had lived on the edges of poverty as a child, and such magnanimous

*Lovely Dorothy Stratten when she was named* **Playboy**'s *1980 "Playmate of the Year."*

attention from an older man dazzled her. After Paul took her to her graduation dance, Dorothy began regularly to slip away to his swanky bachelor's apartment where he would prepare meals for her and later sing and play his guitar. He squired her about town, taking her to the better restaurants and nightclubs. All of it, of course, was an investment from his point of view. He had told a friend: "That girl could make me a lot of money." At the time he did not specify how Dorothy could earn him money but it was not through prostitution. He had bigger things in mind.

Through flattery and cajolery, Snider convinced Dorothy to pose naked, telling her that he was positive that she would be selected as the 25th-anniversary Playmate for *Playboy.* The magazine was then conducting a highly publicized nationwide talent hunt for just such a perfect girl. Snider bought Dorothy a new dress so she would agree to have several nude shots taken of her. At first she covered herself demurely, then gave in to Snider's exhortations and posed provocatively.

Next Snider went to a photographer who regularly worked for the magazine, but the hustler was turned down, told that since Dorothy was underage, she would require her mother's written permission to pose naked for *Playboy.* Paul went to Mrs. Hoogstraten and met with little success. Dorothy's mother adamantly refused to have her daughter's body exposed to the glare of floodlights and cameras. Snider worked on her, telling the mother that this was Dorothy's one golden opportunity. Never again would the five-foot-nine-inch Dutch blonde have such a chance at fame and fortune. Mrs. Hoogstraten finally gave in and signed the release form. Snider himself then mailed off the *Playboy* application form, and in August 1978 he boarded a plane with Dorothy—her first plane ride—and headed for Los Angeles, where tests were made.

To the delight of *Playboy* staffers, Dorothy proved to be exceptionally photogenic. Her natural beauty caused her to be selected as one of sixteen finalists for the post of the anniversary Playmate. Though she lost out to another girl, she was selected as the August 1979 Playmate, and her appearance in the magazine caused a sensation. By then she was no longer Dorothy Hoogstraten. She was Dorothy Stratten and she was quoted in her *Playboy* biography, which accompanied photos of her statuesque, well-curved body, as being "a sucker for the romantic approach.

Romance is very effective for me because I'm a very sensitive person. I'm a faithful one-man woman. It might sound old-fashioned but I have to concentrate my love on just one man."

That man, of course, was Paul Snider. While *Playboy* prepared its new Playmate for fame, he had kept busy in Hollywood by promoting a disco featuring nude male dancers and assorted sideshow attractions like wet T-shirt contests. He was really banking on Dorothy's future, not his own, and to make sure she was in his hip pocket, he proposed marriage to her in May 1979.

Dorothy had been warned by friends not to marry the hustler, but she felt obligated to him and depended on him. He was lover, friend, counselor, guide, and manager. She accepted and the couple were wed in Las Vegas on June 1, 1979, two months before Dorothy became a *Playboy* centerfold.

As Snider expected, after the *Playboy* appearances offers for movies and other important glamour jobs came to his attractive wife. Dorothy had already begun to appear in small roles on TV, being a guest star on the *Buck Rogers in the 25th Century* TV series, which prompted the innocent ingenue to blurt: "Seeing my name in the TV Guide was the most exciting thing in my life."

She appeared as the lead actress in a low-budget Canadian film, *Autumn Born*, but was less than enthusiastic about the part, telling a reporter that she spent most of her time in the movie getting "beat up." The parts, however, improved with appearances in films like *Americathon* and *Skatetown, U.S.A.*; again these were low-budget films, but Dorothy began to emerge as an actress with a genuine talent.

When *Playboy* chief Hugh Hefner selected Dorothy as the 1980 Playmate of the Year, her star really went into its ascendancy. With this honor went more than $200,000 in gifts from furniture to jewelry. She became the toast of Los Angeles, and scores of photographers, hairdressers, designers, coaches, managers, and mentors followed her about, sweeping her away from the control of Paul Snider.

Snider became resentful, accusing Dorothy of shutting him out of her busy life. He raged about his being asked not to attend *Playboy* functions at Hefner's mansion when Dorothy was in attendance. The fact that all Playmate husbands were treated similarly did not mollify him. He had tried to get close to Hefner repeatedly to work his own shady deals, but the *Playboy* chief kept

Right: *A publicity still of Dorothy Stratten just before beginning her motion picture career.*
Left: *Dorothy celebrating her twentieth birthday party with her one-time lover and
promoter, hustler Paul Snider. (UPI)*

him at arm's length, telling intimates that he thought Snider
"sleazy."

Dorothy's first starring movie role was in *Galaxina,* a science
fiction film in which she played a beautiful robot who tells one
of the space-crew members: "I have programmed myself for
love." (This movie was released only a few weeks after Dorothy
Stratten died.)

It became grimly apparent to Snider that he was being left
behind. Dorothy began to move inside the power circles of Beverly Hills, meeting persons who controlled the movie and TV
industries. He argued with her incessantly, until she separated
from him. He went to live in a stucco bungalow in West Los
Angeles near the freeway. Dorothy went to New York to appear

as a featured player in Peter Bogdanovich's new film, *They All Laughed,* which would star Audrey Hepburn and Ben Gazzara, a real movie with real movie stars and Dorothy would be one of their number, entering the golden circle.

While shooting on location in New York, Dorothy began a romance with director Bogdanovich. They were discreet and no gossip leaked about the affair, although Snider called Dorothy every night, suspiciously questioning her. Her conversations with him were halting, and she never responded to him when he closed with "I love you."

Upon her return to the Coast, Dorothy met with Snider and told him that she was in love with Bogdanovich and that she would make any reasonable settlement with him in a quiet divorce. She offered $7,500, and Snider laughed at her. Dorothy then told Snider that she would be living apart from him. Some days later she moved in with Bogdanovich.

Snider, ever the obnoxious bully and braggart, told one and all that he would correct the situation, he would *make* his wife move back with him. Hadn't he created her career, guided her moves, made her a sex goddess?

Snider, however, must have realized that he had lost out completely and would never make his big score, at least not through Dorothy Stratten. He hired a private detective to dog his wife's trail and to gather evidence that could later be used against her in court. He learned that his wife had moved into Bogdanovich's Beverly Hills home, which enraged him. A later account had it that he thought to kill the director and even promised that he would murder Bogdanovich, but this report went unsubstantiated.

At the end of his hustler's rope, Snider apparently forgot the film director. It was Dorothy who had betrayed him and his own financial future. It was Dorothy who would pay for that betrayal. He called his wife and asked her to meet him on Thursday, August 14, at the West Los Angeles bungalow that he shared with two others. They would finalize plans for their divorce, he told her quietly.

The following day, Wednesday, Paul Snider bought a 12-gauge shotgun. He stopped by a photographer's studio to examine nude photos of his new protégée and cryptically remarked to the photographer that "sometimes Playmates get killed and when that happens it brings about chaos."

Dorothy Stratten arrived at Snider's bungalow at about noon on August 14, the appointed hour. She spent some time, perhaps a few hours, with her estranged husband in the living room where her open purse was later found, inside of which was a note from Snider demanding money. Snider's new girl friend and protégée arrived at 5 P.M. to find her lover's bedroom door shut. She left, thinking he wanted to be alone with his "queen." A few hours later Snider's roommate, a doctor, knocked on the hustler's door. Getting no response, he opened it and looked inside. The sight that met his eyes caused him to wince and get sick. Both Paul Snider and Dorothy Stratten were dead. The bedroom walls were flecked with blood. Her beautiful, naked twenty-year-old body was half on the bed; her face had been shot away. Snider was on the floor, also naked, his bleeding body having fallen upon the shotgun he had used to kill his wife and end his own life.

Shock waves reverberated through the Hollywood community when the killings were made public. The movies had been robbed of a potential star, Hefner a Playmate, and Bogdanovich a wife. It was apparent to all that Paul Snider had decided that if he could not have Dorothy as a wife and meal ticket, no one would have her or see her again except as a heap of dead, pulpy flesh. It was in keeping with Snider's egomaniacal personality that he would make sure to destroy that incredibly striking seraphic countenance, that his last gesture would be to eradicate the beauty he had once touted to the world.

Bogdanovich was thoroughly shattered by the murder-suicide. Some days later he arranged for Dorothy's cremation; her ashes were placed in an urn that he could later visit. This was followed by a formal statement from the director which read:

Dorothy Stratten was as gifted and intelligent an actress as she was beautiful, and she was very beautiful indeed—in every way imaginable—most particularly in her heart. She and I fell in love during our picture and had planned to be married as soon as her divorce was final. . . .

There is no life Dorothy's touched that has not been changed for the better through knowing her, however briefly. Dorothy looked at the world with love, and believed that all people were good down deep. She was mistaken, but it is among the most generous and noble errors we can make.

There were no moving statements concerning Paul Snider. His body was shipped back to Vancouver and buried in an inexpensive plot. There were little or no good memories of him unlike the exquisite woman he had killed, but some of his words were recalled. "I will kill myself before I go to jail," he had said. This statement, more than any other, was remembered. And one could easily imagine Snider saying that line to himself after he had murdered Dorothy Stratten, saying it aloud and then turning the shotgun on himself.

# 1980

## EVERETT CLARKE
### MURDER
### ON THE STAGE

Everett Clarke had played the scene many times during his forty-some years behind the microphone: The threat of death, an approaching killer, a violent struggle, and a shriek of desperation as the victim succumbed. He had played the role on radio, chiefly over Chicago stations, acting out parts in countless murder mysteries. His greatest successes, where his bass voice sent shivers up the spines of millions of listeners, were on such programs as "The Shadow" and as the voice of "The Whistler."

Clarke added to his stellar radio reputation as the announcer for WGN Radio's "Chicago Theater of the Air" during the 1940s and 1950s. He went on to become the star of many radio soap operas and children's shows before he went into semiretirement. The announcer took studios in Chicago's Fine Arts Building and, for forty years, established himself as one of the city's leading drama coaches.

On the afternoon of September 9, 1980, painter Ann Lang, whose studio was next to Clarke's, heard loud noises, then a man's voice shout: "No, Paul! God, no, Paul!" Then she heard what sounded like "books falling, almost as if they were being thrown." The painter shrugged, and went back to work. She thought it was another acting lesson being given by Everett Clarke, not an unusual outburst in the Fine Arts Building, which housed scores of singers, composers, painters, actors, and drama teachers.

In fact, one of the great experiences in Chicago is to take a rickety old elevator in this ornate building up several floors and stand near the giant open-air shaft to listen to the incredible cacophony reverberating and echoing from the hundreds of offices. Each day, all day long, singers are bellowing and screeching, hitting notes never thought humanly possible. Unseen actors

*Everett Clarke, Chicago drama coach and one-time voice of "The Whistler," who was murdered on his own stage, September 9, 1980. (Wide World)*

shout and thunder their lines. Composers bang away at ancient pianos. The listener will hear a hundred instruments of all kinds, from violins to French horns, piercing the air. There is no such thing as a strange noise in Chicago's Fine Arts Building.

Painter Lang, of course, was used to such noises, including what appeared to be the sound of a much-respected drama coach instructing a student in the manner of a terrified person, say, about to meet violent death. As she glanced out her window, Ann Lang did think it a bit strange to see a young man climb out of Clarke's window and onto a fire escape, but, again, that might have been an improvisational exit. She forgot about the incident and resumed painting.

By 8 P.M. that Tuesday night the Fine Arts Building was quiet, its shrieks and screams and its grunts and groans of the day passed into artistic history. One elevator rattled its way upward to the tenth floor and stopped. Friends of Clarke's, alarmed that he had missed a dinner date, went to his office studio to check on him.

They found Clarke there, in the middle of his small practice stage, lying faceup, blood oozing from four stab wounds. He was dead. It had not been an acting lesson after all, police concluded following a talk with Ann Lang. Everett Clarke had been brutally murdered. The drama coach who had helped scores of actors to success, even aiding many of them to get scholarships when they were short of funds (his most recent protégé of acting fame was Robert Urich, star of ABC-TV's *Vegas*) had been stabbed three times in the chest and once in the jugular vein in the left side of the neck.

The killing was a less than classic case for police, however. The murder weapon, a bloody scissors, was found a foot from the body. The window leading to the fire escape was still open. After talking to other tenants the following day, the police heard the name "Paul" from Ann Lang. They quickly checked Clarke's appointment book and found the name Paul DeWit, who lived in an apartment on North Lake Shore.

DeWit, a twenty-two-year-old drama student, was promptly arrested and charged with murdering his drama coach. At the time, the motives were obscure, but they were provided by DeWit's defense counsel at his trial. Lorna Propes told a jury that her client was the youngest of four children and had had a long history of behavioral and emotional problems, which had developed in recent months before the killing into uncontrollable "paranoid schizophrenia." DeWit, who was known to neighbors as a "nice, quiet man who sometimes threw parties in his apartment," had only two months earlier been put on probation after pleading guilty to a charge of male prostitution.

Since that time, claimed lawyer Propes, DeWit felt that everyone was out to "get him," and that included his theatrical mentor, Everett Clarke. "The total consequence of all that," Propes told a jury, "is that Paul DeWit took the life of Everett Clarke by stabbing him."

The prosecution argued that the would-be actor was not only mentally fit to stand trial but that he was sane at the time of the murder. DeWit's whereabouts on the day of the murder was firmly established. (A tenant next door to Clarke, violin restorer Mahlon Rhoades, had ridden up in an elevator with Clarke to his floor at 2 P.M. on the day of the murder, to see DeWit waiting for Clarke and walking with the drama coach into his office.)

The jury, after a short deliberation, agreed with the prosecution and found DeWit guilty of murder. He was later sentenced to twenty-two years in prison. It was ironic that Clarke, a wholly gentle and generous man throughout his long and illustrious career, had invariably played the role of the villain during his radio heyday, never the victim. This typecasting would not be reversed until the last moment of his life.

# 1980

## MICHAEL J. HALBERSTAM
### THE GENIUS-TO-
### GENIUS MURDER

Michael J. Halberstam and Bernard C. Welch, Jr., had never met until the night of December 5, 1980, when one took the life of the other. As the facts were later revealed, both men, irrespective of their pursuits in life, were strikingly similar; they were driven by unrelenting ambition and were workaholics. Each was a genius in his own right: one, Halberstam, for the positive forces in society; the other, Welch, a dedicated and incorrigible thief, representing high crime.

Halberstam was born on August 9, 1932, in The Bronx, and raised by his physician father, Charles Halberstam, and his teacher mother, Blanche, in the small mill town of Winsted, Connecticut. He was taught the value of work and developed early a keen sense of competition and experienced the joys of accomplishment. After graduating from Roosevelt High School in Yonkers, Halberstam went on to Harvard as a premedical student but showed a strong bent for literary work, becoming an editor for the student newspaper, the *Crimson*. Such talents were widespread in the Halberstam family; Michael's brother, David, was to go on to prominence as an author and a Pulitzer prize–winning journalist for *The New York Times*.

Michael received his degree from Boston University in 1957 and immediately went to work for the Public Health Service, working in such remote areas as Point Barrow, Alaska, and on an Indian reservation in New Mexico. A man with energy to squander, Halberstam's natural interests in writing, medicine, and politics led him to choose Washington, D.C., as a city best suited to his ambitions. He married Linda Medalsohn, had two sons, then divorced in 1974. Two years later Halberstam married journalist Elliott Anna Jones.

The physician established a busy and lucrative practice in the

nation's capital, specializing in cardiology. When not in the examining room, Halberstam was at his typewriter producing nov-
els that showed considerable promise. He also wrote articles that
appeared in *Modern Medicine* magazine, for which he was the senior medical editor. His physical energies were boundless, and he
wore out dance partners in disco cabarets and ran ragged on the
basketball court men twenty years his junior. The tall, muscular
Halberstam was, given all his interests, passionately involved
with medicine. As his brother David was to comment following
Michael's death: "He was a doctor, and as a doctor, he had an
abiding sense that medicine is as much humanity as it is science."

Halberstam appeared indefatigable, and certainly felt that he
was equal to any challenge, even that of facing down a burglar
who had entered his Washington house overlooking the Poto-
mac, at 2806 Battery Place, on the night of December 5, 1980. The
doctor and his wife had returned home from a cocktail party at
8:45 P.M. Halberstam entered the house alone, his wife waiting on
the porch. He was going to let out his two dogs so that Mrs.
Halberstam could walk them.

The moment he switched on the lights, Halberstam saw a man
dressed in black coming out of his living room. Instead of fleeing,
Halberstam followed his instincts and advanced upon the burglar, grappling with him. The intruder suddenly produced a
handgun and fired five quick shots, two of which struck the
physician in the chest. The burglar fled, and moments later Halberstam ran from his home with blood on his shirt. The forty-
eight-year-old doctor did not appear to be seriously injured. He
and his wife hurried to their car, and the doctor slid behind the
wheel.

"Let me drive," said Mrs. Halberstam.

"Get in," ordered the doctor.

She did and they were off, racing down the street toward Sibley
Hospital. After going only a few blocks, Halberstam saw a figure
crouching on the sidewalk. "There he is!" he shouted to his wife,
and drove his car onto the sidewalk, aiming for the burglar,
striking the man and sending him flying against a brick wall.
Halberstam kept going, trying to reach the hospital. His head
began to bob downward.

"Only then," Mrs. Halberstam later said, "did I realize how
seriously he had been shot. I told him, almost irritatingly, to back

*Dr. Michael J. Halberstam. (Teresa Zabala/The New York Times)*

up, but then I saw him slumping. He lost control and we crashed into a tree." Passersby summoned an ambulance, and Halberstam was rushed to a hospital emergency room, where he died minutes later. The killer had by then been picked up by police as he lay injured on the sidewalk where Halberstam had struck him. He was treated for minor cuts and bruises but would tell police nothing. His pockets were empty and he had no identification whatsoever. As officers took his fingerprints, the six-feet-one-inch, 170-pound burglar, a darkly featured man who had said not a word up to that point, suddenly blurted: "You're going to be surprised." With that he remained silent, and would do so through the coming months up to the time of his trial for murder.

Police were indeed surprised to receive the report on the burglar's fingerprints. The killer was none other than Bernard Charles Welch, Jr., who had escaped from the Clinton correctional facility in Dannemora, New York, in 1974. Welch had been on an FBI "wanted" list for five years on a charge of illegal flight to avoid confinement. The prisoner, it was slowly discovered, had been living a life of luxury under the name of Norman Hamilton in Great Falls, Virginia, with his wife, Linda Susan Hamilton, and their three children.

The home in which the Hamiltons lived on Chesapeake Drive was a sprawling structure of seemingly endless living rooms, bedrooms, ornate kitchens, and baths; it also had an enormous indoor swimming pool with seven giant glass skylights. A huge environmental room provided varying degrees of heat and humidity that simulated both Saharan and Arctic conditions. There was a three-car garage housing three expensive sports cars, including a $40,000 Mercedes-Benz.

Surrounding this fabulous home was a security system that would have been the envy of the Central Intelligence Agency, whose headquarters was only ten miles away from the Welch-Hamilton dwelling. Welch had purchased the home in the summer of 1978, paying $245,000 in cash for it, and then immediately adding expensive wings and improvements. One of the costlier "improvements" was the home's security system, which included a battery of remote-control closed-circuit television cameras capable of sweeping the lawn areas in every direction. Microphones had been implanted in the outside walls of the house, and weight sensors had been embedded in the lawn. Floodlights that could expose the entire estate had been secretly planted in trees and shrubbery and could be controlled from within the house. All of this equipment created an enormous power-drain, but Welch was never worried about a blackout making his security system inadequate. He had installed a powerful auxiliary generator for just such an emergency.

The inside of the house was tastefully furnished, but, one neighbor noticed and later told police, "There wasn't much of it and they had no antiques." The antiques, of course, and much, much more were in the basement of the large house, fifty-one boxes of stolen loot estimated by investigators to be worth more than $3 million and representing about 3,500 burglaries committed by the energetic Bernard Welch. (This Smithsonian-like collection of more than 13,000 items was later exhibited in an enormous hall, to which flocked more than 4,000 burglary victims in hopes of identifying their property, which required 20,000 pages to catalog.)

Anything and everything of value was found in the Welch basement—dozens of mink and sable coats; expensive jewelry; silver flatware; antique brooches, pins, and necklaces; watches; Oriental ivory, porcelain, and jade; vases; candelabras; and antique dolls. Hundreds of rare coins were found, along with many gold ingots worth $10,000 apiece that had been created by Welch himself in melting pots he had had installed. He also possessed an enormous and expensive collection of weapons, chiefly handguns. The very Smith & Wesson revolver Welch had used to shoot Michael Halberstam had been stolen by the superburglar from an FBI agent when Welch burglarized the agent's apartment.

Ironically, Halberstam was a dedicated foe of firearms and had made many TV appearances on behalf of a drive for enactment of federal legislation to control handguns. He had appeared on TV only a month prior to his death to state: "Let's put some of the same energy and urgency into controlling handguns as we put into controlling muscular dystrophy. Start now. Don't wait until someone you love and someone you respect has been murdered by a psychopath with a grudge against society and a .32 special in his pocket."

Welch was no psychopath with a grudge against the social system in which he lived; he was an insatiable collector, an acquisitive shark feeding ravenously from that system. His frenzied burglaries, committed usually between November and April when nights were longer and darker, could at first be likened to pure gluttony. Further, police realized after discovering the enormous loot in Virginia that they had undoubtedly captured the Standard Time Burglar who had struck Washington-area homes between 6 P.M. and 10 P.M. for five years. This vexing master thief —it was certainly Welch—had not only robbed thousands of homes with alacrity but terrified dozens of residents, whom he had hog-tied and threatened with handguns, even raping three female victims, one a woman of seventy-four. He was dangerous when trapped, but police who had been searching for him had all but given up ever catching him.

"We became fatalistic," said Maryland Detective Sergeant James King, "that we'd ever catch Welch by known investigative techniques . . . this guy was better than any fictional character. He was hitting three or four houses every night. But his claim to fame was not how much stuff he stole, it was how he lived after stealing. He wasn't your typical junkie. He took his money and invested it. The guy had imagination."

He was also imaginative in converting his stolen goods to cash. Another police official, when referring to Welch's modus operandi, stated: "The smart burglar lives in one police jurisdiction, burglarizes a different jurisdiction, and fences his loot in yet a third."

Welch burglarized the wealthy bedroom communities of Washington, D.C. He lived in Virginia, and he fenced his loot in the Midwest, traveling with his family to Duluth, Minnesota, to spend the summer in another luxury split-level home (also equipped with security systems and sirens), for which Welch had paid $102,000—again in cold, hard cash. It was here that Welch sold his rare antiques and coins through legitimate dealers. To his neighbors in Virginia, Welch was a man who had gotten rich through clever stock manipulations; to his neighbors in Duluth, he was a millionaire real estate broker. In reality, he was one clever thief.

Duluth was not only the Welch family's summer home but the birthplace of Linda Susan Hamilton, whose father, Russell Hamilton, lived there and was a former crane operator for United States Steel. After Welch's arrest the father hastened to tell au-

*Super burglar Bernard C. Welch, Jr. (Wide World)*

thorities that Welch "was no relative of mine," but added, as most who knew him did, that "he's a decent fellow, polite and considerate."

Welch, to anyone who was not his victim, had been a "nice guy," quiet, easygoing, a man of mysterious riches, which was in keeping with his formula for life, one that he had developed years earlier when he began his long career as a "one-man crime wave."

Born on April 28, 1940, in Rochester, New York, Welch attended the Churchville School but left at the age of sixteen to learn the plumbing trade. His choice of trades may have had to do with the fact that as a child he moved with his family to Spencerport, New York, and there was no indoor plumbing in their ramshackle house. His father worked for Eastman Kodak as a machine operator and spent most of his time drinking and gambling his small salary away. Welch's mother was a recluse who spent decades developing an international pen-pals network. Left on his own, Welch dropped out of school to spend his youthful days hunting skunks and foxes; he sold the skins of these animals to keep himself in pocket money. He developed an early sense of independence and an inflated egotistical opinion of his own importance. "I got away with murder as a child," he was later to tell authorities. "I did everything and never got caught. I thought I could go through life and do the same thing."

From 1958 to 1962, Welch worked as a loner, a plumber by daytime when he would "case" homes pinpointed for robbery, a burglar at night looting those very homes. In 1962, Welch married a local girl and not only took Anne Marie along with him on his nocturnal raids but also dragged along the first of their three children. The wife and child would wait in the car while Welch crept into a darkened house to ransack it.

The apprentice burglar was so successful for two years that he was able to buy a "cute little home" on Brick Schoolhouse Road in Hamlin, a suburb of Rochester. He paid cash for the house, as would be his lifelong habit. In late 1964 police arrested Welch for a burglary in Madison, New York. He posted bail, then packed up his family and the loot from many robberies and drove to Berkeley Springs, West Virginia, a small resort town where he opened an antique store that served as a clearing house for the items he had stolen and continued to steal.

Welch was an active shopowner, too active for a suspicious

county sheriff named James Batt, who noted that Welch worked his shop alone and would appear behind the shop like clockwork at 3 A.M. to unload goods from a flatbed truck. The sheriff checked with out-of-state authorities and learned of outstanding warrants for Welch's arrest. Within days Welch was picked up and returned to New York. His wife, Anne Marie, who would divorce him in 1971, received a suspended sentence for cooperating with police. She rattled off the number of burglaries she knew her husband had committed; there were scores more she had not known about. "He thought he was smart to get away with it," she later commented.

Welch was sent to prison for five years, serving four years in the Elmira correctional facility. Released in 1968, he worked as a pipe fitter in upstate New York but could not resist home invasions and was picked up for burglarizing a residence in Wellsville. Again he jumped bail, and went on a crime spree, burglarizing hundreds of homes in Allegany, Ontario, and Wyoming counties. He fenced his stolen goods in Delaware and in Miami, Florida, driving truckloads of antiques to dealers in these states for resale. He had by then become somewhat of an expert in the antiques field, knowing exactly what worthwhile items to steal and how much they would bring on the open market. A suspicious dealer finally turned in Welch in 1971, and he was sent back to prison after being convicted of a dozen counts of burglary and illegal entry. This time his sentence was stiff: ten years in Attica, the state's toughest, meanest prison. He arrived there just in time to witness its most bloody inmate revolt. After three and a half years Welch was transferred to the Clinton correctional facility, a minimum-security prison.

Though he was eligible for parole in 1975, a year short of this time Welch decided to make a break with another prisoner, Paul David Maturano. The prisoners hid beneath bleachers on the grounds after a softball game; in the cover of darkness they climbed a twenty-five-foot fence and escaped, running to a house only seven miles from the prison, where they stole money, clothes, and a car. Their flight was right out of a 1930s Warner Bros. movie.

Police had set up roadblocks within a thirty-mile radius of the prison, but they failed to stop Welch. The fugitive approached one roadblock in the stolen car and, instead of coming to a stop, jammed his foot on the accelerator, smashing through wooden horses blocking the way and ducking behind the wheel as a half-dozen officers let loose with a fusillade of bullets at the fleeing car.

Officers leaped into squad cars and gave chase for several miles, but Welch, an experienced driver, led them in a wild chase on dirt roads cutting through the deep forests of the Adirondack State Park where he had hunted as a boy. Finally he lost them. He and Maturano drove to Richmond, Virginia, and there began robbing houses, the pair working successfully for almost two years until Maturano grew disgusted with Welch's greed. He quit the criminal partnership and was picked up in 1976. He later stated: "Welch was burglarizing everything in sight. Then we met broads, and he liked to slap them around. I didn't like that."

By the time Maturno departed, Welch had taken up with a Richmond schoolteacher but he abandoned this woman when he moved to Washington, D.C., in 1976 to begin his thousands of burglaries in the surrounding communities. This was the same year, ironically enough, that another D.C. resident, Michael Halberstam—the man Welch would murder four years later—married his second wife, Elliott Jones. Two years went by in which Welch gained fabulous riches through burglary. Then, in early 1978, the superthief met attractive Linda Susan Hamilton.

Then working as a government secretary, Linda Susan Hamilton was impressed with this tall, quiet man with thick brown hair and hazel eyes. He had plenty of money and told her that he was a successful antique and rare-coin dealer.

He also informed Linda that, though he loved her, he could not marry her because his wife refused to give him a divorce. Moreover, he asked to take her last name so that they could live as common-law man and wife. That way he could avoid cruel alimony payments. She agreed, and the couple set up housekeeping in Falls Church, Virginia, where Welch purchased a three-bedroom house, paying for it with cash, as usual. They lived quietly but Welch's occasional extravagances aroused some suspicions. He once gave a local teen-ager $150 to feed his cats while he took his wife on a Caribbean cruise.

A neighbor, William Tomlinson, an agent for the Federal Drug Enforcement Agency, wondered about "Hamilton's" income and ran a routine check on him to see if he had ever been charged with drug violations. The answer was negative, and Tomlinson thereafter accepted his neighbor as an upstanding citizen.

A sixth sense of danger, however, must have been working for Welch, for he soon decided to move, first buying the home in Duluth in 1978, and then purchasing the opulent house in Great Falls, Virginia, in that same year. The Hamiltons spent the summers of 1978, 1979, and 1980 in Duluth. For Welch, these were working holidays. He would arrive with his family in a large moving van and spend weeks unloading his stolen goods at night, unseen by his Minnesota neighbors. This was the loot he had stolen from the Washington, D.C., area, which he fenced in Minnesota.

He hired a seamstress to cut out labels and monograms of hundreds of fur coats that he transported from his Duluth home to her workshop. The labels were from stores in New York, Washington, and Philadelphia, but the seamstress asked no questions. She later told police: "He told me he was a fur dealer and who was I to know the difference? I didn't know anything about him."

Welch went to many midwest coin and antique dealers to sell off his stolen goods. His polished manners and expensive attire disarmed one and all from thinking that his merchandise was anything but legitimate. To Jerry Rose, a Minnesota gallery owner, Welch-Hamilton was a real estate tycoon. "He acted and looked like a millionaire," Rose said later. "I had no reason to question his integrity." Rose auctioned off a reported $300,000 in goods for Welch.

Police later learned that Mrs. Hamilton was identified as the woman who had brought many rare coins to local dealers who, in turn, sold them for the Hamiltons. (Linda Hamilton was apparently operating on good faith, believing her common-law husband to be a genuine dealer; she was never charged with any crimes.) Linda delivered coins to a dealer named Stan Sunde, according to one report, and he quickly sold the rare coins and sent on checks to the Hamiltons. Then Welch-Hamilton himself appeared with coins for Sunde to handle. Sunde also invested confidence in his new customer, later commenting: "He dressed well and he knew what he was doing. Once I asked him where he got the stuff—coins, rings, cuff-links. When he told me that he bought estates, I said, 'I wish I could get estates like that.' He said, 'You have to know the right people.' "

Duluth neighbors thought the Hamiltons an ideal couple. Their children seemed normal and played with other neighborhood children. Linda, old friends said, had been a shy girl who had grown up in the poor section of the West End in Duluth. She had dated little while attending Denfield High but had worked on the high school yearbook. She attended her high school's tenth-year reunion with Welch, introducing him as her husband. On her finger was a huge diamond wedding ring.

The poor girl had, like her husband, neighbors believed, lived a rags-to-riches story, one that inspired those who knew them in the community of Hidden Valley (aptly named, given Welch's circumstances) rather than raised doubts about their income. Robin Seiler, who lived across the street from the Hamiltons, spent time with the soft-spoken Welch talking "about the land . . . I guessed he was in real estate. . . . He seemed to meet the requirements of a good neighbor. He didn't beat his wife, he paid his bills on time and he didn't make trouble."

There was only one trait that made Welch stand out, according to Seiler. "He did like to brag about what he had. He was always talking about things like his two Mercedes and when he planned to sell one or buy another." Perhaps this, more than anything else, revealed the motive for Welch's incredible nonstop drive, his willingness to assume greater and greater risks in his marathon burglaries.

Perhaps, as police later believed, he was not merely wallowing in greed. (He had, by the time of his arrest, already acquired goods and bank accounts that ran into the millions.) He had passed the point of mere survival years earlier. He could not or would not quit and retire on his vast, ill-gotten fortune, as many a practical-minded criminal before him had done.

The clue to Welch's ambitions lay in his remarks to his neighbors. The normally closemouthed burglar conformed to the necessary social images except one. He bragged about his possessions. And that meant an abiding lust for status. He would not only be accepted in an economic peer group of upper-class Americans, he would exceed their life-style achievements. Quite simply, Bernard Charles Welch, Jr., who had grown up without the benefit of indoor plumbing, would outdo the Joneses or die in the attempt, a typically American ambition gone unchecked into mania. It was a desperate status-seeker who had murdered Michael Halberstam on December 5, 1980, not merely a cat burglar accidentally caught with an expensive vase in his gloved hands.

Of course, once in custody Welch would admit to nothing, let alone discuss his motives for the burglary and Halberstam's murder. "He'll never tell us," complained one detective who had vainly grilled Welch for hours. "His attitude has been: 'You've got me and you're probably going to put me away, but I'm not going to do or say one thing to help you.' "

On April 10, 1981, Welch was found guilty of murdering Michael Halberstam by a jury of nine women and three men who took only two hours to decide on the verdict. He was sentenced on May 22, 1981, to fifteen years to life. Throughout his trial and at his sentencing Welch maintained a quiet composure. He said nothing, and as the "one-man crime wave" was led from court en route to prison, he had no remarks for reporters. Undoubtedly the persistent American dream of success was much on his mind, and still is today.

# 1980

## JOHN LENNON
## THE SLAYING OF
## A SUPERSTAR

**D**espite his desperate attempts for a decade to disassociate himself from The Beatles, John Winston Lennon, up to the time of his violent death at age forty at the hands of an unhinged fan, was umbilically linked with the singing foursome that became the world's most popular rock group. As the years ebb and flow that image will probably never change. It was no accident that Lennon arrived and departed the public eye inside of mass mania, even though this exceptionally talented man, called a musical genius by many, fought against just such a fate.

Lennon was born on October 9, 1940, into an unhappy Liverpool family. His father, an itinerant seaman, deserted him and his mother when John was three. Though his mother also deserted him, leaving him in the care of her sister, Lennon reserved a special hatred for his father. Years later, when the elder Lennon suddenly appeared at his son's door, the then super rock star took one look at him and, without a word, slammed the door in his face. He later said with a great deal of bitterness: "I don't feel I owe him anything. He never helped me. I got there by myself."

Such self-confidence sometimes ran to megalomania with John Lennon, even when he appeared to be joking. At one point when The Beatles were working their way to the zenith of worldwide public acclaim, Lennon remarked: "We're more popular than Jesus now; I don't know which will go first—rock'n'roll or Christianity." He was to regret the comment and considered it a moment when his pride jumped his wit. He made a public apology on August 12, 1966, in Chicago, saying he "was sorry that he opened his mouth about Jesus Christ."

Lennon had been shown the error of false pride by his fans, who undoubtedly prompted the apology; after his "Jesus" remark thousands of fans gathered to publicly smash and burn Beatles albums. Had not the commercially minded Lennon made his retraction, he and his three partners might have seen their fabulous careers go up in smoke.

Those careers and the enormous success attending them proved Horace Greeley's belief that young men could make their fortunes by "going west," only in this instance it was traveling west from England to America, the land that lined the pockets of The Beatles with more gold than they could ever spend.

The idea for the group slowly took form when fifteen-year-old John Lennon met Paul McCartney in 1955 at a Liverpool party. This was at a time when rock'n'roll was an embryo, with singing stars such as Buddy Holly, Bill Haley, and Elvis Presley just beginning to emerge. McCartney and Lennon began to talk about music, and a year later Lennon formed his first band, The Quarrymen, which McCartney promptly joined. The name derived from Quarry Bank High School in Allerton, a suburb of Liverpool, which Lennon attended.

Lennon's autocratic ways soon alienated most members, who came and went, but McCartney stayed and George Harrison later joined the group, Ringo Starr being the last permanent member to join up. That John Lennon was always the recognized leader of the foursome was reflected in some of the names used for the group: Johnny and the Moondogs, and Long John and the Silver Beatles, the latter name used in 1959. Finally it came down to the Silver Beatles, and then just The Beatles.

In the beginning Lennon was thought of as a talented up-and-comer in England but a sarcastic type who would rather deliver a wry insult than a compliment. His first wife, Cynthia, with whom Lennon had a son, Julian, was to comment in her book *A Twist of Lennon:* "I think he was the last stronghold of the Teddy Boys [British street thugs]—totally aggressive and anti-establishment." Critic Stanley Reynolds, who knew Lennon and his group long before they cut their first album, later remarked: "John Lennon was the hardest, toughest kid I ever met. He had an uncompromising attitude that would never give an inch. He was completely unbending and it shocked you meeting him because he was, after all, a young fellow and a civilian—so why was he at war? The truth was he was at war with the whole world."

The group nevertheless caught on, and in February 1963 the

*The Beatles in 1968, when they were already tired of their success—(left to right) Paul McCartney, John Lennon, Ringo Starr, and George Harrison. (UPI)*

first Beatles album, *Please Please Me,* began to climb the charts in England. A year later, on February 8, 1964, the group appeared for the first time on the Ed Sullivan TV show, and from that point onward The Beatles became a household word in America, whether the older generation wanted to hear it or not.

McCartney supplied the masterful tunes and Lennon the brilliant lyrics for the group. All the members supplied quips or puns by the score to a public eager for any word they cared to drop. Their songs, style, and personae became a vogue that lasted for six years and continues to linger like a stubborn ghost. Lennon led the way. If he changed his style of clothes, tens of thousands of fans changed from suits to casual wear. When he donned dark, grainy glasses—he was always myopic—identical glasses appeared on the faces of the faithful. He grew a thin droopy mustache. Thin droopy mustaches became the rage.

Meanwhile, Beatles albums came out with crescendo at the cash register—*A Hard Day's Night* (1964), *HELP!* (1965), *Sgt. Pepper's Lonely Hearts Club Band* (1967), *Yellow Submarine* (1969), *Let It Be* (1970). Millions of dollars rolled in from their records and millions more from their films and personal appearances. The stage appearances toward the end of the group's career became so hectic that the members were almost torn to pieces by uncontrollable, emotional fans.

John Lennon grew to hate the very throngs that raved about him and his group. He had to run police gauntlets through which fans grabbed, clutched, tore, and scratched for souvenirs, especially fanatical girls gone berserk to have a shred of clothing from their idols. Lennon would arrive home scratched and bruised, his necktie or scarf torn from his throat, his clothes in tatters, to collapse on a bed exhausted with the ordeal. "Christ, Cyn," he told his wife once, "we'll have to get out of this death trap before they kill me. I had no idea it was going to be like this. It's like a bloody madhouse out there. We deserve every penny we get."

Lennon's dissatisfaction with the fierce fans and the demands of albums and appearances began early; by 1966, the year he met artist Yoko Ono, he was thinking of quitting the group and striking out on his own to create a "more classical" kind of music. Not until 1970 did Lennon and the rest of The Beatles break up, however, each going his own way with only Paul McCartney and The Wings having any kind of success similar to that enjoyed by the original group. Yoko Ono, of course, for whom Lennon left his first wife, was a great influence in his life. It was Yoko who persuaded Lennon to concentrate on his own creativity and discovery of self. He, like the other Beatles, spent the 1970s experimenting with self-analysis, drugs, and a search for gurus with all-knowing answers. Such self-indulgences might be expected of four young men who had, perhaps, too early in life been deluged with fame and riches.

It was also Yoko Ono who convinced Lennon to live in New York City, where the couple and their small child moved into the posh Dakota apartments. Oddly enough, he told a British interviewer three days before his death, he felt "secure" by living in New York. "It was Yoko who sold me on New York," Lennon said. "I fell in love with New York." Another irony was that the very violence that his own songs damned took his life. *Double*

*John Lennon with wife, Yoko Ono, a photo used on the singer-lyricist's last album, "Double Fantasy," in 1980. (UPI)*

*Fantasy,* his last album, done with Yoko, plaintively asked how long society would tolerate its own destruction.

Toward the end Lennon had turned almost mystical, introspectively examining himself and the world about him. He was also fatalistic, believing that he would be destroyed by a nuclear holocaust long before reaching old age. He talked of this eventuality at great length with his son Julian.

Only hours before his end came, Lennon was interviewed by RKO Radio Network, telling interviewers: "We're going to live, or we're going to die. If we're dead, we're going to have to deal with that; if we're alive we're going to have to deal with being alive. So worrying about whether Wall Street or the Apocalypse is going to come in the form of the great beast is not going to do us any good today."

At 5 P.M. that night, December 8, 1980, Lennon and Yoko left the Dakota en route to a recording session. Several fans who habitually stood outside the swanky apartment complex pushed forward to get Lennon's autograph. One of these was a cherubic young man with a copy of *The Catcher in the Rye* jutting from his jacket pocket. Lennon gave him his autograph and then climbed into a waiting limousine after his wife. The couple returned to the Dakota at 11 P.M. They got out of the limousine at curbside and began to walk toward the Dakota's courtyard.

The same young man with the cherubic face and thick mop of black hair who had gotten Lennon's autograph six hours earlier suddenly appeared, coming up from behind the couple and shouting: "Mr. Lennon!"

Lennon turned about slowly to see the man suddenly drop into a military crouch, his legs spread apart as he aimed a .38 Charter Arms revolver at the singer-composer. Without another word he fired off five shots, which struck Lennon in the chest, back, and left arm. He took about six steps, crying out to Yoko: "I'm shot." He collapsed. His assailant calmly dropped the revolver as if he were throwing away a half-eaten hot dog, then sauntered to the side of the Dakota and sat down, pulling out the J. D. Salinger novel and reading it avidly.

Patrolman Jim Moran who was detailed to keep fans from getting too close to the Dakota—it was the home of many celebrities, including Lauren Bacall, Leonard Bernstein, and Gilda Radner—ran forward. He helped the wounded singer to his squad car,

*The Dakota Apartments in New York, residence of John Lennon and the site of his murder. (UPI)*

placing him in the back seat, then jumped behind the wheel, heading for a nearby hospital. "Are you John Lennon?" Moran asked. Lennon was in acute pain and could not answer. He only nodded and groaned. By the time Lennon was taken into the emergency room at Roosevelt Hospital, he was dead from his multiple wounds.

The killer was quickly identified as a former mental patient named Mark David Chapman. The twenty-five-year-old murderer, who offered no resistance to police taking him from the scene of the killing, was a resident of Hawaii. In his pockets police found fourteen Beatles tapes, the Salinger novel, and $2,000. He offered no explanation for the murder.

The public reaction to the killing was one of national shock and sorrow. Hundreds of Lennon's fans gathered outside of the Dakota to sing and pray, offering condolences to Yoko. Mayor Edward Koch heard of the killing and immediately called for nationwide gun control of handguns. President-elect Ronald Reagan called the singer's death "a great tragedy," and President Jimmy Carter paid tribute to the genius and music of John Lennon, saying: "His spirit, the spirit of The Beatles—brash and earnest, ironic and idealistic all at once—became the spirit of a whole generation."

Within twenty-four hours the hawks of commerce descended. Lennon's albums were being sold faster than stores could stock them. Hundreds outside the Dakota were wearing brand new T-shirts inscribed: "John Lennon, 1940–1980, rest in peace."

The killer had also advertised his love for The Beatles, police later learned. In the past Chapman had pinned buttons to his shirt that read "John Lennon." As his defense attorney later pointed out, however, he was not proudly advertising his support for Lennon as a loyal fan; he thought *he was* Lennon. Mark Chapman was decidedly a mental case. The twenty-five-year-old had tried to commit suicide in Hawaii in 1977 and once again in New York, only two weeks before he shot and killed the man he once thought to be a god on earth.

Chapman was born in Fort Worth, Texas, on May 10, 1955, the year John Lennon and Paul McCartney first met. He was raised in Atlanta and Decatur, Georgia, graduating from high school and going on to DeKalb Community College. He later worked for various charitable organizations such as the YMCA, aiding Vietnamese refugees at Fort Chaffee, Arkansas, in 1975 when he was twenty. By then he had already gone through his own rock band in high school, where he played guitar and emulated The Beatles. He had collected every record the group cut.

Slowly, authorities learned how Chapman's obsession with the chief Beatle had led him to stalk John Lennon for several days until he killed him. Hours before he shot Lennon, Chapman was photographed as Lennon autographed an album for him.

As the facts emerged it was clear that Chapman's background was unnervingly similar to that of his victim. He, too, had come from a broken home; his parents divorced only two years before he murdered Lennon. He had struck out on his own as a "wild and fantastic kid," according to one YMCA coworker who labored alongside Chapman to rehabilitate Vietnamese refugees. Chapman had taken an oath never to touch drugs and was a "born again" Christian. He was remembered as being a rabid Beatles fan, but became extremely upset whenever anyone mentioned Lennon's remark about being more important than Jesus. "Who in the hell are they to compare themselves to Jesus?" he would ask over and over at such times.

Chapman lived a nomadic life through the mid to late 1970s, working in Arkansas and Tennessee and traveling to Hawaii and Switzerland, studying various religions but seeming to get nowhere. In 1979 he met an attractive travel agent, Gloria H. Abe, a woman four years his senior and of Japanese descent (as was John Lennon's Yoko Ono). The couple wed in June, moving to Oahu, Hawaii, where Chapman worked in a print shop at the Castle Memorial Hospital near Kailua. He later got a job as a security guard in a Honolulu condominium.

It was while living in Hawaii that Chapman began to lose control of himself. He forbade his new wife to read newspapers or watch TV and insisted she break with all her old friends. Chapman at this time began calling the Church of Scientology, whispering: "Bang, bang, you're dead!" He was working as a security guard in a building directly across from the church, whose members remembered him standing outside it and shouting abuse. "He was a very very strange character," said one parishioner.

A friend of those days watched Chapman deteriorate to the point where he became "a jerk, a creep, just a negative person"

*John Lennon's mentally deranged killer, Mark David Chapman. (Wide World)*

who spent most of his time playing Beatles records or visiting art galleries to argue with spectators over the values of Salvador Dali and Norman Rockwell. Chapman was a kind and gentle person to other people who had never seen the vicious side of his character. He was later to tell police: "I couldn't help myself. I've got a good side and a bad side. The bad side is very small, but sometimes it takes over the good side and I do bad things." To one friend in Hawaii, Chapman was nothing more than an innocuous soul "who ate a lot of peanuts."

In the fall of 1980 the five-feet-eleven-inch Chapman left his wife. He removed his name tag from his security guard uniform and substituted the name "John Lennon." He abruptly quit his job on October 23, 1980, going to the employee logbook to sign out for the last time. He signed the name of "John Lennon," then scratched it out.

By then Chapman was definitely two people, according to psychiatrists, a complete schizoid personality that had lost itself to the image of Beatle John Lennon, so much so that he began to take on the singer's powerful identity. "Chapman probably came to see himself as the real John Lennon," reported Dr. Robert Marvit of Honolulu. "He probably felt he could find his rightful place as John Lennon if he got rid of the imposter."

To Chapman, Lennon's retreat from the public eye, his rebuttal of the brash and wild image of his former days, represented a cowardly withdrawal from an anti-establishment posture. John Lennon was a sell-out, a drop-out, a person who no longer fought the good fight (whatever that fight might have been). He took to calling Lennon "a phony, a fake," and, in these remarks, he apparently began to substitute himself for the aggressive, take-charge John Lennon that was no more.

Four days after quitting his job Chapman went to J&S Enterprises, a shop only one block distant from Honolulu's main police station, and purchased a .38 caliber snub-nosed Charter Arms pistol, known as an "undercover special," used by detectives. Chapman was granted permission to buy the weapon since he had no police record at the time.

Next, Chapman borrowed $2,500 from a credit union and flew to New York on Saturday, December 6, 1980. He stayed at the West Side YMCA that night and the next day, checked into an

$82-a-night room in the Sheraton Centre Hotel. Then he began to keep his daily vigil for Lennon outside the Dakota, briefly talking to other Beatle fans who stood about for long periods in hopes of catching a glimpse of their idol.

On December 8 he approached amateur photographer Paul Goresh, who was hoping to catch a few candid shots of Lennon.

"Are you waiting for Lennon?" he asked Goresh.

"Yes," replied the photographer.

"I'm Mark," Chapman told Goresh, "I'm from Hawaii."

"Where did you get that accent?"

"I'm originally from Atlanta, Georgia."

"Where are you staying in New York?"

At that Chapman bristled. "Why do you want to know?"

Chapman walked away, then returned to say: "Sorry. I'm staying at the Sheraton. I've spent the last three days trying to see Lennon. I want him to autograph his new album."

Then Chapman's fallen idol appeared with Yoko Ono. He timidly approached the great entertainer and held out the album *Double Fantasy,* an ominously revealing title, given Chapman's strange aberrations. The star wrote on the album the words: "John Lennon, 1980," and walked off with Yoko to a waiting limousine. Chapman then turned to Goresh and said in amazement: "John Lennon signed my album. Nobody in Hawaii is going to believe me." Goresh also had a Lennon album, but it had not been signed.

Goresh stayed for two more hours, then decided to leave. Chapman asked him: "Why don't you wait until they come home? He should be back soon. Then you can get your album signed."

"I can get it another day."

"I'd wait," Chapman said. "You never know if you'll see him again."

"What do you mean? I always see him."

Chapman shrugged: "It's possible he could go to Spain or somewhere tonight, and you'll never get your album signed."

Goresh left. Mark Chapman stayed behind to wait. A few hours later John Lennon was dead.

While awaiting trial, Chapman was guarded day and night. It was thought that he would attempt to take his own life, but he remained a docile prisoner. At his initial hearing he pled not guilty. His lawyer, Jonathan Marks, announced that he would present an insanity defense.

Psychiatrists came forward to testify that Chapman certainly was insane, "a chronic paranoid schizophrenic," according to Dr. Daniel Schwartz, who had examined Chapman in his cell. Schwartz claimed that Chapman's own miserable life with all its shortcomings was so unacceptable to him that he "killed himself psychologically" when he murdered John Lennon. Further, to survive the thought that Lennon, his god, was a "phony," Chapman was compelled to make an "abrupt break" with the singer.

At a hearing on June 22, 1981, Chapman told a judge that he had spoken to God and that God had instructed him to confess to the murdering of John Lennon. As his shocked lawyer stood by, Chapman pleaded guilty to second-degree murder.

On July 24, 1981, Chapman was sentenced to serve twenty years to life in prison for the murder of the top Beatle. His only response was to stand up and read a passage from J. D. Salinger's novel *The Catcher in the Rye,* about confused adolescence. At the time, the killer was wearing a bulletproof vest under a blue pullover shirt.

"Thousands of little kids," droned Chapman as he read the passage concerning the book's hero, Holden Caulfield, and how he envisioned having to save hordes of children playing dangerously close to a cliff, "and nobody's around—nobody big, I mean —except me. And I'm standing on the edge of some crazy cliff. What I have to do, I have to catch everybody if they start to go over the cliff—I mean if they're running and they don't look where they're going I have to come out from somewhere and catch them. That's all I'd do all day. I'd just be the catcher in the rye."

The passage had great significance to Chapman, his lawyer later stated. For the convicted killer it meant that the world is phony and "children should be saved from adulthood."

These were the last words Mark David Chapman would utter to the world. Reported lawyer Jonathan Marks: "And he said he does not plan to talk anymore." With that Chapman left the court for Sing Sing.

John Lennon, however, goes on talking and singing in his albums, which continue to earn more than $10 million each year.

He left an estate to Yoko Ono and their son, Sean, along with his other son, Julian, valued at more than $235 million. He also left his family a promise that he would try to contact them, especially Yoko, from "the other side."

Said his son Julian recently: "I'm convinced Dad will contact Yoko because their minds were in tune . . . he said that if anything happened to him, he'd send a sign back to us that he was okay. He said he'd make a feather float down the room.

"Ever since his death I've been waiting for that sign. Every time I'm alone in a room, I find myself staring round, looking for the feather."

# 1979–1980

## CLAUS VON BULOW
### INJECTING
### THE BIG SLEEP

C laus von Bulow was a determined man. For most of his adult life he had maintained an envious life-style inside the cream of international high society, power, and wealth. He had enjoyed the company of glamorous, attractive women including his millionairess wife, Martha "Sunny" Crawford. He went on enjoying beautiful women after his marriage, and when Sunny withdrew into her old-money memories and decided to abstain from sex, Claus took a mistress and a call girl. The mistress demanded marriage and gave Claus a deadline. At the end of that deadline was murder.

For Claus Cecil von Bulow such an act could be seen as an expedient necessary to preserve his lovelife and his bank account. His wife Sunny had made provisions in her will to leave him approximately $14 million out of her $75 million estate upon her death, a death the cunning von Bulow would conveniently bring about through his wife's addiction to sweets, or so he thought. The plan von Bulow put into action in late 1979 was clever, even diabolical, but perfectly in keeping with a man who had lived a successful life through his wits, a man who took a great pride in his ability to outthink others.

Born in 1926 in Denmark (his original name was Borberg) of a prestigious German family of aristocrats, Claus was sent away as a child to a boarding school in Switzerland, returning to Denmark in 1937. The eleven-year-old was surrounded by wealth and power that made an indelible impression upon him. His grandfather, Fritz von Bulow, was Denmark's minister of justice and controlled the country's treasury. It was from this stern Victorian that Claus came early to appreciate the value and power of money.

In 1942, two years after the Nazis had invaded Denmark, Claus escaped to England, where his mother was living. His father, Svend, stayed behind and was later tried for collaborating with the enemy but was acquitted. Claus stayed in England to study law at Cambridge, and following the war he attended the Sorbonne. He became a student of languages and mastered many, especially French, German, and English. Returning to England, Claus donned a bowler hat and went to work as a junior executive at London's Hambro Bank before practicing as a barrister—a trial lawyer—for Lord Hailsham.

As his fortunes grew through well-connected clients, von Bulow lavished a luxurious bachelorhood upon himself, moving into a swanky apartment in Belgrave Square and several times a week throwing parties where champagne flowed and beautiful women adorned his bedchamber. London's elite invited Claus into their manor homes, and he was soon a fixture of high society. His standing in the legal profession, coupled with his high office contacts, moved billionaire businessman J. Paul Getty to solicit his services in 1959. Getty insisted that von Bulow give up the law and devote his considerable energies to his empire, which Claus did. Most believed that it was von Bulow's passion for money that propelled him into Getty's megabucks world, and most were correct.

It was von Bulow's job as chief executive assistant to the tycoon to fly about the world putting together business deals for the Getty interests. (Getty himself refused to fly.) Claus, almost on a weekly basis, jetted to Saudi Arabia and Denmark, creating mergers, buying out companies, establishing refineries for Getty Oil. The diplomatic von Bulow became so important to Getty that he was brought into the tycoon's inner circle, and all expected that he would some day take over as the chief executive of Getty's vast empire. There was nothing Claus would not do for his chief, including keeping the peace between the billionaire and his sons, which he did and did often.

On one of his jaunts for Getty in 1960, Claus was introduced to Martha "Sunny" Crawford von Auersperg, a lithe, attractive blonde who was worth a great fortune. At the time, she was married to an impoverished Austrian prince, Alfred von Auersperg. Claus met her again in 1964 at a dinner party and once more in 1965. By then she had left her husband, and Claus

courted her vigorously for almost a year. They were married on
June 6, 1966.

Von Bulow was at first ebullient about his bride, telling one
and all that "I've finally found the right girl." What he had really
found was a fortune of old money. Sunny Crawford had known
nothing but wealth and luxury all her life. Born in 1932, Sunny
was the only child of George Crawford, chairman of the board of
Columbia Gas and Electric Company. The utilities czar died when
she was only three, and Sunny was left in the care of her grandmother, Mrs. Martha Warmack, and her mother, Annie-Laurie,
who later married Russell Aitken.

Like most rich girls of her class, Sunny attended very private
schools, such as New York's Chapin School and St. Timothy's in
Maryland. The tall, sweet blonde made her debut into high society in 1951 and embarked on the traditional European grand tour
a few years later.

Sunny, in spite of her breathtaking fresh-as-daisies beauty,
was a shy, almost retiring young woman who fell easily in awe
of European aristocrats. The continental manners of a particularly
handsome royal young man, Prince Alfred von Auersperg, utterly
captivated her. He was an Austrian blueblood, but his family was
poor. He worked as a tennis instructor in an Alpine resort. They
were married in 1957 and their union produced two children,
Alexander and Annie-Laurie, called Ala.

By the early 1960s Sunny was tiring of polished European
manners and pauperous royalty. She had met Claus von Bulow
several times before her divorce and began to see him after her
marriage ended. Von Bulow, unlike von Auersperg, was a successful man in his own right as well as having come from a
distinguished European family. And he was every inch the figure
of authority, self-assurance, and distant worldliness. He exuded
an aura of wealth in keeping with Sunny's ideas of the upper
class.

Physically, Claus was a towering man of six feet four inches
with a large head and thinning hair, a long, thin nose, and a
resolute jaw jutting beneath thin tight lips. He was all shoulders
and chest, a man who stood ramrod stiff in tailor-made double-
breasted suits. He was the perfect traveling companion.

Oddly enough, the successful von Bulow quit Getty to become
Sunny's full-time escort following their marriage in 1966. He told

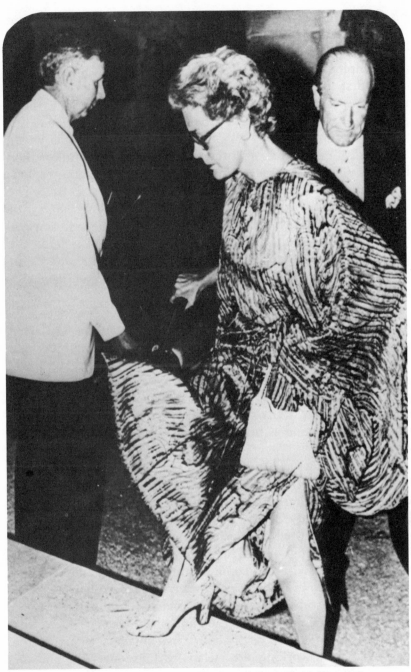

*The beautiful heiress Martha "Sunny" von Bulow with her husband Claus in the background at right in 1979, just before Sunny's first mysterious coma. (Wide World)*

his friends that his wife insisted he devote all his time to her, but it was later obvious that the heiress grew more and more displeased with her loafing spouse and encouraged him to find high-level employment.

The first ten years of the von Bulow marriage were tranquil, sometimes spectacularly joyous. The couple had a child, Cosima, now fifteen, and spent most of their time in their luxurious Fifth Avenue co-op in New York, a fabulous suite of rooms where servants catered to their slightest whims. Sunny von Bulow then began to flex the muscles of her millions, purchasing a resplendent mansion in Newport—Clarendon Court—for a fortune. The square, towering Victorian mansion had been built in the days of Diamond Jim Brady and squatted on a huge beach acreage. (Sunny took one look at her new ocean view and ordered the grounds lowered to improve the watery vista.) Clarendon Court had the added glamour of being the site where the film *High Society* was made in 1956.

Sunny's new extravagance included expensive improvements on the Newport mansion, redecorating its vast rooms, enlarging its pool and gardens. Everywhere were the priceless antiques and curios the von Bulows collected. Sunny and Claus began to give parties, magnificent affairs catered by hosts of servants and complemented by orchestras, where guests strolled through the luxury of Clarendon Court sipping champagne as if the heyday of the Vanderbilts and Whitneys had somehow miraculously returned.

The von Bulows at Newport were surrounded by the cream of East Coast high society and enjoyed their roles as arbiters of taste. Only a short distance away was Hammersmith Farm where Jacqueline Kennedy Onassis had been raised and was later married. But all was not utter bliss in this sumptuous paradise. Sometime in 1979, Sunny and Claus began to drift apart. Claus later claimed that his wife had come to him saying that she was "no longer interested in having sex." Sunny's perspective was different, according to her devoted maid, Maria Schrallhammer, who had been with Sunny since the time she was married to von Auersperg. Maria later testified that her mistress thought "the marriage wasn't working out." Claus was very nervous, and she thought that he might be having a nervous breakdown.

As court records later revealed, Claus was not having a nervous

*The Von Bulow estate at Newport, Rhode Island, Clarendon Court. (Wide World)*

breakdown but had simply increased his sexual activity. He spent most of his time in 1979 at his private New York club, the Knickerbocker. He began seeing Alexandra Isles, a thirty-three-year-old socialite-actress whose father had been von Bulow's friend in Denmark and who had been a regular on the TV soap opera *Dark Shadows*. Mrs. Isles was divorced and had a young son. Further, Claus regularly visited a New York prostitute, forty-three-year-old Leslie Baxter. If von Bulow was suffering from a case of the jitters, it had to do with physical exhaustion, not psychological apprehensions.

Von Bulow began complaining to Sunny's grown children, Ala and Alex, that their mother was making him feel like a cheap gigolo and that not only was he losing the respect of his onetime business associates but neighbors in Newport were becoming outwardly hostile toward him, thinking that he was nothing more than a parasite sponging from his wife.

Claus kept active, however, by backing Broadway plays, one of which was *Deathtrap*, which proved to be enormously successful and was later sold to Warner Bros. for $1.5 million, plus a percentage of the gross. Ironically, the play profiled a man and wife involved in a murder plot.

Meanwhile, von Bulow pursued his romance with Alexandra Isles, talking to her by phone every other night and dining with her two or three nights a week. He sent her books and flowers. The actress later said that she understood the von Bulow marriage was an unhappy one, that "Claus was energetic and outgoing and his wife was the private person."

More and more von Bulow talked of leaving Sunny, who he claimed had become a hopeless recluse, withdrawing from the world to spend her time reading books and eating sweets. He asked the family physician, Dr. Richard Stock, whether Sunny could stand the trauma a divorce might bring. There was an air of desperation about Claus von Bulow as he continued to carp about his unhappy situation. By late 1979 he had come to a decision.

Alexandra Isles was later to state that she had given Claus a deadline for marrying her. The deadline was before the end of 1979. During the Christmas season, as was their habit, the von Bulows moved to Clarendon Court in Newport. On December 26 the von Bulows and their children enjoyed some of Sunny's homemade eggnog, a rich drink that suited Sunny's sweet tooth. The heiress's penchant for sweets had increased over the years, and she consumed great amounts of ice cream topped with a homemade caramel sauce prepared by her cook, Irene Silvia. There were always several quarts of this sauce on hand. In addition, Sunny drank ice cream sodas like water. All of this caused her to gain many unwanted pounds.

Sunny had several sodas and dishes of ice cream with caramel topping at dinner on December 26 before retiring to her bedroom. Her butler, Robert L. Biastre, brought her several glasses of eggnog, and she asked for a large bottle of ginger ale before going to sleep. Sunny's confidante and maid, Maria, entered her bedroom to see her "lying on her bed . . . I thought she was asleep." Von Bulow was in the bedroom and asked Maria to leave.

The next morning von Bulow went to Maria and told her not to disturb Sunny, that she was still asleep. Claus later claimed that his wife had had the flu for two days and that the large intake of eggnog had not helped her. Maria, who had long thought that von Bulow's actions were suspicious, ignored his instructions and

*Soap-opera actress Alexandra Isles, Claus's lover, testifying at his murder trial. (Wide World)*

went into her mistress's bedroom. Sunny was unconscious and von Bulow was lying next to her. Maria tried to wake Sunny but found it impossible.

"She's unconscious," Maria told Claus. "You should call a doctor."

"No," von Bulow said. "She's sleeping."

Maria again tried to wake Sunny, but nothing could rouse the heiress. Maria grabbed her hand, saying loudly: "Madam, wake up!" There was no response.

"She's sleeping," Claus repeated. "We haven't slept for two nights and we're tired."

Maria left the room but returned again to find her mistress still unconscious. Again von Bulow shrugged off his wife's condition, insisting that she was sleeping. This scene was repeated half a dozen more times throughout the morning, with Maria begging Claus to call a doctor. Von Bulow adamantly refused to call anyone, insisting that his wife "needed the rest."

Von Bulow finally succumbed to the maid's persistence and called Dr. Janis Gailitis of Newport Hospital. Maria later claimed that Claus distorted the reasons for her mistress's deep sleep, telling the doctor that "my wife has an alcohol problem, and the night before was one of those nights. I'm not really concerned about it. I'll watch her carefully and if this gets worse, I'll call you back."

Responded Dr. Gailitis: "Well, it's all right, you know, given the two nights of insomnia. If there's any change, call me back."

Alexander returned from a tennis match at about 4:30 P.M. and was immediately met by the frantic maid, who told him that "something was very wrong" with his mother. "I went directly to my mother's room," Alex later told police, "and found that she was lying on her bed. I shook her, tried to arouse her, and there was no response at all."

At this point, according to Alex, Claus appeared and said to him: "What should I do?"

"Call the doctor," insisted Alex.

Von Bulow went to the phone and summoned Dr. Gailitis. Waiting for the physician to arrive, Claus examined his wife and noticed that "suddenly her breathing changed from a normal deep sleep, quiet, no snoring, just normal sleep—and suddenly there was a kind of rattle."

Maria picked up her mistress, holding her by the shoulders. "She couldn't breathe anymore . . . and I was really afraid that she would die before the doctor arrived."

Dr. Gailitis arrived to find Sunny comatose. She stopped breathing as he began his examination. Gailitis gave her mouth-to-mouth resuscitation and pressed her chest to revive her. The physician later told police that he was certain that Sunny von Bulow was only "ten to fifteen minutes from death" by the time he arrived. The heiress was promptly taken by ambulance to Newport Hospital, where physicians pondered the puzzle of her coma. Seeing that her blood sugar was extremely low, they pumped glucose into her, but her blood sugar fell even lower. Somehow the heiress slowly recovered. Gailitis and other doctors originally thought that the woman was suffering from hypoglycemia. Later, Gailitis, thinking over what Claus had told him on the phone, blamed alcohol for the coma. Liquor and enormous amounts of barbiturates, Claus had said, had caused his wife to fall into her deep sleep.

Gailitis later told investigators: "I continued to believe this until several weeks later when I received the transcripts of the report from Newport Hospital indicating that the blood alcohol level on admission was zero and that Mrs. von Bulow had not taken any alcohol." Tests to determine barbiturates in the heiress's system also proved negative.

Before her release Sunny firmly insisted to doctors that she never overindulged in drugs or alcohol, but thanks to von Bulow's earlier statements, she was not believed. All through 1980 the heiress's condition seemed to worsen. She appeared dazed and weak to her family and servants and seemed lethargic to doctors who examined her in April and June 1980, when she underwent tests at New York's Columbia-Presbyterian Hospital. It was determined that Sunny had reactive hypoglycemia, low blood sugar, but most physicians agreed that such a condition would not have produced the coma Mrs. von Bulow suffered in 1979. Dr. Phillip Felig of Yale New Haven Hospital, an expert in the field, would later testify that "people with hypoglycemia may have symptoms in the form of weakness or irritability or fatigue, but they do not go into comas."

Claus went on telling friends how sad it was that his wife overindulged in alcohol and drugs, informing one friend that "one feels so disloyal . . . my wife was a very private and rather nervous person." Mrs. Aitken, Sunny's mother, later had a different story to tell, one wherein she portrayed her daughter as "a very calm woman. She wasn't the type who leaned on drugs in any way, shape or form." Mrs. Aitken added that "before 1979 she was extremely healthy except for a sinus condition that gave her headaches. She was very shy, but she took exercise classes every day. She was very strong physically."

By mid-1980 Sunny was no longer strong; in fact, she could not remember anything that happened just before her coma. She was suffering from retrograde amnesia and could recall nothing of events leading up to her comatose, near-death state. Her maid Maria began to think that Claus not only was negligent in his care of Sunny but might have caused her illness. Maria's early anxieties were summed up in a letter to a friend in which she wrote: "Sometimes I am not feeling well thinking what is going to happen next. Mrs. trusts her husband blindly and is totally dependent. He of course has a girlfriend. Their whole life has changed. No more parties and they don't go out either. She gained a lot of weight and is very unhappy about it."

Maria's relationship with von Bulow became strained. When Sunny got sick one day, Maria practically ordered Claus to call a doctor. Von Bulow exploded, shouting at her: "Either you get out of here or I do!"

The maid retreated, defiantly answering: "Well, maybe you forgot December the twenty-seventh [of 1979], but I didn't." Maria, alarmed over Sunny's increasing spells, began to go through Claus's things, finding in his closet a small leather black bag. Inside of this she discovered syringes and drugs. She took three samples of the drugs—a pill, a vial of liquid, and some paste —giving these to Ala, who in turn took them to Dr. Stock. The physician reported that all the samples were forms of Valium, although he was perplexed after studying the paste, reporting that no pharmacy would prepare the drug in such form.

Maria continued to keep an eye on von Bulow's black bag and regularly inspected its contents. On Thanksgiving, 1980, Maria found a small bottle labeled "insulin." She showed the bottle to Alexander, asking "What for insulin?" He didn't know the reason for the insulin, which Maria promptly returned to the black bag but which was later made shockingly evident.

So hostile did Sunny's maid of twenty-three years become toward Claus that, on December 8, 1980, she wrote a friend: "Bulow and I are at daggers' points already." When the family prepared to go to Newport for the 1980 Christmas season on December 19, Maria again noted that Claus was taking his little black bag. She even carried the bag for Claus to the elevator in the Fifth Avenue home, checking its contents and finding a needle and a bottle labeled "insulin." Maria asked Sunny if she could accompany the family. Von Bulow curtly told her: "No, you cannot go to Newport. You are too tired."

Sunny, Claus, and Cosima left for Newport and were joined by Alex, who traveled from Providence where he was a student at Brown University. Sunny was not in top physical condition. Only three weeks earlier, on December 1, 1980, Claus reportedly found her on the bathroom floor of their Fifth Avenue apartment and had called an ambulance. She was rushed to a hospital, where she was treated for "aspirin poisoning." (Von Bulow's defense attorney would later make much of this event, point out that Claus, at the time, had every opportunity to allow his wife to die but instead called for help.)

On December 20, following an early dinner, the von Bulows went to a movie. Upon returning home, Sunny sat in the library talking to Alex as she sipped a rich soda. "Her speech started to grow weaker," Alexander later remembered. She slurred her words and the soda glass slipped from her hand. Claus appeared, bringing his wife some hot chicken soup. Sunny then became so weak that Alexander had to carry his mother to bed.

Claus was up early the next morning. He took a walk along the beach and later made two phone calls, both to Alexandra Isles. About 11 A.M. Claus said over breakfast that he was surprised Sunny had not risen. He said he would check on his wife. Von Bulow later insisted that he returned to the dining room within a minute or two. Alexander stated that von Bulow did not return for at least *fifteen* minutes, and when he did, it was to motion Alex into Sunny's bedroom. The heiress was unconscious on the floor of her bathroom. It was 1979 all over again, with Sunny being rushed to the hospital; but this time doctors could not pull her out of her coma, one that persists to this writing as Sunny lies in a bed at Columbia-Presbyterian Hospital.

Physicians examining the heiress found that she had low blood sugar and an alarmingly high insulin count. Again they were baffled. Dr. Fred Plum, a specialist in coma, was consulted, and he announced that Sunny von Bulow would never recover, although she might go on living for years if properly cared for. Such a prospect was unthinkable to Claus, who told Dr. Stock that, for mercy's sake, his wife, who had been turned into a "vegetable," should be allowed to die. Said Stock later: "He knew his wife would not want to be sustained in a helpless coma and that in England they know how to deal with this kind of situation."

Von Bulow also suggested to both Alex and Ala that their mother be removed from her life-support systems. Claus was firm in his idea, too firm, Sunny's adult children thought. They had no intention, however, of pulling the plug on their mother. Instead they took their suspicions about their stepfather to Richard Kuh, a former Manhattan state's attorney. Kuh then hired Edwin Lambert, a private detective, to investigate von Bulow.

On January 23, 1981, Lambert and Alex went to Clarendon Court. There, in Claus's closet, they found the black bag Maria Schrallhammer had inspected several times. Inside was a used syringe, and this the sleuths took to be analyzed. Found on the needle were traces of Diazepam, Amobarbital, and insulin, the latter already having been determined as the cause of Sunny's deep sleep.

The case was turned over to the Rhode Island State Police, and officers embarked on a six-month investigation into the affairs of Claus von Bulow. Claus during this period was enjoying the company of Alexandra Isles, first at the exclusive Lyford Cay Club in Nassau in the Bahamas, with Mrs. Isles's son, staying in a two-bedroom cottage and incurring $3,500 in expenses, and later in Florida, where Cosima joined her father and Alexandra and her son. The bills for these chic vacations were discovered by the ever-ferreting maid, Maria, and turned over to Alexander, who gave them to investigators.

Rhode Island State Police officers arrived at Clarendon Court to question von Bulow on April 21, 1981. The next day Maria Schrallhammer quit her job, an act that did not upset Claus one bit. All was calm until July 6, when Claus was indicted on two counts of assault with attempt to murder. He was released on a $100,000 bond, and his Danish passport was revoked.

The von Bulow trial in Newport, beyond the vast fortune involved, was all the more sensational in that it was televised for millions of viewers, who gaped as the secret lives of high society figures were revealed. Von Bulow, through his lawyer, main-

*Claus hears his guilty verdict with his usual emotionless air on March 16, 1982. (UPI)*

tained from the beginning that Sunny was simply a spoiled, neurotic, and self-destructive woman, one who habitually overdosed herself with barbiturates, sweets, and alcohol.

New York lawyer Herald Price Fahringer, who conducted von Bulow's defense, depicted the heiress as an irresponsible rich woman who "took large amounts of aspirin, barbiturates and tranquilizers. In later years she shunned contact with people outside the family and became reclusive."

A bevy of witnesses, including Alexander, Maria Schrallhammer, and even Alexandra Isles, took the stand to describe the actions of Claus von Bulow. The defendant himself never took the stand. His appearance in court was one of aloofness, almost uninterest. He did not look at those testifying against him and only glanced at Alexandra Isles as she spoke haltingly of her relationship with him. At the time she was asked if she was in love with von Bulow, the actress-socialite paused dramatically, then slowly said "I don't know."

Irrespective of the dismal portrait the defense drew of Sunny von Bulow, Fahringer could not escape the hard medical fact that the heiress's permanent coma had undoubtedly been caused by insulin, and not the amount of insulin normally produced by the human body. Questions were raised by reporters covering the trial concerning the possibility of Sunny administering the insulin to herself, abusing herself for some perverted reason or another, or possibly attempting to commit suicide. Yet the fact that no notes were left by her and that no needles were found seemed to rule out suicide attempts.

The focus of the prosecution narrowed down to Claus von Bulow. He owned the little black bag, and it was inside this bag that the insulin and insulin-coated needles and syringes were found. The insulin, several physicians testified, had to have been injected. Dr. H. Harris Funkenstein, a Boston neurologist who had treated Sunny from the beginning of her last coma, stated that the "only viable cause" of her condition was the administration of insulin "by either intramuscular or intravenous routes." Only insulin injections could have been responsible for Sunny's deathlike sleep, echoed Dr. George Cahill of the Harvard Medical School. Dr. Gerhard Meier testified that he had found "an incredibly high insulin level" in Sunny's system after she arrived in a coma at the Newport Hospital on December 21, 1980.

These witnesses, more than any other, undoubtedly convinced a jury of seven men and five women that von Bulow was guilty of attempting to murder his wife. The presence of insulin in Sunny's body and inside von Bulow's little black bag, which he never bothered to explain, sealed the dapper socialite's fate. He was found guilty on March 16, 1982, but remained free on bond, pending his sentencing.

The jury's decision seemed to surprise the packed courtroom. There were noticeable gasps from spectators after the foreman read the verdict. Each jury member was twice polled separately. As he heard the word "guilty" repeated twenty-four times by the jury members, not a flicker of emotion showed on the immobile face of Claus von Bulow.

The prosecutor, Stephen Famiglietti, turned to his boss, Susan McGuiri, Deputy Attorney General of Rhode Island, and said:

"My God, we've done it." To the press an elated Famiglietti later said: "It's not a whodunit anymore."

Oddly enough, spectators had taken the stoic von Bulow's side throughout most of the trial. Famiglietti had been repeatedly booed when entering the courtroom, and when von Bulow left the courtroom, a throng of people outside applauded and cheered him, shouting: "Free Claus! Free Claus!"

As Famiglietti stepped outside and began to descend the courthouse stairs, members in the crowd chanted: "Not guilty! Not guilty!" He was booed and hissed. The prosecutor gave the crowd a short wave and smiled.

# BIBLIOGRAPHY

The research for this book was performed in libraries and archives throughout the United States, in addition to national correspondence and interviews. Scores of newspapers and periodicals were also consulted; specific dates for newspapers were too numerous to cite herein. Some of the most helpful published sources follow.

## Books

Allen, Frederick Lewis. *Only Yesterday.* New York: Harper & Brothers, 1931.

————. *Since Yesterday.* New York: Harper & Brothers, 1940.

Allsop, Kenneth. *The Bootleggers.* London: Hutchinson, 1961.

Amory, Cleveland. *Who Killed Society?* New York: Harper & Brothers, 1960.

Asbury, Herbert. *Sucker's Progress.* New York: Dodd, Mead, 1938.

————. *Gem of the Prairie.* New York: Alfred A. Knopf, 1940.

Atwell, Benjamin H. *The Great Harry Thaw Case.* Chicago: Laird & Lee, 1907.

Bacon, James. *Hollywood Is a Four-Letter Town.* New York: Avon Books, 1977.

Barnes, David. *The Metropolitan Police.* New York: Baker & Godwin, 1863.

Bell, Arthur. *King's Don't Mean a Thing.* New York: William Morrow, 1978.

Berger, Meyer. *The Eighty Million.* New York: Simon & Schuster, 1942.

Bierstadt, Edward Hale. *Curious Trials & Criminal Cases.* Garden City, N.Y.: Garden City Publishing, 1928.

Boettiger, John. *Jake Lingle.* New York: E. P. Dutton, 1931.

Bolitho, William. *Murder for Profit.* London: Jonathan Cape, 1926.

Bontham, Alan. *Sex Crimes and Sex Criminals.* New York: Wisdom House, 1961.

Boucher, Anthony (ed.). *The Quality of Murder.* New York: E. P. Dutton, 1962.

Brearley, H. C. *Homicide in the United States.* Chapel Hill: University of North Carolina Press, 1932.

Bright, John. *Hizzoner Big Bill Thompson.* New York: J. Cape & H. Smith, 1930.

Burns, Walter Noble. *The One-Way Ride.* Garden City, N.Y.: Doubleday, Doran, 1931.

Busch, Francis X. *Prisoners at the Bar.* Indianapolis: Bobbs-Merrill, 1952.

Butterfield, Roger. *The American Past.* New York: Simon & Schuster, 1947.

Casey, Robert J. *Chicago Medium Rare.* Indianapolis: Bobbs-Merrill, 1932.

Cassity, J. H. *The Quality of Murder.* New York: The Julian Press, 1958.

Chafetz, Henry. *Play the Devil.* New York: Clarkson N. Potter, 1960.

Chapin, Charles. *Charles Chapin's Story.* New York: G. P. Putnam's, 1920.

Chenery, William L. *So It Seemed.* New York: Harcourt Brace, 1952.

Churchill, Allen. *A Pictorial History of American Crime.* New York: Holt, Rinehart & Winston, 1964.

Clarke, Donald Henderson. *In the Reign of Rothstein.* New York: The Vanguard Press, 1929.

Clinton, Henry Lauren. *Celebrated Trials.* New York: Harper & Brothers, 1896.

Cohen, Lewis H. *Murder, Madness and the Law.* New York: World, 1952.

Collins, Ted (ed.). *New York Murders.* New York: Duell, Sloan and Pearce, 1944.

Connable, Alfred, and Silberfarb, Edward. *Tigers of Tammany.* New York: Holt, Rinehart & Winston, 1967.

Corder, Eric (ed.). *Murder My Love.* Chicago: The Playboy Press, 1973.

Crane, Milton (ed.). *Sins of New York.* New York: Boni & Gaer, Inc. 1947.

Crouse, Russel. *Murder Won't Out.* Garden City, N.Y.: Doubleday, Doran, 1932.

De Ford, Miriam Allen. *Murderers Sane & Mad.* New York: Abelard-Schuman, 1965.

De Rham, Edith. *How Could She Do That?* New York: Clarkson N. Potter, 1969.

Dobyns, Fletcher. *The Underworld of American Politics.* New York: Fletcher Dobyns, 1932.

Dorman, Michael. *King of the Courtroom: Percy Foreman for the Defense.* New York: Delacorte Press, 1969.

Douthwaite, L. C. *Mass Murder.* New York: Holt, 1929.

Duffy, Clinton T. *The San Quentin Story: As told to Dean Jennings.* Garden City, N.Y.: Doubleday, 1950.

————, with Hirshberg, Al. *88 Men and Two Women.* Garden City, N.Y.: Doubleday, 1962.

Duke, Thomas S. *Celebrated Criminal Cases of America.* San Francisco: James H. Barry Co., 1910.

Emery, J. Gladstone. *Court of the Damned.* New York: Comet Press, 1959.

Erbstein, Charles, E. *The Show-Up: Stories Before the Bar.* Chicago: Pascal Covici, 1926.

Farley, Philip. *Criminals of America.* New York: Philip Farley, 1876.

Farr, Finis. *Chicago.* New Rochelle, N.Y.: Arlington House, 1973.

Fenichel, Otto. *The Psychoanalytic Theory of Neurosis.* New York: W. W. Norton, 1945.

Fowler, Gene. *The Great Mouthpiece.* New York: Covici-Friede, 1931.

————. *Skyline.* New York: Macmillan Books, 1962.

Furneaux, Rupert. *The Medical Murderer.* London: Elek, 1957.

Geisler, Jerry (as told to Pete Martin). *The Jerry Geisler Story.* New York: Simon and Schuster, 1960.

Gilbert, Paul Thomas, and Bryson, Charles Lee. *Chicago and Its Makers.* Chicago: University of Chicago Press, 1929.

Hamer, Alvin C. (ed.). *Detroit Murders.* New York: Duell, Sloan and Pearce, 1948.

Harrison, Carter H. *Stormy Years.* Indianapolis: Bobbs-Merrill, 1935.

Hirsch, Phil (ed.). *Hollywood Uncensored.* New York: Pyramid Books, 1965.

Holmes, Paul. *The Candy Murder Case.* New York: Bantam, 1966.

House, Brant (ed.). *Crimes That Shocked America.* New York: Ace Books, 1961.

Houts, Marshall. *They Asked for Death.* New York: Cowles, 1970.

Hynd, Alan. *Murder, Mayhem and Mystery.* New York: A. S. Barnes, 1958.

Irving, H. B. *A Book of Remarkable Criminals.* New York: George H. Doran Company, 1918.

Jackson, Joseph Henry (ed.). *The Portable Murder Book.* New York: Viking Press, 1945.

Jesse, F. Tennyson. *Murder and Its Motives.* New York: Alfred A. Knopf, 1924.

Johnston, Alva. *The Legendary Mizners.* New York: Farrar, Straus & Young, 1953.

Josephson, Matthew. *The Robber Barons.* New York: Harcourt Brace, 1934.

Juergens, George. *Joseph Pulitzer and the New York World.* Princeton, N.J.: Princeton University Press, 1966.

Kahn, E. J., Jr. *The World of Swope.* New York: Simon & Schuster, 1965.

Katcher, Leo. *The Big Bankroll.* New York: Harper & Brothers, 1958.

Kingston, Charles. *Remarkable Rogues.* New York: John Lane, 1921.

Kobler, John. *Some Like It Gory.* New York: Dodd, Mead, 1940.

Langford, Gerald. *The Murder of Stanford White.* Indianapolis: Bobbs-Merrill, 1962.

Laurence, John A. *Extraordinary Crimes.* London: Sampson, Low, 1931.

Lawes, Lewis E. 20,000 Years in Sing Sing. New York: The New Home Library, 1932.

Lawson, John D. *American State Trials.* St. Louis: F. H. Thomas Law Book Co., 1914.

Lewis, Alfred Henry. *Nation-Famous New York Murders.* Chicago: M. A. Donohue & Co., 1912.

Lewis, Lloyd and Smith, Henry Justin. *Chicago: The History of Its Reputation.* New York: Harcourt Brace, 1929.

Logan, Guy B. H. *Rope, Knife and Chair.* London: S. Paul & Co., 1930.

Lord, Walter. *The Good Years.* New York: Harper & Brothers, 1960.

Lunde, Donald T. *Murder and Madness.* San Francisco: The Portable Stanford Series, 1976.

Lustgarten, Edgar. *The Murder and the Trial*. New York: Charles Scribner's Sons, 1958.

Lyle, John H. *The Dry and Lawless Years*. Englewood Cliffs, N.J.: Prentice-Hall, 1960.

Lynch, Denis Tilden. *Criminals and Politicians*. New York: Macmillan, 1932.

McComas, J. Francis. *The Graveside Companion*. New York: Obolensky, 1962.

McConaughy, John. *From Caine to Capone*. New York: Brentano's, 1931.

MacDonald, John M. *The Murderer and His Victim*. Springfield, Ill.: Charles C. Thomas, 1961.

Mackenzie, Frederic A. *Twentieth Century Crimes*. Boston: Little, Brown, 1927.

———. *The Trial of Harry Thaw*. London: Geoffrey Bles, 1928.

McPhaul, John J. *Johnny Torrio*. New Rochelle, N.Y.: Arlington House, 1970.

Merriam, Charles E. *Chicago*. Chicago: University of Chicago Press, 1929.

Merz, Charles. *The Dry Decade*. New York: Doubleday, Doran, 1931.

Millar, Mara. *Hail to Yesterday*. New York: Farrar & Rinehart, 1941.

Mills, James. *The Prosecutor*. New York: Pocket Books, 1970.

Minot, G. E. *Murder Will Out*. Boston: Marshall Jones, 1928.

Mizner, Addison. *The Many Mizners*. New York: Sears Publishing Co., 1932.

Myers, Gustavus. *History of the Great American Fortunes*. New York: Modern Library, 1936.

Nash, Jay Robert. *Bloodletters and Badmen: A Narrative Encyclopedia of American Criminals from the Pilgrims to the Present*. New York: M. Evans, 1973.

———. *Hustlers and Con Men*. New York: M. Evans, 1976.

———. *Murder, America*. New York: Simon & Schuster, 1980.

———. *Look for the Woman*. New York: M. Evans, 1981.

———. *People to See*. Piscataway, N.J.: New Century, 1981.

Nash, Jay Robert (ed.). *Almanac of World Crime*. New York: Doubleday, 1981.

Neustatter, W. L. *The Mind of the Murderer*. London: Johnson, 1957.

Noble, John Wesley, and Averuch, Bernard. *Never Plead Guilty*. New York: Farrar, Straus & Cudahy, 1955.

Nuetzel, Charles. *Whodunit? Hollywood Style*. Beverly Hills: Book Company of America, 1965.

O'Brien, Frank M. *Murder Mysteries of New York*. New York: W. F. Payson, 1932.

O'Connor, Richard. *Courtroom Warrior*. Boston: Little, Brown, 1963.

Orth, Samuel P. *The Boss and the Machine*. New Haven, Conn.: Yale University Press, 1920.

O'Sullivan, F. Dalton. *Crime Detection*. Chicago: F. Dalton O'Sullivan, 1928.

Owen, Collinson. *King Crime.* New York: Holt, 1932.

Pasley, Fred D. *Al Capone.* Garden City, N.Y.: Garden City Publishing Company, 1930.

Pearson, Edmund L. *Studies in Murder.* New York: Macmillan, 1924.

———. *Murder at Smutty Nose.* Garden City, N.Y.: Doubleday, 1927.

———. *Five Murders.* Garden City, N.Y.: Doubleday, 1928.

———. *More Studies in Murder.* New York: H. Smith & R. Haas, 1936.

Pierce, Bessie Louise. *As Others See Chicago.* Chicago: University of Chicago Press, 1932.

Pinkerton, Matthew W. *Murder in All Ages.* Chicago: A. E. Pinkerton & Co., 1898.

Pollack, O. *The Criminality of Women.* Philadelphia: University of Pennsylvania Press, 1950.

Porges, Irwin. *The Violent Americans.* Derby, Conn.: Monarch Books, 1963.

Porter, Garnett Clay. *Strange and Mysterious Crimes.* New York: MacFadden, 1929.

Quimby, Ione. *Murder for Love.* New York: Covici, 1931.

Quinn, John Philip. *Fools of Fortune.* Chicago: W. B. Conkey, 1890.

Radin, Edward D. *Crimes of Passion.* New York: Putnam's, 1953.

Rammelkamp, Julian S. *Pulitzer's Post-Dispatch 1878–1883.* Princeton, N.J.: Princeton University Press, 1967.

Reckless, Walter. *Vice in Chicago.* Chicago: University of Chicago Press, 1933.

*Remarkable Trials of all Countries.* New York: S. S. Peloubet & Co., 1882.

Reynolds, Ruth. *Murder 'Round the World.* New York: Justice Books, 1953.

Rodell, Marie F. (ed.). *New York Murders.* New York: Duell, Sloan and Pearce, 1944.

Ross, Robert. *The Trial of Al Capone.* Chicago: Robert Ross, 1933.

Roughead, William. *Malice Domestic.* New York: Doubleday, Doran, 1929.

Rowan, David. *Famous American Crimes.* London: Frederick Muller, 1957.

Runyon, Damon. *Trials and Other Tribulations.* Philadelphia: Lippincott, 1926.

Samuels, Charles. *The Girl in the Red Velvet Swing.* New York: Fawcett, 1953.

———. *Death Was the Bridegroom.* New York: Fawcett, 1955.

Sandoe, James (ed.). *Murder, Plain and Fanciful.* New York: Sheridan, 1948.

Sann, Paul. *The Lawless Decade.* New York: Crown, 1957.

Seagle, William. *Acquitted of Murder.* Chicago: Henry Regnery, 1958.

Sinclair, Andrew. *Era of Excess.* New York: Harper & Row, 1964.

Smith, Edward Henry. *Famous American Poison Mysteries.* New York: Dial Press, 1927.

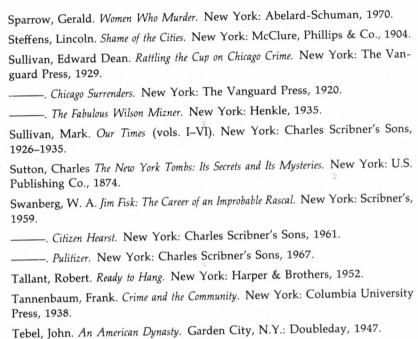

Sparrow, Gerald. *Women Who Murder.* New York: Abelard-Schuman, 1970.

Steffens, Lincoln. *Shame of the Cities.* New York: McClure, Phillips & Co., 1904.

Sullivan, Edward Dean. *Rattling the Cup on Chicago Crime.* New York: The Vanguard Press, 1929.

———. *Chicago Surrenders.* New York: The Vanguard Press, 1920.

———. *The Fabulous Wilson Mizner.* New York: Henkle, 1935.

Sullivan, Mark. *Our Times* (vols. I–VI). New York: Charles Scribner's Sons, 1926–1935.

Sutton, Charles *The New York Tombs: Its Secrets and Its Mysteries.* New York: U.S. Publishing Co., 1874.

Swanberg, W. A. *Jim Fisk: The Career of an Improbable Rascal.* New York: Scribner's, 1959.

———. *Citizen Hearst.* New York: Charles Scribner's Sons, 1961.

———. *Pulitizer.* New York: Charles Scribner's Sons, 1967.

Tallant, Robert. *Ready to Hang.* New York: Harper & Brothers, 1952.

Tannenbaum, Frank. *Crime and the Community.* New York: Columbia University Press, 1938.

Tebel, John. *An American Dynasty.* Garden City, N.Y.: Doubleday, 1947.

Thaw, Harry K. *The Traitor.* Philadelphia: Dorrance, 1926.

Thompson, C.J.S. *Poison Mysteries in History.* Philadelphia: Lippincott, 1932.

Train, Arthur. *True Stories of Crime from the District Attorney's Office.* New York: McKinley, Stone & MacKenzie, 1908.

Triplett, Colonel Frank. *History, Romance and Philosophy of Great American Crimes and Criminals.* Hartford, Conn.: Park Publishing Co., 1885.

Tully, Andrew. *Era of Elegance.* New York: Funk and Wagnalls, 1947.

Van Every, Edward. *Sins of New York.* New York: Frederick A. Stokes, 1930.

Waldrop, Frank C. *McCormick of Chicago.* Englewood Cliffs, N.J.: Prentice-Hall, 1966.

Walker, Stanley. *The Night Club Era.* New York: Blue Ribbon Books, 1933.

Walling, George. *Recollections of a New York Chief of Police.* New York: Caxton, 1887.

Wecter, Dixon. *The Saga of American Society.* New York: Charles Scribner's Sons, 1937.

Weinberg, Arthur (ed.). *Attorney for the Damned.* New York: Simon & Schuster, 1957.

Wellman, Manly Wade. *Dead and Gone.* Chapel Hill: University of North Carolina Press, 1955.

Wendt, Lloyd, and Kogan, Herman. *Lords of the Levee.* Indianapolis: Bobbs-Merrill, 1943.

————. *Big Bill of Chicago.* Indianapolis: Bobbs-Merrill, 1953.

Whitelaw, D. *Corpus Delicti.* London: Geoffrey Bles, 1936.

Williams, Jack Kenny. *Vogues in Villainy.* Columbia: University of South Carolina Press, 1959.

Wilson, Colin. *A Casebook of Murder.* New York: Cowles, 1969.

Woollcott, Alexander. *While Rome Burns.* New York: Viking Press, 1934.

————. *Long, Long Ago.* New York: Viking Press, 1943.

Wren, Lassiter. *Masterstrokes of Crime Detection.* Garden City, N.Y.: Doubleday, Doran, 1929.

Wright, Sewell Peaslee (ed.). *Chicago Murders.* New York: Duell, Sloan and Pearce, 1945.

## Periodicals

"Allard Lowenstein, R.I.P." *National Review,* April 4, 1980.

Alpern, David M., with Michaud, Stephen G. "The Call of the Wild." *Newsweek,* December 22, 1975.

"America and the Sixth Commandment." *The Outlook,* February 16, 1907.

"Analytical Chemistry of Murder." *Current Literature,* March 1906.

"Andy and Claudine." *Ladies' Home Journal,* June 1977.

"Andy & Claudine & Spider & Co." *Time,* April 5, 1976.

"Another Day of Death." *Time,* December 11, 1978.

"The Armored Lady." *Time,* February 4, 1966.

Asbury, Herbert. "Days of Wickedness." *American Mercury,* November 1927.

"Assassination of an Assassin." *The Ring.* March, 1972.

"Aunt Candy." *Newsweek,* January 31, 1966.

Banay, R. S. "Study in Murder." *Annals of the American Academy of Political and Social Science,* 284, 1952.

"The Baseball Scandal." *The Nation,* October 13, 1920.

Beck, Melinda, with Shabad, Steven. "Harris: I Only Want to Die." *Newsweek,* March 9, 1981.

————, with Reese, Michael. "Night of Gay Rage." *Newsweek,* June 4, 1979.

Bell, Daniel. "Crime as an American Way of Life." *Antioch Review,* June 1953.

Bent, Silas. "Newspapermen—Partners in Crime?" *Scribner's Magazine,* November 1930.

Berger, Meyer. "Lady in Crepe." *The New Yorker,* October 5 and 12, 1935.

Blackman, N., Weiss, J.M.A., and Lambert, J. W. "The Sudden Murderer." *Archives of General Psychiatry,* 8, 1963.

Blanshard, Paul. "Who Killed Jake Lingle?" *The Nation,* July 2, 1930.

Bogdanovich, Peter. "The Murder of Sal Mineo." *Esquire,* March 1, 1978.

"The Bonded Blonde." *Time,* August 20, 1965.

"The Candy Trial." *Newsweek,* March 14, 1966.

Carpenter, A. "Pattern for Murder." *Science Digest,* June 1947.

"Case of the Heiress's Coma." *Newsweek,* January 18, 1982.

"Chicago as Seen by Herself." *McClure's Magazine,* May 1907.

Cole, K. E., Fisher, G., and Cole, S. S. "Women Who Kill." *Archives of General Psychiatry,* 19, 1968.

Collins, F. L. "Mistakes That Trap Murderers." *Science Digest,* June 1947.

Creel, George. "Unholy City." *Collier's,* September 2, 1939.

Crovant, B. A., and Waldrop, F. N. "The Murderer in the Mental Institution." *Annals of the American Academy of Political and Social Science,* 284, 1952.

"Death of the Diet Doctor." *Time,* March 24, 1980.

"Death Takes No Holiday in San Francisco, As a Shocked City Mourns Two Murdered Leaders." *People,* December 11, 1978.

"Detroit's Murderous Election Climax." *Literary Digest,* August 9, 1930.

"Easy Times for Murderers." *Literary Digest,* October 4, 1924.

"Emotional Insanity." *Independent,* August 27, 1908.

Flynn, John T. "These Are Our Rulers." *Collier's,* July 6, 1940.

"Four Murders." *Time,* July 14, 1961.

"Gangland's Brazen Challenge to Chicago." *Literary Digest,* June 21, 1930.

Geis, Gilbert. "Crime and Politics." *The Nation,* August 14, 1967.

"Getting Off?" *Time,* May 28, 1979.

Gibbens, T.C.N. "Sane and Insane Homicide." *Journal of Criminal Law,* 49, 1958.

Goldberg, H. "Crimes of Darkness." *Cosmopolitan,* April 1959.

Greenacre, P. "Conscience in the Psychopath." *American Journal of Orthopsychiatry,* 15:495, 1945.

Grinnell, C. E. "Modern Murder Trials and Newspapers." *Atlantic Monthly,* November 1901.

Gross, Karl. "The Paranoiac Murderers." *Journal of Criminal Psychopathology,* 1:66, 1939.

Haden-Guest, Anthony. "The Headmistress and the Diet Doctor." *New York,* March 31, 1980.

Harlan, H. "Five Hundred Homicides." *Journal of Criminal Law,* 40:736, 1950.

Hill, D., and Pond, D. A. "Reflections on 100 Capital Cases." *Journal of Mental Science,* 98:23, 1952.

Hoffman, F. L. "Murder and the Death Penalty." *Current History,* June 1928.

"Homicide as an Amusement." *The Independent,* October 11, 1906.

Howe, William F. "Some Notable Murder Cases." *Cosmopolitan,* August 1900.

Irwin, Will. "The First Ward Ball." *Collier's,* February 6, 1909.

James, M. "Annals of Crime." *The New Yorker,* December 6, 1941.

Jenkins, Herbert. "My Most Bizarre Murder Case." *The Atlanta Journal and Constitution Magazine,* August 22, 1971.

Kahn, M.W.A. "Superior Performance IQ of Murderers as a Function of Overt Act." *Journal of Social Psychology,* 76, 1968.

Kennedy, John B. "Lords of the Loop." *Collier's,* April 3, 1926.

Labich, Kenneth, with Reese, Michael. "He Hated to Lose." *Newsweek,* December 11, 1978.

Landesco, John. "The Criminal Underworld of Chicago in the Eighties and the Nineties." *Journal of the American Institute of Criminal Law and Criminology,* May–June 1934, March–April 1935.

Langberg, R. "Homicide in the United States." *Vital Health Statistics,* 20, 1967.

Langdon, Dolly, Reilly, Patricia, and Smilgis, Martha. "The Killing of Scarsdale Diet Doctor Herman Tarnower Leaves a Single Haunting Question: Why?" *People,* March 31, 1980.

Leacock, S. "Such Fine Murders We're Having!" *Collier's,* November 1, 1924.

Lunde, D. T., "Our Murder Boom." *Psychology Today,* November 1975.

"Lust for Blood as an Incentive to Murder." *Current Literature,* August 1909.

MacDonald, J. M. "The Threat to Kill." *American Journal of Psychiatry,* 19, 1970.

Mathews, Tom, with Lubenow, Gerald C. "Day of the Assassin." *Newsweek,* December 11, 1978.

Maynard L. M. "Murder in the Making." *American Mercury,* June 1929.

"Mesmerism in Miami." *Time,* March 18, 1966.

"Millions and Murder." *Literary Digest,* July 31, 1915.

Morganthau, Tom, with Shannon, Elaine. "A One-Man Crime Wave." *Newsweek,* December 22, 1980.

——, with Kasindorf, Martin. "The Sal Mineo Case." *Newsweek,* February 26, 1979.

"Murder and the Law." *The Nation,* April 13, 1913.

"Murder in New York." *The Nation,* August 12, 1931.

"Murder in Philadelphia." *Time,* December 22, 1975.

"Murder Mysteries." *The Survey,* May 15, 1932.

"Murders by Poison." *Harper's Weekly,* November 8, 1902.

"Newspaper Criminals in Chicago." *The Nation*, July 23, 1930.

Park, R. E. "Murder and the Case Study Method." *American Journal of Sociology*, November 1930.

Peters, W. "Why Did They Do It?" *Good Housekeeping*, June 1962.

Player, Cyril Arthur. "Gangsters and Politicians in Detroit." *The New Republic*, August 13, 1930.

Radin, E. D. "Invisible Clues That Trap Killers." *Science Digest*, September 1950.

Randolph, Colonel Robert Isham. "How to Wreck Capone's Gang." *Collier's*, March 7, 1931.

Riis, Jacob A. "How the Other Half Lives." *Scribner's Magazine*, January 1937.

Robinson, Archie. "Murder Most Foul." *American Heritage*, August 1964.

Robinson, Paul. "Gays in the Streets." *The New Republic*, June 9, 1979.

Rolph, C. H. "Those Who Murder." *The Nation*, May 14, 1960.

Rosenblatt, Roger. "Plato Dies." *The New Republic*, March 6, 1976.

Rousseau, V. "Lawless New York." *Harper's Weekly*, December 26, 1908.

"Safest of all Crimes." *The Independent*, January 27, 1903.

Salmans, Sandra, with Gram, Dewey. "Death in Aspen." *Newsweek*, April 5, 1978.

Saltis, E. "Champion Poisoners." *Cosmopolitan*, February 1902.

Schilder, P. "The Attitudes of Murderers Toward Death." *Journal of Abnormal and Social Psychology*, 31, 1936.

Sellers, Pat. "Skull-duggery Detective Work Is the Diet for Scarsdale Defense." *Us*, July 8, 1980.

"Sentimentality in Murder Trials." *Review of Reviews*, November 1908.

Shipley, M. "Crimes of Violence in Chicago and in Greater New York." *Review of Reviews*, September 1908.

"Squeaky Sweeney." *National Review*, April 4, 1980.

"Stale Candy." *Newsweek*, March 14, 1966.

"The Strange Case of Sunny and Claus." *Newsweek*, July 20, 1981.

"The Talk of the Town." *The New Yorker*, March 31, 1980.

Teale, E. "Is it Murder?" *Popular Science*, September 1940.

Tharter, Celia. "A Memorable Murder." *The Atlantic Monthly*, May 1875.

"Thaw, Becker, *et al.*" *The Independent*, August 9, 1915.

"A Tragic End of a Long March." *Newsweek*, March 24, 1980.

Turner, Guy Kibbe. "The City of Chicago. A Study of the Great Immoralities." *McClure's Magazine*, April 1907.

Wakefield, E. "Brand of Cain in the Great Republic." *Living Age*, January 2, 1892.

Waldron, E. "Murder Tour of the Midwest." *Holiday,* August 1961.

Waldrup, F. C. "Murder as a Sex Practice." *American Mercury,* February 1948.

Weiss, Michael J., and Mills, Barbara Kleban. "A Suburban D.C. Family Man Turns Out To Be a Suspected Killer and Robbery Baron." *People,* January 19, 1981.

Wertham, Fredric. "It's Murder." *Saturday Review of Literature,* February 5, 1949.

Weymouth, Lally. "Sleeping Beauty." *New York,* January 11, 1982.

"Who Is the Real Murderer?" *Literary Digest,* December 15, 1931.

Wilkinson, S., and Toland, J. "Why They Killed the People They Loved." *Cosmopolitan,* March 1960.

Williams, Dennis A. "The Lady and the Doctor." *Newsweek,* March 24, 1980.

———. "The Outcast." *Newsweek,* February 23, 1976.

———. "It's All Claudine's Fault." *Newsweek,* January 17, 1977.

Wolf, W. "Poison Murders Solved by Test Tube Sleuths." *Popular Science,* August 1935.

# Bulletins, Documents, Pamphlets, Reports

*Address of Hon. Lyman Tremain to the jury on the final trial of Edward S. Stokes for the murder of James Fisk, Jr.* New York: George F. Nesbit & Co., n.d.

*An Authentic Life of John C. Colt.* Boston: S. N. Dickinson, 1842.

Barnhart, K. E. "A Study of Homicide in the United States." *Birmingham Southern College Bulletin,* 5:25, 1932.

Chicago Crime Commission: *Annual Reports,* 1919–31.

*Chicago Police Problems.* The Citizens Police Committee, 1931.

*Chicago Vice Commission Report,* Chicago, 1912.

*Full Particulars of the Assassination of Albert D. Richardson, the Libertine, shot by the injured husband, McFarland.* New York: N.p., n.d.

*James Fisk, Jr., His life and death.* New York: N.p., n.d.

Ledyard, Hope. *Articles, speeches and poems of Carlyle W. Harris.* New York: J. S. Ogilvie, n.d.

*Life, adventures, strange career and assassination of Col. James Fisk, Jr.* Philadelphia: Barclay & Co., 1872.

*Life, career and assassination of James Fisk, Jr.* New York: N.p., 1872.

*Life, Letters and Last Conversation of John Caldwell Colt.* New York: New York Sun, 1841.

*The Life of Col. James Fisk, Jr..* New York: W. E. Hilton, 1872.

*Life, trial and conviction of Edward Stokes, for the assassination of Jas. Fisk, Jr.* Philadelphia: Barclay & Co., 1873.

Mansfield, Helen Josephine. *The Truth at Last! Life of Col. James Fisk, Jr.* New York: N.p., n.d.

*The Murder of James Fisk, Jr..* New York: Thames O'Kane, n.d.

*The Richardson-McFarland Tragedy.* Philadelphia: Barclay & Co., 1870.

*Summing up of John Graham, Esq., to the jury, on the part of the defense, on the trial of Daniel MacFarland* [sic]. New York: W. A. Townsend & Adams, 1870.

*Testimony, as reported by Coroner Nelson W. Young, in the case of James Fisk, Jr.* New York: George MacNamara, 1872.

*The Trial of Carlyle W. Harris.* New York: N.p., 1892.

*The Trial of Carlyle W. Harris for poisoning his wife, Helen Potts.* New York: N.p., 1892.

*The Trial of Daniel McFarland for the shooting of Albert D. Richardson, the alleged seducer of his wife.* New York: American News Co., 1870.

## Newspapers

Atlanta: *Constitution, Journal;* Boston: *Globe;* Chicago: *American, Daily News, Evening Journal, Herald Examiner, Sun-Times, Tribune;* Detroit: *Free Press, News;* Kansas City: *Star;* Los Angeles: *Examiner, Herald-Examiner, Times;* New York: *American, Daily News, Evening Journal, Herald, Mirror, Post, Times, Tribune, World, World-Telegram;* Philadelphia: *Daily News, Evening Bulletin, Inquirer;* St. Louis: *Globe-Democrat, Post-Dispatch;* San Francisco: *Chronicle, Examiner.*

# INDEX